> Dear John,
> I wish Manifest Everyone's for
> The common element is of your dreams.
> Much aloha,
> Diane Scheurell
> July 28, 2014

Manifesting Paradise

Diane M. Scheurell

No part of this book may be reproduced without the author's prior written permission.

Copyright © 2014 Diane M. Scheurell

All rights reserved.

ISBN-10: 1499618182
ISBN-13: 978-1499618181

DEDICATION

To my husband and daughters

CONTENTS

	Preface	v
	Acknowledgments	viii
	Map of the Big Island	x
1	Getting There	1
2	Settling In	23
3	Celebrating the Holidays	46
4	Creating a New Life in a New Year	59
5	Rethinking the Chicken and the Egg and Other Meaty Matters	84
6	Relishing an Auspicious Birthday	102
7	Choosing Your Attitude	123
8	Looking Back	139
9	Experiencing Hawaiian Politics	164
10	Growing Deeper Roots	181
11	Manifesting Happiness	196
12	Finding My Passion	226
	Diane's Dictionary	250
	Diane's Transformation Tools	254
	Cast of Characters	262
	Bibliography	265
	About the Author	266

PREFACE

Aloha. This is a memoir of my journey to find my truth and to live authentically, to transform from stressed-out executive to relaxed malahini. That's Hawaiian for newcomer. Yes, I now live on an island with five volcanoes, three of them active, surrounded by lush tropical vegetation (my husband says jungle), enjoying plentiful avocados and oranges from my yard, swimming in the ocean and at the local pool year round and relishing the rich cultural diversity that is Hawai'i. But first I had to struggle.

I spent years drinking the Corporate Kool-Aid, trying to climb the success ladder, only to realize after two decades that I no longer wanted that. Maybe I never did. I was a product of the late '60s and early '70s, a member of the generation that believed we could change the world. Earth Day. Civil rights. Women's liberation. We were all about doing what's right. What happened? How did I wind up in the corporate uniform of skirted power suit, pantyhose and high heels?

My journey back to my former ideals distressed me at times, digging deep inside, revisiting tough times and learning difficult lessons. But with the help of tools that my mentors and life coach taught me, as well as those I discovered on my own, I slowly climbed out of the hole I had dug. These tools changed my life and I am happy to share them with you. They include positive thinking, journaling, vision boards, gratitude, being present, meditation, even hypnosis! The kuleana, the responsibility, that goes along with good fortune is to pass it on.

This memoir also contains stories of my new life here in paradise. As we settled into our new home on the Big Island, I was as consumed by unpacking and remodeling as an executive on a timeline. It took a few months before the easy pace of living on an island took hold. And it was fun for me to notice when that executive style popped out again. I soon made new friends and found my place in this community. I looked around and truly noticed the beauty, sacred spaces, local cultures and unique brand of politics here. As a newcomer, I easily spotted the wonderful and sometimes frustrating quirkiness of Hawai'i.

But I also observed the anxiety this huge change had on my family. My teenage daughters were not keen on this move. And one of the main reasons for leaving corporate life early was to reconnect with Jade and Faye before they went off to college. Could I succeed given that they were Daddy's girls? My husband, BG, wasn't completely convinced that this was the right move either, especially for the girls.

Looking back on the 15 months that frame my story, what I appreciated most was my continued growth. I had a new quest: looking inward to determine the passion that would sustain me for this new chapter in my life. I started the search with what got me here in the first place, my transformation tools. I am grateful that I found my new passion.

My journey did not end with this book. I continue to share my story at www.ManifestingParadise.com. I invite you to check out my blog.

Five editorial notes:

- These essays describe real events, though I took liberties with the timeline; some incidents might have happened sooner or later than described. I also gave the people mentioned the option of using a pseudonym. The historic documents are also authentic. I wrote them on the dates listed.

- You will find a map of the Big Island featuring places described in the book. It is by no means complete, but portrays our world for the first 15 months.

- At the end of the book, I appended a small dictionary of words that may not be familiar to you, as well as a list of my transformation tools and where they're referenced or demonstrated in the essays. I also included a cast of characters.

- If you want to see pictures that accompany the essays, you can view them on my website, www.ManifestingParadise.com. From the top of the Home page, click on "Book Photo Album." This album also contains additional commentary and even some recipes related to the story.

- For those readers who prefer to focus on the bottom line, you can skip right to Chapter 11 for a discussion of my main transformation tools. But I'd urge you to relax a little and let the rhythm of the story reveal not only the tools, but the magic that is Hawai'i. This story is about the destination as well as the process.

I hope you enjoy sharing my journey. Perhaps it will help you with your own life quest. With luck, you won't have to struggle the way I did. Thank you, or as we say in Hawai'i, mahalo.

May 27, 2014, Honoka'a, Hawai'i

ACKNOWLEDGMENTS

Thanks to my email and blog readers, and especially to those who provided me with feedback, encouragement and stories of their own: Dr. Chantelle Beal, Dr. Barbara Cavalier, Sue Daniel, Amy Haines, Rita Hyland, Rox-Anne Klemetsen, Dr. Barbara Perry, Nancy Pozorski, and Tom Rosholt.

My new friends in Hawai'i accepted me into their lives with open arms: Seny Bynum, Anita and Bob Cawley, Stacy Disney, Dianne and Mitch Evans, Julia Fairchild, Thomas Gyrion, Kristan Hunt, Lillian and Peter Jefferson and their daughter, Sandy Jilton, Ana Jones, Lois Keb, Deacon Ritterbush, Alvita Soleil, Teri Sugg, Judy Syrop, Dolores Whaley, Louli Yardley and Kim Ziegler.

I am grateful for the mentors and teachers who shaped my life: Shahadah Frederick, Dr. Norman Hollies, Dr. Charles Sontag, and Wynn Wacker; and especially the women who coached, cajoled, and loved me into finding my authenticity, accepting myself, and creating my future: Dr. Barbara Cavalier, Rita Hyland and Dr. Barbara Perry.

Thank you to the supportive people who reviewed my manuscript in its many forms: Amie Best, Sue Daniel, Cindy Dumlao, Dianne Evans, Lynn Fraher, Amy Haines, Jean Kelly, Amanda Lawrence, Nancy Pozorski, and Deacon Ritterbush.

Special thanks go to my editors, Tom Peek, who encouraged me at the beginning, and Deb Russell, who examined every comma and colon at the end of this process.

I also thank my web designer and business systems implementer, Julia Fairchild; my graphic designer, Michael Zack; and my publishing coach, Eliza Cahill. I thank Deacon Ritterbush who gave me the courage to self-publish; I am a proud indie author.

Thanks to my nurturing extended family, especially Dad and Mom (I know you're watching from above), and my dear sisters.

Finally, thanks to my wonderful husband and daughters who patiently waited on the important things in their life while I wrote, and who provided so much inspiration for my ponderings. I am truly blessed.

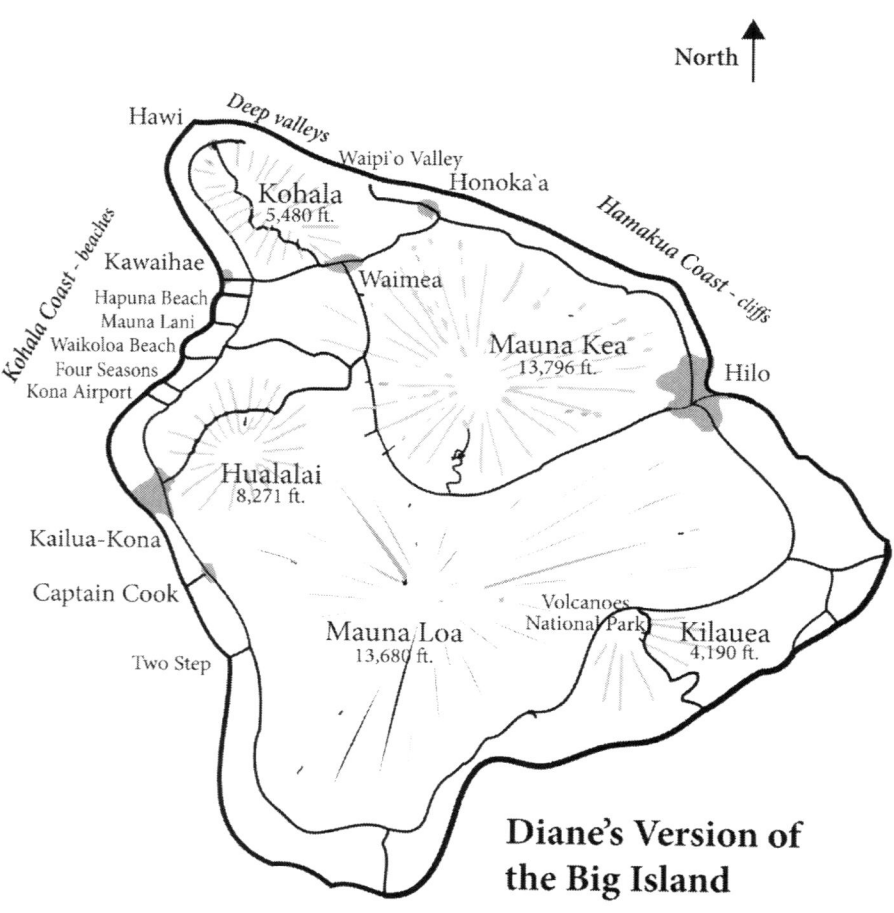

1. GETTING THERE

Moving to Hawai'i!

August 1. Racine, WI. After living my whole life in conventional locales, I'm going exotic. Okay, there were the seven years I lived in Maryland, gripped inside the beltway of Washington, DC. I guess that's not ordinary. But twelve years in the suburbs of Atlanta and the rest in Wisconsin, mostly in industrial towns along Lake Michigan, almost define humdrum.

People ask, why Hawai'i? Are they kidding? Two years ago in Racine we had 100 inches of snow. This year we had 60. I hate winter! It's not just the cold, it's the duration, December through March, sometimes later. I hate boots, mittens, scarves, bulky winter coats, overheated malls, streets turned to slop – ugh! I just don't want to live that way anymore.

Over the past six years, we used family vacations to explore places to move. Every place was warm. But that wasn't enough. With Lake Michigan in my bones, I needed water. We kept going back to the Big Island. Jade, Faye, BG – we all liked it. We loved the rich diversity. So many cultures settled there and intermarried.

BG and I will be in the minority, while our adopted Chinese daughters will fit right in. Diversity also extends to plants, birds, food, climate and terrain. It's a lush exotic haven for all senses.

We're moving to a village called Honokaʻa. It's on the north end of the island, on the wet side. Trade winds come in from the east, dropping rain as they rise over the mountains, the old volcanoes. By the time the winds blow to the other side, there's no more moisture to wring out, leaving the western side dry.

The dry side has parched upland pastures and massive lava plains from eruptions in 1801 and the 1850s. Geologically, that's a minute ago. Luckily Honokaʻa is in the safest volcanic zone on the island. This newer lava creates a bleak landscape. Very little grows on it – a few tufts of grass here and there, just enough for wild goats and donkeys to eat and survive. But the dry side's also where the tourists go. It has beaches, resorts, dry weather, cruise ship stops, nightlife, luaus, sunset dinner cruises, a seahorse farm, the Place of Refuge, lessons on surfing, snorkeling, and paddle boarding, helicopter rides, golf, whale-watching excursions, swimming with dolphins and other touristy attractions. We did as much as we could fit in during our vacations here.

But it didn't take us long to discover the wet side of the Big Island. It has its tourist attractions, too. The best is the active volcano Kilauea, home of Pele, Hawaiian goddess of fire. It also has botanical gardens, waterfalls and Waipiʻo Valley. This is where I want to live, on this lush green side. Life is authentic here, not just focused on tourists. You see the real Hawaiʻi, feel the real aloha and meet real people living real lives.

We could've decided to settle in Hilo, second largest city in the whole state, with 47,000 people. Only Honolulu on Oʻahu is bigger, at just under a million. But Hilo gets too much rain for my taste, more than 100 inches every year, and it's nowhere near the school we chose for the girls. You see, we chose the school first. Everything else had to fit around that. The school's in Waimea, but I didn't want to live there, either. At 2500 feet, Waimea is cattle country at the saddle between two dormant volcanoes and on the divide between the wet and dry sides. Rain is abundant and flies sideways because the wind blows all the time, sometimes fiercely. There's nothing to break it except occasional tree lines dividing pastures. And it's cold up there. What's the point of moving to Hawai'i and then living in Wyoming?

Honoka'a is 17 miles east of Waimea at 1000 feet, definitely high enough to avoid a tsunami but low enough to have great weather. The town was at the heart of the Hāmākua Coast's sugar cane industry, with small plantation worker camps all around. When the sugar industry collapsed in 1994, Honoka'a was left to die. But people were loyal, or maybe, like many permanent residents of Hawai'i, too poor to move away. Either way, the town has managed to survive.

I love this charming town. They call it a town, but really it's just a village. Honoka'a is a scene out of the 1920's with untouched older buildings on Mamane, the historic main street. Some buildings display murals. Others have names and the years they were built, like Andrade Building, 1924. Storefronts have signs like Farm Consultant, Ph.D., Asian Food, NeNe's Sewing Corner, Taro Patch Gifts and Honoka'a Filipino Store. Guidebooks describe it as stepping back into the 1950s: no big box stores, no fast-food chains, not even a stoplight. Our post office is tiny. It doesn't even deliver mail in town, so we'll have to pick it up. It's closed at lunch and only opens for an hour on Saturday.

Everything is near us except for the girls' school and church we'll attend. We're within walking distance of the community pool, our bank, the library, a fresh vegetable stand, downtown shops, the town grocery store, a couple of restaurants, my yoga class and the movie theater.

The hardware store looks like a movie set with cement floors worn smooth from decades of use. An old wooden stand of drawers holds individual screws, nuts and bolts. Narrow, crowded aisles are filled to capacity, and tools hang from the ceiling and loft. You almost expect to see a wooden barrel with a checkers game set out, except the third generation owners are Japanese, and they'd more likely set out Go or Mahjong. Despite its small size, it has everything you might want and the now-deceased founder's daughter-in-law, grandson and granddaughter can put their hands right on it.

They even have some things in the front window that a Home Depot or Lowe's wouldn't carry, such as new washboards, just like my grandma used. They still hand-write receipts on pads with carbon paper, total up your purchases with an adding machine and package them in little paper bags. Like the post office, they're closed at noon eating lunch at their home nearby. And even though townspeople do much handiwork on the weekend, they'd better arrive at the store early on Saturday because it closes from noon on Saturday until Monday morning.

A block away, I plan to become spoiled by Ted's Garage where they still pump gas for you. I don't understand why some people do it themselves. There's no extra charge for the service and his gas is always the same price as the brand name station across the street. At Ted's they'll also check your oil and fill your tires for three dollars. What a luxury not to have to do it myself! Ted also conducts the yearly car safety inspections required in Hawai'i, though it's clear he'd rather be under a hood, tinkering.

The town feels safe. The woman who owned our house didn't even have locks on the doors! I had to install them before renting it out. We think we'll be okay with Faye and Jade going to the grocery store or veggie stand alone. That's a big deal to them because we never allow them to walk alone in Racine, not even around the block, and they're 16 and 12!

I bought the house last summer and have been renting it out. It's a vintage 1935 plantation house originally built for the town's postmaster. After dealing with our 1904 home in Wisconsin, BG said he'd never own another house older than he was. That's why I bought it myself. That, and he wasn't ready to commit money to this adventure a year ago. But the day we went back to have a second look and take measurements, he stopped at the hardware store and bought a tape measure and a brass ring. Handing me the ring, he said, "Go for it." He was "in" for the move if I wanted to take the plunge!

It was scary buying a house by myself; still is. I was glad to learn the former owner renovated it including new electrical wiring. It also has a new carport with an 'ohana above. 'Ohana means "family" in Hawaiian, so an 'ohana unit is like a mother-in-law apartment, originally intended for family. The house has two big covered porches called lanais and you can see the ocean from the backyard. The former owner planted lots of exotic (that is, local) plants including oranges, bananas, and grapefruit; eleven coconut trees and several other kinds of palm trees. She owned a garden center in Honoka'a and when it closed she filled her yard. I can't wait to start growing my own veggies year-round.

I'll see if I like village life; Honoka'a has only 2000 people. It's so different from the historic district of Racine and suburbs of Atlanta. But surprisingly, this town feels much like my hometown, Manitowoc, safe, with family values of the '50s and an air of a simpler time. Or maybe it's that my memories of home are stuck in the 1950s. Regardless, I'm looking for simplicity. Life has become too complex.

Moving to an exotic location is one thing, but I'm also leaving corporate life. Retiring before age 60 has been a dream of mine for a long time. Dream isn't the right word. I believe that we can all create our own futures by asking our Higher Spirit or God for help, showing gratitude for blessings and thinking positively. I truly believe that I manifested this new life.

The scary thing now is, what's next? For the past two years, I've focused on ending the last chapter of my life. I haven't spent any time figuring out what I'm going to do now, except to reconnect with the girls before they go off to college. I've been so busy with my career and being the main breadwinner that I've missed much in their lives. And it will be interesting for BG to have the main job, maybe the only job in the family.

BG is certain I'll be bored and looking for a job in no time. I'm not so sure. After decades of trudging in corporate front lines, I'm burned out and ready to go AWOL. Originally a young hippie wanna-be, I've forgotten why I signed up for the stressful corporate gig in the first place. So when I get to Honoka'a, I'm going to relax and spend the first three months on my backside reading novels. But then what? Should I volunteer? Take a job? What's my next life's passion? For decades I defined myself as a manager and now need to do a total mind-shift. At the moment, I have no ideas. My head hurts thinking about it because there's still so much to do before the move. But I know that once settled in, I'll tackle it as another stimulating step on my life journey. I just don't need any more stimulation right now.

Meanwhile, we leave next week to relocate BG and the girls to our new home. The girls start school in two weeks so they have to be set up in the house by then. Unfortunately, I have to come back to my job until the end of September to wrap things up. I also have to pack up the house and send off all the stuff. My grind is not over.

This is actually scary. But I'm so excited! It's the start of our new life. We all ping-pong between anticipation and anxiety. As we get closer to the date, the girls seem almost hostile about leaving friends and cousins behind. Even BG seems like a deer caught in the headlights, slow to make decisions. I wish they'd expressed their reluctance to move sooner, when there was time to change plans, like a year ago. I don't need this right now. I need their help! I hope it's just jitters.

Too young to retire.

August 5. Racine, WI. Actually, who retires anymore? That's just an old corporate idea. We either can't afford to retire, are too afraid to take the leap, or do it and go on to undertake something else. Age-wise I may be too young to retire. Spirit-wise I'm ready to reclaim my youthful ideals and pull out of corporate life. "You can't trust anyone over 30." That's what we said a lifetime ago. Next year I'll be twice that age. Where did the years go? Where did my ideals go?

I was in the high school class of 1970. Some of my friends were already pregnant at graduation, already starting families. I felt women could do more, be more than their mothers. Yet, even though I wanted a career in journalism, and started college with that intention, I later chose Home Economics Education because I didn't want to compete with my boyfriend who also majored in journalism. And my dad told me teaching was a secure profession. Where's the Women's Lib in that choice?!

It was the summer of the Sterling Hall bombing on the University of Wisconsin Madison campus, the last act for campus protestors. The attack absolutely shut down any chance that my parents would let me go to school there, even if I'd had the money. I contented myself with working hard at the local two-year UW campus and found my first mentor, Dr. Chuck. He helped me see things differently and become an adult with my own ideas.

Meanwhile, my boyfriend and I were outraged by what the government was doing in Vietnam, afraid he'd be picked for the draft, and distrusted big institutions, including college! But a new feeling arrived on the second Earth Day, April 22, 1971. It was almost like spring itself rooted in my soul. Yes, I remained angry about the war, but new hope and optimism also bloomed: Earth Day, civil rights, women's liberation. They were all related; do what's right. We could push Congress for clean water and clean air. We could end poverty in America. We could make sure every child on the planet had enough to eat. We could ensure that every baby was wanted. We could end discrimination in all its ugly forms. We could help every person achieve their potential. What happened? How did we go from the generation of "We" to "Me," from "We shall overcome" to "We shall overspend?"

A couple years went by. The boyfriend ditched me. Over my parent's objections, I transferred to UW Madison as a junior, knowing full well that I'd not receive any more money from them.

I was ready, having spent my sophomore year saving my earnings from working four concurrent jobs. Leaving their financial aid behind also meant independence, and I exercised it by moving into a co-op. In the midst of this huge campus, I found a new boyfriend, a graduate student who soon became my husband. He was a genius, and he and his genius friends often asked, "Why's a smart girl like you studying Home Economics?" It embarrassed me, made me feel I had to do something more than teach high school. I gutted out the four semesters to finish the bachelor's degree, but changed majors for my master's degree. I was letting others decide for me again, this time, my new husband.

I went on to get my Doctorate at the University of Maryland, just outside Washington, DC. I wanted to teach college so I could inspire the next generation with the fervor of my ideals. It would be difficult because the country now leaned even further right. Reagan's presidency was evidence of that. We'd have to wait for a different administration more favorable to ending poverty and discrimination.

As I came close to finishing my Ph.D., I received a call from a big consumer products company in Wisconsin, close to family for me and my husband. The man who was to become my boss wanted to know if I'd consider a job conducting consumer research on new product ideas. It sounded like so much fun and paid considerably more than teaching at a university. By this time I was genuinely tired of PB&J sandwiches.

I reasoned that I could take this job for a couple of years, add to my knowledge bank and feed my consumer needs: car, furniture, maybe even a down payment for a house. Then I'd return to academia. I also reasoned that I could use this opportunity to be a role model for other young women who wanted to choose career over homemaker. Was that real or was I justifying this abrupt change in my own path?

But I had stepped onto a slippery slope. After three years, I divorced my first husband and moved to the Atlanta area for a gig with my second big corporation. There I married BG, adopted Jade and Faye and, after 13 years, returned to the first company in Wisconsin. I got caught up in all the fear-based BS that Corporate America preached in the '80s and '90s: "If you're not trying to move up, you're dead." "There are only so many plum jobs to go around." "You won't get those plum jobs unless you sacrifice for the company." The message wasn't overt, at least in the two companies that employed me. They're decent places.

No, it was me, pressuring myself, believing the corporate BS portrayed in the media and replaying in my head. I read the books, I went to the seminars, I dreamed big. I wanted to be the first female Vice President of Research at the Atlanta company. But I didn't stand a chance. I didn't have it in me. Yes, there were external factors that stood in my way. When I became a manager, I looked around at my division peers. *Every* male at my level and higher had a wife who stayed home. Was that coincidence?

But the bigger hurdle standing in my way was that this corporate suit didn't fit me. It restrained me, both literally and figuratively. In the '80s and '90s it was the two-piece skirted power suit with panty hose and high heels. As I wobbled around on those heels I felt just as unsteady inside. I never had a sense of balance or inner peace. I had long ago lost my connection to my God, who could've provided some relief, some shelter, but I wasn't asking.

I was always wary, on guard, and I didn't like it. I chafed at self-imposed rules that were supposed to pay off. I bought into the whole corporate scene. The higher I went, the more wary, guarded and unhappy I became, often to the point of tears. One year a female boss said, "Diane, you need to stop crying at work." That was one of the lowest points. I thought if another woman didn't get it, I was truly lost. The next week I asked my doctor for Prozac. It stopped the crying, but not the gnawing inside that something was wrong.

What did turn me around was a women's leadership seminar. I connected with mentors and, soon after, initiated work with a life coach. All of them helped me see that I could be happy by being authentic. Being authentic meant letting people see the real me, the part I buried for so long, the part I hid. I was scared at first, but began to reclaim my idealism. Realistic enough not to try to change the whole corporation or even the research division, I focused on my department: demonstrate unconditional love, treat people with respect, empower them and build trust. People noticed. Soon employees from other parts of the company came to our area to feel the vibe or get a free hug. I created a safe place for people to be themselves, be authentic and still be highly respected for their work. Tapping into each person's abilities, we grew our responsibilities organically, adding human factors, usability, sensory research, analytics and claims research. The company even asked me to take my function global. Clearly we were doing something right.

I've been choreographing that dance for seven years. I developed an inner peace as I lived by my recovered ideals, but I'm butting heads with my bosses more and more. They don't like the dance, it's too different. Hah. My words just reminded me of something. My very first boss told me in my first performance review that I had to stop running in the halls! Now I'm not only running, but metaphorically dancing and leading a whole department in the art! But my dance has to end. There's only so much Nirvana a person can create inside a corporation. I have to leave. And luckily I can retire, gold watch and all, in just another eight weeks.

That's my story, more like a cathartic confession. I'm not too young to leave corporate life. But, yes, I am too young to retire. I will do something else. I'll find my passion. I just have to figure out what that is and how it connects to my ideals. This time I get to do it my way. We leave in three days.

Waking up to roosters.

August 12. Honokaʻa, HI. We made it to our new house around 9 p.m. on Monday after several long flights. By that time we'd been awake more than 24 hours. Luckily, I hadn't rented out the upstairs ʻohana. I'd set it up as a little hideaway for myself with furniture I bought from the former owner and Stacy, my real estate agent. I used the ʻohana twice: last November with my sister Grace, and in December for the girls' school admission interviews. We had no electricity when we arrived but that didn't matter. We just fell into bed, dead tired.

Because we couldn't use our electric stove, we bought a gas grill on Tuesday. We put it out on the front lanai, even though I felt like a hillbilly cooking meals out there. Being without electricity gets old fast, especially when you're trying to settle in. I'm tired of buying ice; I want my refrigerator! But before we can get electricity, we need an address (post office box) for the billing. To obtain a PO Box, the post office wants documentation (proof of house ownership, passport) that's, unfortunately, at the house in Wisconsin. And we face lots of other annoyances. I swear that if people remembered the hassle of moving, they'd never do it again. On the other hand, we had supper with avocados off our own tree last night.

Everyone is working hard. We have no trouble falling asleep even with coqui frogs blurting their "song." Mornings are a different matter. The damn roosters across the street start their serenade around 3 a.m. I'm sure there's more than one. They seem to call back and forth. Are they talking or challenging each other? I hope it's a challenge; maybe they'll kill each other. The girls are especially irate, sleeping next to the ʻohana window that fronts the street. I think they're plotting coq au vin.

School starts Monday and we barely pulled everything together: books, gym clothes, supplies, book bags and additional clothing to fit the dress code. Both girls are attending Hawaiʻi Preparatory Academy, but at two different locations. Faye is at their middle school in Waimea, while Jade is at the upper school campus just outside town on the dry side. It's laid out like a college with various buildings housing different disciplines and dormitories. Half the students in each class are boarders living on campus. Many are from the Pacific Rim.

Faye is nervous. We found out last week that the school decided to take her Wisconsin principal's recommendation to have her skip a year, so she'll start eighth grade instead of seventh. She's been bored in school for years, so I hope this will finally challenge her. It's a big step, but I have confidence in her ability to adapt, and this is the time to do it while she's in transition anyway.

I hope the girls feel more at home in this multiracial, multicultural melting pot than they did in Wisconsin where there were few Asian kids. Here, they're everywhere. And no one looks twice at our biracial family. It already feels good to be here, though Jade and Faye continue to give me stink eye for moving. I trust that will change.

Meanwhile, I'm practicing a lot of deep breathing to keep myself calm. And we're looking forward to supper tonight – chicken in effigy; I mean on the grill!

Life is getting better – do I have to go back?

August 16. Honoka'a, HI. Blessed relief. The roosters shut up in the rain! And we've had gentle rains every night for a week. This truly is paradise. It rains at night and is sunny during the day. And it's not hot up here at 1000 feet. I get the feeling that this elevation will make a big difference in our comfort. You see, our house has neither heat nor air conditioning. Our only means of temperature control is opening and closing the many well-positioned windows and turning fans on and off.

I've gone over to the dark side. After resisting for years, I finally bought a cell phone and I can't imagine life without it. With the girls 17 miles from home at different campuses, starting and ending at different times, we need lots of coordination, so we all have a phone. Faye will give me texting lessons later today.

I've transitioned from frantic Moving Organizer to Soccer Mom in the space of a week, even going to yoga class, taking time for a bit of self-care. I'm playing chauffeur big time. Thank God I bought that CRV last November when I vacationed here with my sister.

We see lots of cows as we drive past the upland pastures on the way to Waimea. They aren't like Wisconsin Holstein dairy cows, black with white patches or white with black patches. These are small mixed herds of cows with interesting colors, or large herds where the cows all look alike, solid brown and/or solid black. None have the big udders of our dairy herds. I guess it takes someone from Wisconsin to notice cows before anything else.

Actually, I don't mind driving to Waimea. We don't yet have Internet at home, so I use a Wi-Fi hot spot at the Waimea Coffee Company. After dropping the girls off at school, I stop for coffee, croissant and computer access. I could like this routine. It's not fair that BG and the girls get to stay here, and I have to go back to work. And, of course, I have to pack and manage the move as well. Ugh! I'm usually all about relishing the journey, but the only way I'm going to survive this is to focus on the destination.

A clear day on the mountain.

August 19. Honokaʻa, HI. No rain this morning. As I took the girls to school, it was sunny and clear all the way up the volcano. I could see the mountaintop observatories, a somewhat rare sight because the top of Mauna Kea, at almost 14,000 feet above sea level, is usually obscured by clouds, fog or rain. Traffic in Waimea was unusually bad this morning. In addition to heavy school and business traffic, the church we joined was holding a funeral for a young parishioner killed in Afghanistan. Everyone, right up to the Governor, flew in to pay respects. For a moment, I felt sad to think that the absurdity of war and the ensuing family sorrow shows up even in paradise.

We attended this parish a couple of years ago and were astonished to see the altar girls praying the Our Father to hula moves. They still do it that way and the whole congregation now hulas along with them. It's performed in the ancient form of the hula, not the modern form reminiscent of grass skirts and coconut bras. I have much to learn about honoring traditions in Hawai'i, but I'll feel more connected to the island when I do. For now, I've learned this hula. BG's not dancing yet but, then again, he doesn't sing either.

Earlier this week we abandoned the 'ohana and moved into the big house. The girls are happy sleeping on new mattresses in their own bedrooms; no more sharing the sofa bed. BG also paid the mattress delivery guys to haul the two couches and the bed from the 'ohana down to the main house. We're now firmly ensconced in our new home, just without most of our furniture, creature comforts and tools. I find myself looking for a potato masher or carving knife and realize they aren't here yet. Patience has never been my strong suit.

Faye is adjusting well to eighth grade, especially enjoying honors math. She's glued to her new cell phone, calling friends back home. But she's also making friends here and checking out cute boys in class. She's a bit disappointed that Spanish class was full, but so far likes her Hawaiian language and culture class.

Jade is not having an easy transition. She didn't make the varsity volleyball team (they'd been practicing much of the summer), and she can't join the JV team because she's a junior. But she did take a position as varsity team manager. Tonight there's a tournament so I'll make three trips to Waimea: dropping both off in the morning, picking up Faye at 3:10 p.m. and getting Jade at 9:30 p.m. I expect the late ride will be silent. She's not talking to me right now because I've moved her away from "home." I was in a damned if you do, damned if you don't predicament on the decision to move while she was still in high school. We could have waited until after her graduation (make her happy now), but at some point she would have complained that we didn't take her to Hawai'i with us (make her unhappy later). I really couldn't win, so I decided to move away from snow-land earlier.

I leave tomorrow night for the mainland. I'm not sure I accomplished all that I should have, but BG will have to take it from here. I feel guilty sticking him with the new problems that will arise. For example, Jade just mentioned she needs new bras. Why didn't she say something earlier? Still, I'll be back in six weeks. How much can go wrong?

Trip musings.

August 20. Kona, HI. As I sit at the airport waiting to leave, I record some final thoughts on my two weeks in Hawai'i to settle the family.

Most bizarre change of heart: by the end of this trip, I enjoyed the chickens. Once we moved into the main house with bedrooms in the back, it was easier to ignore the rooster noise. It's funny to see these chickens running around free. They *do* cross the road, frequently. And they are all colors: brown, rust, bronze, golden, white and black, some with speckles or patches of blue, red or teal. Some have fancy feather patterns, some have long feather plumes. These aren't your plain white chickens.

Most jolting realization: I'm going to spend a lot of time driving. A round trip to Waimea costs me an hour of time plus gas. And with gas at $4.23 compared to $3.49 in Racine, it hurts. There are substantial gas price differences across the island too. The cheapest is in Hilo – $4.09; the most expensive is Kona – $4.54. The closer you get to tourists, the more you spend on gas. But here's an example of my good luck: Honokaʻa is about equidistant between Hilo and Kona, so we have a choice of going to either for our big-box store shopping. People from Kona rarely go to Hilo and vice versa because it's too far.

Most amusing dilemma (if only it didn't happen to me): the post office wouldn't give us a PO Box because we didn't have proof of residence (mortgage documents were in Wisconsin, and we didn't have a utility bill with a Hawaiʻi address). The electric company wouldn't give us service because we didn't have a PO Box. The logjam cleared when the Water Board (the water company, not the torture method, though you couldn't tell by me) gave us service because we paid the $50 deposit. Their receipt had our physical address on it. I returned to the post office and got the PO Box, allowing us to obtain electric service. Apparently logistical issues like this happen all the time in Hawaiʻi. I'm not looking forward to obtaining local driver's licenses. I hear those are the worst.

Most valued fast food: A couple years ago, we'd read about the famous Big Island Loco Mocos in one of our guide books, then found them at Tex Drive In in Honokaʻa. Now we can eat them any time. It's a timesaver to make a quick stop on our way home from errands and buy a lunch I know everyone will eat, including my picky 12 year old. They also serve malasadas, which are small Portuguese sweet breads. I can't wait to continue sampling all the new foods available on this island – so many cultures to taste!

Most useful Hawaiian words: I'm learning some practical Hawaiian words. Mauka means towards the mountain, and makai means toward the sea. I find these two words very useful because I'm often asking for directions. The concept reminds me of my upbringing along Lake Michigan. There we said "toward the lake" and "away from the lake," because you always knew where the lake was. So mauka and makai are comfortable directional words for me because I always know where the mountain and ocean are. Maybe using that directional language as a child is the reason I still don't know left from right, or maybe it's my form of dyslexia.

Most appreciated local: Stacy, my real estate agent, loaned us three tables so that everyone could set up a work area. She gave us a printer, too, but BG decided to buy a new one despite his moaning about running through money like it was water. She also gave Faye gym clothes for Middle School and much advice about getting settled. She's becoming a friend.

Most changed person: Faye. She's turned into a responsible and grateful tween. Is that an oxymoron? She completes tasks I assign to her without grumbling and mostly when I tell her. More amazing still, she says thank you when it's correct to do so, often with a big smile. Perhaps it's because I gave her a house key (something she didn't have in Racine), or a cell phone (ditto). Or maybe I gave her those things because she's shaped up in a big way in a few short weeks. It's a nice spiral in a positive direction.

Most satisfying thought: I love my new house! I can't wait to turn it into our home. After owning it for a year on legal documents, I can now own it in my heart. It's better than I imagined. I love the 1930's plantation character, the yard's lush feel, the old avocado tree, the big lanais and of course, its location, location, location. Holy cow, this is really happening! Thank You, God!

Ditching my rock.

September 9. Racine, WI. Movers show up in two weeks and I'm still packing! Rita, my life coach, called to say goodbye and wish me luck. I can't thank her enough for helping me change my life. My boss sent me to her after he gave me a bad performance review. He thought I'd need support. He was right. Now I joke that I'm her new marketing director because I've convinced several people at work to hire her, and I sponsored a bunch of my people to consult her as well. It helps everyone in my department; we call it Rita Run-off.

We reminisced for a bit, talking about our time together. She asked, "Looking back on it all, which tool was your favorite?" That was a difficult question. She taught me many, and each helped at a different time for a different purpose. But I settled on an early exercise, identifying and getting rid of my unsupportive limiting beliefs – the stuff I carried around that prevented me from reaching my goals. That was necessary before she could help me create new beliefs. Rita asked me to write them all down, then burn the piece of paper in a purging ceremony. I decided to add my own twist: instead of paper, I found a large, flat rock in my garden. I brought it inside and cleaned it up properly. This was to be my offering. Using something solid from my own yard made the whole process more tangible. As I worked with Rita to uncover unsupportive things I'd been saying to myself, I carefully printed each on the rock:

- I'm not good enough.
- I'm a bad mother.
- I'm a fraud and "they" will find me out.
- I'm selfish to take time for self-care.
- I'm handcuffed to this job because I don't have enough money saved.

- I'm a failure if I don't get a promotion.
- I don't have time to explore other options for my life.
- I'm a traitor to my generation – I went corporate.

And others . . . they came out in our conversations, one by one. Soon the rock was full, so I flipped it over and started on the other side. There was satisfaction in uncovering the belief, working through it with her and writing it down. This was heart wrenching, sometimes gut wrenching, emotional work. I shed many tears over that rock hidden in my closet. It's hard to face your demons, examine them and purge them.

By the following summer I was ready to ceremonially rid myself of these beliefs and my rock. I brought it Up North to the lake we've been visiting every year since I was two. About midweek I asked my brother-in-law, Vitmer, to take me out on the lake in his pontoon boat. Ever the supportive rescuer type, he agreed and didn't raise any questions about the bag I brought on board and set at my feet. He has a depth finder, so I asked him to take me to the deepest spot out there. It was an overcast day and the lake surface reflected the gray of the sky. Fitting, I thought.

When we arrived I removed the rock from the bag and read each statement on it one more time, this time negating each phrase (I *am* good enough; I'm *not* a bad mother). I ritually heaved that rock into the lake where it presumably sits today, 32 feet down. Vitmer looked at me quizzically, but said nothing. As we turned around, the sky brightened, and I saw sparkles on the water. Thank you, Rita. Thank You, God. We motored to the cottages in silence. After my ceremony I felt good. So good that I spent the rest of the day with a great sense of relief and liberation. So good that I was sure I'd put some, if not all, of the statements to rest. So good that I started work on my plan to retire and move to Hawai'i. So good that I had a hard time remembering them for this essay. That's good.

Remember, you can look at pictures related to the essays on my website at www.ManifestingParadise.com/bookphotos.html.

2. SETTLING IN

Going out with a bang.

October 6. Honoka'a, HI. I did retire. I do love it here.

My last day at work was September 30 and I jumped on a plane the next morning, still cleaning and fussing right up to the last minute. Exhausted, I slept most of the flight. But as the plane prepared for landing, I could hardly contain my joy and exhilaration. I was so happy to see Jade, Faye and BG at the airport. We hugged long and hard and, of course, I cried.

My farewell party was a hoot. One person said he'd been to about two dozen retirement coffees and heard more laughter at mine than all the rest put together. I insisted that we call it a retirement "roast;" a "coffee" is just so Midwestern. What I didn't tell people was that I'd roast them as much as they roasted me. I was counting on humor to keep me from blubbering.

I've always been a bit too far out there to fit comfortably into the corporate mold. I'm too liberal, too loud and working class, too expressive and feeling. In earlier years, I tried to repress "me," but that only meant it popped out like a pimple under pressure at inconvenient times. I've slammed my fist down in a meeting full of peers. I've told a roomful of pompous gray-hairs that what they were doing was "bullshit." And many other examples, even more embarrassing to remember. But after working with Rita, I came to embrace "me" and relish being my authentic self. It didn't result in fewer embarrassing moments, but at least they were intentional and not of the angry variety. This is probably why I never made Vice President, and I came to realize that I didn't even want that. Being authentic with your truest desires does that to a person.

This roast was the moment to go all out. What were they going to do, fire me? I wore a full length, fully sequined, fire-engine red dress. I had my brunette hair highlighted with a lot of blonde the night before, something I'd wanted to do for years but was too chicken. I figure this will be the easy way to go gray. No more dying my hair; I have no intention of fussing now that I'm retired. My sister Grace doesn't think I'll stick with it. We'll see.

My favorite people roasted me with much loved stories. They also recorded the whole thing, a first at work as far as I know. There's something about a microphone that gets my juices going. I read the assembled group a true essay about the time I almost killed the current CEO and Chairman of the Board. This was a near accident, with him in the backseat of a car I was driving. It may have been one of the scariest incidents of my life, but I had the crowd roaring.

I revealed favorite quotes from each boss. Here's some of the best:

- "Diane, I never really thought of you as a woman." (He meant it as a sincere compliment.)

- "When I think of Scheurell, I smell money." (What was I supposed to say to that? Does that mean I should bathe more or less often?)

- "Diane, we don't swear." (Said on my first day at work.)

- "Your department is the crack cocaine of the rest of the research division." (He didn't mean it as a compliment.)

I've had some great bosses and I've had some doozies over the years. I eventually learned to stop taking comments like these personally.

I even sang a new verse I'd written for the song, *Oh Lord, Won't You Buy Me a Mercedes-Benz*, and then had the whole crowd joining me in the first verse. This is usually a staid Midwestern group, but not at *my* party. We had so much fun and I didn't even cry! That was the biggest surprise, because I've even been known to cry at Kleenex commercials. I guess that means I'm not looking back but forward.

At the end, a few stragglers asked me how I was able to put the corporate BS behind me. I told them I couldn't answer that question in a sentence or two, though I did say that tapping mentors and using a life coach were critical to rethinking my life because I became accountable to them. Rita helped me find the beliefs that drove my behavior at work and at home. If the belief still served me, we left it alone. For example, it's import to me to keep family ties strong. If anything, I'm even closer to my sisters now that both of my parents have passed.

If the uncovered belief didn't serve me, we worked to change it, using various exercises to attack it from different perspectives. The most difficult for me was "I'm not good enough." It started in my teens and intensified in college when I constantly compared myself to my genius first husband. It accelerated from there.

The stragglers were good friends, so I shared an exercise I wrote in 2007 that surfaced while cleaning out my computer files. This letter to myself explains the "not good enough" belief, and my struggle to purge it. I'd like to say that I'm cured, but it remained an issue for some time, and there are moments when I fear it could return. But authentic gratitude for my new life keeps it in check.

Killing the "I'm not Good Enough" Demon 11/03/07

Diane, it's time to address why I carry this falsehood that I'm not good enough. Part was being raised Catholic. Part was my dad's expectations. As a child, I learned that things are black or white, good or bad, success or failure.

Over many years I've addressed the black/white, good/bad dichotomy. As I became an independent adult, I didn't have the same definitions of good and bad as the Church. We diverged on many points but I made peace with my viewpoint on these issues. I was happy to rejoin the church after 35 years being away because, regardless of my personal beliefs about the church, I know I'm a good person. Instead, it's about taking time weekly to praise God in a community of caring people. The priest is a teacher. I listen to his sermons for inspiration, as much as I look to books that Rita recommends as a jumping-off point for thinking about issues. I see the true relationship is between God and me, a God who is loving and merciful, not judgmental. My reestablished relationship with God is a cornerstone to the peacefulness I've achieved and my belief that the Universe (God) listens and provides.

So let's tackle my beliefs on success and failure. All the work I've done in the past year prepared me to understand WHY I have these beliefs. First, my Catholic upbringing framed my definition. I could not both succeed and fail. Second, WHO decides the definition of failure? I looked to external figures (Dad, priest, school advisors) to decide. During my work life, I let the good old boys define my success. Did I make VP? No. Was it partially because of the glass ceiling for females in Research & Development? Yes. Was it partially because I didn't want to do the technical and manufacturing work required to succeed in their world? Yes. So OWN THAT.

Was it also because I knew I'd have to play the man's game? That I'd have to act and think differently? Yes, so own that too, and be proud! I chose not to lose my feminine compassion, my intuitive, feeling side. And frankly, would I want to be VP? No. I hate playing political games. OWN THAT!

So the external factor on why I wasn't "good enough" was the use of others' definitions of success. But here's the internal factor: I also believed and used their measuring stick to define my success. This self-assessment substantiated my fear that I was not good enough. I've been beating myself up to meet a standard I now do not accept as true, and using a measuring stick that I no longer believe is valid. Going deeper, I had told myself I'm not good enough because it served me. It made me "fail" in a system where, subconsciously, I didn't want to succeed. How convenient! I know in my gut and heart that had I "succeeded," I would not be living authentically.

The real learning is that I don't want to live by that thought process anymore. I don't want to continue wounding myself. I OVERTLY ACKNOWLEDGE THAT I DO NOT BELIEVE IN THE STANDARD DEFINITION OF SUCCESS. Now I get to create my own definition and my own measuring stick, where I cannot fail and I'm always good enough, even perfect, and certainly whole. I now choose to live differently, to be authentic, and to manage my department differently.

I'm more than good enough for my definition of success, which is that empowered people are formidable forces for moving goals forward, whether those are company objectives or social objectives. I believe that people who feel safe, nurtured and loved will spread that love to others. I believe that unconditional love moves mountains. I believe that diversity is crucial, especially diversity of thought. My work with the people in my department reflects that.

"I'm not good enough" no longer serves me. I don't need that crutch anymore. I can be an even more potent force for good if I relish my strengths. Face it, Diane, I'm in a powerful position. I am free to quit work. That means I can speak my truth. I can be true to the way I think, including feminine intuition, the way I feel and the way I pursue my team's needs. I am good enough. Own that!

Lazy living – interrupted.

October 13. Last weekend we conducted our home smudging. Our neighbor from Racine, a Buddhist priest, sent us a stick of incense to conduct the ceremony. It burned with a lovely scent as we walked through the main house, 'ohana, carport and yard, chanting the words that he'd given us. Our household is now blessed.

BG works during the day up in his office, the girls go to school, and I've been napping, reading and trying new foods. The old gent down the street asked if he could have some breadfruit off the tree in our yard. Since we didn't know what to do with it, we said yes. He brought me a cooked sample and told me how to prepare it. It was delicious. Since then I've boiled it, put it in soup, and fried it in butter. Unfortunately, no one else likes it. Too bad. It would be nice to use what we have growing in our own yard. Jade planted rosemary, oregano and basil a couple weeks ago in the back flower garden, but it's still a bit young to pick. We can't wait to savor her lasagna made with her own herbs.

I'm also eating and appreciating our oranges because I caught Faye's cold. No wonder I'm napping so much. Our avocado supply is still abundant, though one tree has finished its annual fruiting. Having never bought avocados in Georgia or Wisconsin, we enjoy experimenting with ways to prepare them.

Amy, my Racine neighbor, asked me, *"Are you sleeping on the lanai, with palm and banana branches waving nearby?"* Sorry to dash her vision, but I'm napping in my bed. However, I do hear lots of outside sounds, because my windows stay open day and night. Palm tree fronds make interesting sounds, clicking when the wind is a whisper, and clacking when it's strong. The first time I noticed this was a couple of years ago, when we stayed at the Waikoloa Beach Marriott during a night storm. I thought the noise was shells clattering together as they washed up on shore. At dawn, I hurried down to the beach and, to my surprise, I saw no shells. I finally realized it was the wind rustling the stiff palm fronds together.

Local birds also add to my nap music though, until I learn each call, their song will just be one blended melody. I hear a cow mooing makai, an occasional turkey and, of course, the roosters across the street. As for waving banana branches, I'm more interested in the fruit than the lulling rustle of leaves. We have five green bunches and I'm using the Internet to investigate when and how to harvest them. The instructions say to wait for one of the bananas to turn yellow, then chop the whole stalk down. Each stalk only makes one big bunch of bananas.

On Tuesday a good news/bad news call interrupted my lazy living: our household goods made an earlier boat from the west coast. So I'm suddenly scrambling to paint the dining and living rooms before our containers arrive. I don't want to paint while dancing around furniture and boxes.

Faye wants her bedroom blue. That's next. Jade doesn't know if she wants to make changes in her room. She still hasn't acknowledged this as home. I just discovered that she's mad at me because she had to go bra shopping with her dad while I was back in Racine. She was embarrassed to death because BG took her to the power tools check-out where a macho young local rang up her purchase. Naturally, that's my fault.

This afternoon I ran out of paint so tomorrow I have to run to Kona to buy another gallon at Home Depot. That's more than an hour each way. On the other hand, I can gas up at Costco while I'm there. We finally broke down and joined because they have mainland prices on goods and somewhat reduced prices for gas. It costs us about $7.00 round trip to take the girls to school. With different pick-up times, that's more than $100 in gas every week just for school runs. Ouch. One does pay a price to live in paradise. Until I moved here, I didn't know that these are the most remote islands on Earth, and certainly far from Mideast oil fields. On the other hand, we have no air conditioning or heating bill and our water is solar heated. So, pick your poison . . . or paradise.

Our first earthquake!

October 19. The walls of the dining and living rooms were dark mustard yellow but I painted them light green – very calming. Good thing I got it done, because the first container of our household goods arrived today. I'd boxed up and inventoried all my stuff and the girls' belongings, so I knew what boxes went where. With luck, this is the last time in my life that I have to be so organized. BG didn't make time to pack, so his stuff was unlabeled except for the moving company's stickers. They hoisted multiple heavy boxes upstairs to the 'ohana where he set up his office. They pushed, dragged and shoved others into the carport and stacked them four boxes high, including two large metal milk crates full of rocks. Don't ask.

The crew leader, Kalani, and I were in the middle of matching my box numbers with the moving company's stickers, when the whole house shook. I heard and felt a low rumble, and the old paned windows rattled in their frames. We stopped talking, stood still and looked at each other in surprise. "Earthquake," Kalani murmured, his eyes darting around, as if he could see it. I knew right away what it was – my *first* earthquake! It was over before I could react, so I can't say I was scared. We felt one aftershock, though Faye informed us there were two, according to a website her classmates checked after emerging from beneath their desks. She thought it was cool. Jade was unsettled and distressed. I thanked God neither was harmed.

The movers kidded BG, "Brah, must be fault line under 'ohana. Da kine prob'ly cause da quake." Da kine boxes full of stuff, indeed! I wish BG had purged before we moved, but just convincing him to stop picking up treasures on trash day was difficult. As I predicted, he has only pig-paths through the carport and 'ohana, and the second container load comes tomorrow! Anyway, I have something I can cross off my bucket list. Did you hear that God? You don't need to send any more earthquakes!

Pumpkin Patch volunteer.

October 23. Today was the school's fall fundraising festival, the Pumpkin Patch. I helped Stacy with the Caesar Salad booth. Yesterday, at her house, we washed, chopped and bagged 100 pounds of donated organic baby greens of all kinds and colors. The tequila, chips and artichoke dip she served helped us work faster as the afternoon wore on, and no one lost a finger.

Then, today, we hustled to the school after Mass. Faye's Hawaiian class opened the ceremonies, reciting a chant and dancing a traditional Hawaiian hula. They looked great with synchronized moves and their prayerful arms and far-seeing eyes lifted to east and west. Even their forceful movements matching powerful sections of the chant appeared graceful. They pointed and arched bare feet with precision. Faye seems to like her Hawaiian class. She can translate some words already and corrects our pronunciation of street names.

Jade volunteered her time selling cotton candy and musubi, a local delicacy of grilled sliced Spam on top of rice, all rolled in seaweed. Faye loves them. I worked on the other end of campus. In our booth, we used a motif of Halloween and cowboys; Waimea is paniolo (cowboy) country. We wore black cowboy hats with gold skulls on them and Stacy found bandanas at Mama's Thrift Shop. We hawked our product so successfully that, of all the food booths, ours sold out first. Yeah! I'm afraid the spirit of aloha has not yet curbed my competitive spirit.

Now we're finally home. I'm pooped and ready to sit. Only it's hard to unwind with so many boxes stacked up around me. I'd try a nap but I'd be down for the night, so I'm off to push some boxes around. I hope they don't push back.

Aloha is real.

October 24. I've referenced "the spirit of aloha" a couple of times. I'm not just spitting out a cliché, though one does hear the word quite often. I see bumper stickers encouraging us to Be Aloha, Live Aloha and Practice Aloha, so it's clearly more than hello and goodbye. The real aloha isn't just a greeting, but a way of seeing the world, a fellowship mindset. I felt it often as we visited and it drew me here. Aloha is about doing the right thing, especially for the 'āina – the land. It's about relationships and spiritual awareness. Someone told me that practicing aloha is actually a state law!

We experienced aloha directly just before our goods and second car arrived. I needed to pick up the girls but found the CRV battery dead. Yelling to BG to come down and look at the car, I ran over to Ted's gas station. But Ted and his bright blue truck were gone. The nice guy who fills my gas tank said, "I can't leave. But take this battery starter." He didn't even ask for a credit card as collateral! So I grabbed the starter and quickly marched home.

Someone who had been gassing up while the attendant and I talked drove past the house just as I got there. He rolled down his window. "You need help?"

"Oh, thank you so much. But we think we're good now." We smiled and waved him on his way too soon. The battery charger unit itself was dead. Rats. So while BG ranted at the car, I ran back to Ted's. "The charger's dead. Do you have another?"

The attendant, a local, called over to someone filling his tank. "Hey, Brah, you got jumpers?"

"Ya, what you need?"

"Can you jump this lady's car? She live roun' da corner."

"Ya, no worries." Turning to me, he said, "Jump in."

I waivered for a moment. All our lives Dad warned us to stay away from strangers, and certainly never get into a car with one! But I spied his toddler in the back seat and she waved at me sweetly. How dangerous could a daddy be? So off we went, my dad's ashes probably swirling in his box. The guy pulled his jumpers from the back of his car, hooked them up and our CRV roared back to life. I was so grateful. I grabbed a twenty out of my wallet and handed it to him as I thanked him profusely.

But he backed away. "I don't need that."

"Oh, please take it. You helped me so much." I was worried that I had insulted him.

After a pause, he grinned and said, "Okay, I buy ice cream for her," motioning to his daughter. Most Wisconsinites are helpful to neighbors, but this was three different people offering aid, and two of them were complete strangers!

People here smile at visitors, say hello on the street, do things for others and generally act a bit more graciously, some would say more slowly. Recent transplants and tourists joke about "island time," but I like the warm feeling that goes along with this leisurely pace. I already know some of the shopkeepers and people at church who inquire after the girls. I never took time for chitchat back on the mainland, but here I stop and talk. I'm enjoying the receiving end of aloha, but I also have a responsibility to change my ways and practice it. I'm trying.

Living the dream.

October 26. The girls are the closest to being unpacked and they have fully claimed their rooms. Both are adjusting now that the newness has worn off, though they still give me stink eye. They've made friends, but talk frequently with old pals back in Racine. Jade went to her friend Audrey's house over the weekend to decorate t-shirts for a school event. Audrey's family has a hobby farm and they raise horses. Jade even rode one. Faye was gone Saturday, too, joining others from her class to work on a science project. I'm grateful that they're fitting in.

It's hard to believe I've been here almost four weeks. I'm still saying "pinch me." Unfortunately my bruises are not from that, but from unpacking and banging into boxes. For weeks I complained that I didn't have any of my stuff. Now that our belongings are here, I can't get at the stuff I want because boxes remain piled precariously high in many rooms. I pushed my way through the living room boxes, but nothing is arranged, just randomly put on shelves. The kitchen needs major work, but I can maneuver enough to cook. I've assumed the cooking job again. I thought BG and I were going to fight over it, but it's been a peaceful transition. We're both good cooks, making most dishes from scratch and avoiding processed foods. But he cooks with a lot of oil and butter and I want to maintain or even improve my weight loss after all the work I did preparing for the move.

The last thing I want is to bring on diabetes just as I begin living among all these new sweet fruits. One of them is passion fruit. No, it's not named that because it makes one amorous. Its flower shape reminded missionaries who "discovered" it of the Passion of Christ. In Hawaii, it's called lilikoi. Tart and sweet, crunchy and slippery, no amount of explaining will do it justice. It doesn't grow in my yard, but my yoga teacher has an abundance and readily shares. I need to plant some myself because I can't find them in grocery stores or at the farmer's markets. I think the plant's so ubiquitous that no one thinks to sell them.

Last week, as I walked around my yard, I spotted a flower with the most wondrous shape and colors: a pink fan flanked by purple petals. This is a fantasy flower worthy of any child's free-form coloring. It's called Tallandsia Cyanea. I have a botanical garden right in my yard. I used to say "life is good" but that phrase isn't *big* enough anymore. I've switched to "living the dream."

Still talking to God.

November 4. I'm closer to God now than ever before. Her hand is everywhere in this lush tropical wonderland, and a quick thank you is never far from my lips. We choose to worship in Waimea because the Catholic church there is a larger parish than the one in Honoka'a and has a bigger class of teens preparing for Confirmation. I want Jade in that larger class. Initially I worried that I wouldn't love my parish here as much as I did St. Richard's in Racine. I didn't think anyone could match the warm, down-to-earth sermons of Father Ron or Father Jack before him. Father Jack helped me come back to the church after 35 years.

I truly believe that God, my Higher Spirit, the Universe, whatever you want to call Her, has guided me in the last eight years, and that I wouldn't be here today if it weren't for my prayers and affirmations. While unpacking, I found a prayer I wrote, stuck in a book of daily readings. I thoroughly enjoyed reading it again.

> Dear Holy Spirit, 6/16/07
>
> Thank You for all Your blessings over the past few years. Thank You for bringing me back to the church, December 2003. I'm thankful that my children have the opportunity to live consciously in the grace of God. I'd forgotten how important it was for me to live in a community of worship. Thirty-five years was a long time to be lost. Thank You for never abandoning me.
>
> You guided Rita into my life in 2004. Through her, I healed my wounds, reflected deeply and came to a new understanding of myself and the world around me. I took up the spirit of unconditional love to the best of my ability and continue to evolve. I learned that loving first, without expecting anything back, wasn't a sign of weakness. I learned to trust the Universe, another name for You. I learned to "feel the fear and do it anyway." I finally

understood the meaning behind St. Francis of Assisi's words: "Preach the Gospel always; use words if necessary." At last I'm living an authentic, loving, and turn-the-other-cheek kind of life.

Now Rita is back in my life again, this time helping me focus on being happier. She gives me the courage to really examine my life and decide to do something different with it. To *decide* – to consciously *choose* a better life is the first step. It would be so easy to stay on my old path. But Your wisdom helped me realize that I only have so many years on earth and I want to spend them blissfully. So I'm embarking on a journey to find joy and contentment. Now I have to take the next steps. I appreciate your guidance. You've always been there for me. I only had to listen.

Your loving daughter, Diane

Isn't that cool? And a written prayer is better than a spoken one because it truly cements the intention. Now I'm responsible for paying my good fortune forward to others.

Winter in Hawai'i.

November 15. Surprisingly, we do have a winter season – late October to March – and it's rainier than summer. Right now morning temperatures start out in the mid 60s, cool enough to need socks, pants, a sweatshirt and sometimes even a hat. As the day warms up, I take off the hat, remove the sweatshirt and, finally, exchange pants for shorts. With no heat or AC, we've learned to change clothes frequently to match fluctuating temperatures. The high may reach 80°F. Afternoons are sticky if the trades stop blowing, a good time to nap. At night I sleep with a down comforter but windows are open.

It's dark around 5:30 p.m. at this time of year, though that beats 3:30 in the dead of winter in Wisconsin. It's light by 6:30 a.m. This is a nice change, though I'm guessing I'll miss the longer daylight hours of Wisconsin in summer. Hawai'i doesn't switch to Daylight Savings Time. We're close enough to the equator that we don't need to save daylight and apparently we don't give a damn about what the mainland does.

I can't relate to reports of 19° F in Wisconsin and I've only been gone since October first. When my sister and I visited the island last November and the temperature hovered around 70°, we saw a woman working in a local shop wearing a turtleneck sweater, corduroy jumper and heavy tights. We laughed about it when we got back to the car. I can now see how I might be that way in a couple of years. Maybe sooner!

This weekend we ate turkey. The two big Waimea grocery stores are in the midst of a turkey war. Foodland started with an offer of a turkey for $6.00 if you buy $25 worth of groceries. That's $6.00 for the whole turkey! KTA shot back with $2.99 for a whole turkey. Then Foodland offered a *free* frozen turkey with a "Product of the Week" coupon. We've been accumulating coupons, so we picked up three, each 15 to 16 pounds, and all free! If we could fit another in the freezer, we'd have four! Many families are depending on the food pantry this year so I used our remaining coupons to donate turkeys to the pantry. I lugged four frozen birds over there last week and another this morning.

On the other end of the wealth spectrum, last weekend Faye attended a classmate's party at the Hualalai Four Seasons Resort. I needed directions so I checked out the realty section of the website. It was full of phrases like luxury villas, distinguished addresses, multimillion dollar homes, 40 miles of pristine coast, and exquisite luxury. I was almost afraid to show up! The classmate lives there and her parents rented the residents' Canoe Club complete with bar loaded with pupus, a large pool, and a hot tub covered by a thatched roof. They also hired trainers to teach Zumba; the winning team won $10 iTunes cards. Faye said there were complimentary hairbrushes in the changing locker. Yikes.

Impressive but, to my taste, the atmosphere was artificial. The resort's several communities consist of villas and big houses that look the same, on tiny lots that look the same, amid oases of perfectly manicured golf greens interspersed among lava fields. All the streets look the same. We got lost even *with* directions. It's a great environment for a week's vacation, but I can't imagine living there. No church, bank, school, post office, library, farmer's market or roosters. It's a sterile place, though wild goats do live on the nearby lava. An acquaintance said she often sees them browsing on the resort's manicured grass.

I'm not making a judgment about people who choose that lifestyle, just reconfirming it's not for me. I prefer the real town where I live with real people, mostly working class, from many backgrounds and cultures. The divide between wet and dry sides is more than geography. I'll take our one-and-only four-way stop instead of fancy resort roundabouts any day.

It finally stopped raining.

November 18. After unrelenting rain for seven days, everything inside is damp. Paper in our printer droops, the air smells humid, surfaces in the bathroom feel clammy, even the wool runner in the hallway seems to squish. Today is sunny with a dry breeze. Thank God! I've been here in November and December, but never experienced this kind of rain.

We'd planned to leave all the dehumidifiers with the house in Racine, but the movers packed one by mistake. We're glad to have it. We plugged it in yesterday, and it dried out the house a bit and warmed it up, too. It's been around 66°F but, with no heat, that gets old after a while. My feet are especially cold with all the wood and tile flooring. A local told me that November is the wettest month, so I'm hoping the worst may soon be over.

Jade recently turned 17 and Faye turns 13 in December. We'll celebrate both birthdays spending a night at the Waikoloa Marriott over the Thanksgiving break. It will be warmer there, maybe even hot – a nice escape. I'm grateful that the girls are doing well. Both made first quarter honor roll, both have close friends, and no one is talking about seceding from the union any more, though they still take any opportunity to grump about the move.

In fact, as Jade begins narrowing college choices, she's discovering that a Hawaiian address will help her. At least that's what the school's college counselors say. She's considering colleges in Oregon and Wisconsin. It kills me that we might be paying out-of-state tuition to a Wisconsin school after paying so much in taxes while a resident. But we'll pay out-of-state tuition wherever she goes. I love the clever essay she developed for UW-Madison: "My address says Hawai'i, my face says China, and my name says Ireland, but I'm a Cheesehead at heart."

I've found almost everything that went missing during the move. It will all turn up. We still have many boxes to empty. Luckily, they all fit in the carport; we're no longer dancing around them in the house. So life approaches normal, though I'm not sure what that is because I have a new title: "retired."

I'm regularly attending yoga class. I walk to the post office and see people I know. I have a State of Hawai'i library card and I get books once a week. (Quaint local note: our library still checks books and videos out by stamping a date on a card pasted on each. I haven't seen that in a long time.) I'm looking for a place to volunteer, checking out my options. I think there are lots of places where I can apply my talents. I just have to find one that can sustain my passion.

Planned for retirement. (do your homework)

I've been retired about six weeks, and I don't miss any aspect of the corporate environment. No "buyer's remorse." It's been such an easy transition, probably because I planned it for so long. I stepped off the plane and into my new life. Like the athlete who mentally goes through her event time and again, when she finally runs the race, she pulls it off flawlessly. Muscle memory carries her across the finish line. I'm that athlete pulling off retirement. Still living the dream.

Taos women's seminar.

November 20. I just received a reminder about a seminar that I attended twice in New Mexico, called Passion for Leadership, Voice for Change. It's possible I'd be ready to go to Taos again in May, but I doubt it. I need time to process all the big changes in my life before I work through anything new, although I am starting to fret about what's next. What *is* the focus of my life now? The two seminar organizers, Dr. Barbara P. and Dr. Barbara C. sent along a personal note that advised me to take time to "shed the layers." I wrote about that in my journal last night. I can see myself shedding layers every week. Eventually I'll rediscover the "stripped down" me, though I don't think it'll take too long. I've been working on being authentic ever since I attended their seminar the first time, back in September 2004.

I'm sure glad I knew one of them before that seminar – someone to vouch for me. Considering that it was a women's leadership class, I wasn't exactly in the right frame of mind; a week earlier my boss gave me a "needs development" rating on a performance review. I arrived with an attitude: ashamed, withdrawn and stony faced, worried I'd be shunned, and anxious that I might have to reveal my dirty little secret. My perspective was so corporate-twisted. Then I started listening to other women's stories about being fired or losing husbands to death or divorce. One even described having a heart attack. We all cried with her. My story of "not being good enough" was so small compared to these remarkable women.

That seminar turned me around, not only in recovering from the poor performance review, but in finding myself again. We did exercises that allowed me to express my anger. I learned that self-care is not selfish, but important to maintaining balance. Their message that women must "find their voice" hit me hard. I had never thought of myself as a weak woman, but I realized that I had lost my voice on occasion. We talked about being authentic, being ourselves even in a corporate world. It was the first time I had thought about authenticity. Now I'm living it.

A by-product of that seminar was discovering the existence of sacred spaces. Taos reverberated with an energy I didn't know existed. Being in that sacred space fueled my healing. I came away wanting to live in a place like that. At the time, I thought it meant finding a different place to work, but now I know it led me here, to Hawaiʻi.

On a lark, I went back to my journal entry on the day I returned:

> Dear God,   Monday, September 27, 2004
>
> I feel energized. I am good enough. I am worthy. I am a very good manager. I know now that the company has no intention of firing me. I am going back to my old department where I can succeed. The performance review rating was only a "needs development." While I could hardly say the words last week, I have internalized that it's just a one-year label, something to improve upon.
>
> What I now know is that I don't care whether I ever become a director, ever join "the club." This will likely create different behavior in me. If I cannot improve my relationship with that higher-level committee, it's okay. It only means that my way of doing things is not compatible with theirs. It does not mean that my way is wrong. I just have to find a management group with whom I can feel congruent, even harmonious. I know now that I can choose to leave this company or stay. It's my choice.
>
> I also realized that I need to live in a sacred space. I either need to find a new job located in sacred space or buy weekend property in a sacred space so I can escape to it.
>
> Knowing all these things, and feeling as good about them as I do today, are two different things. I'll have to work to keep this perspective, unless it's a paradigm shift – that would be too easy! I came to work joyful today, instead of dreading it. I hope this is not a passing mood. Amen.

I didn't understand the acuity and profoundness of that last paragraph when I wrote it. I realize now that it *was* a paradigm shift. Dr. Barbara P. and Dr. Barbara C., along with my coach, helped me achieve my dreams. I began working with Rita immediately after that seminar and we built off my new insights.

Five years later, when I took their seminar again, I went with a far different intent. I listened to my aspirations, decided to *believe* the retirement calculations on my multiple spreadsheets, and cemented the plan that brought me to Hawai'i. I chose to trust that I could manifest my paradise. That was an important tool Rita taught me. Decide and take action. "Be a bold decision-maker." By combining Rita's tools with the Barbaras' powerful message, it was bound to happen. All I had to do was implement the plan.

Remember, you can look at pictures related to the essays on my website at www.ManifestingParadise.com/bookphotos.html.

3. CELEBRATING THE HOLIDAYS

Feeling closer to God.

November 27. My favorite time of year at church is celebrating Christmas and the activities leading up to it. For our church's Thanksgiving Mass, people of all ethnicities wore their traditional native dress and brought cultural foods for Father to bless. I didn't make the trip up the mountain just to have Father Bob pray over my sauerkraut. Besides, the closest I have to a Czech outfit is a Renaissance wench costume, probably not appropriate for Mass.

That's not the only special event our church held this month. To celebrate All Saint's Day, Father Bob commemorated all 13 people from the parish who died this past year, aged 19 to 90, including the 21-year-old killed in Afghanistan in August. As he read each name, the church bell tolled and two ladies lit a candle for each person. After Mass, Father invited family members to take the candles with them. It made me cry. The next week he commemorated Veterans Day by inviting all the parish veterans to come up and give their names (such an abundance of diversity) and their branch in the armed services. They had served in everything from WWII, the Korean War and Vietnam, to Coast

Guard duty off Hawaiian waters. Women were well represented too; the choir director was in the medical corp.

I enjoy this parish. They mark special days and draw us together as a community, making sure we know each other as people, not just faces. It's practicing aloha at the parish level. I love Father Bob. His sermon gives me something new to chew on every week. He's articulate and never loses me or puts me to sleep. Deacon Larry speaks from his heart. He's 72 and has a big booming voice which he commands with perfect intent. He makes us laugh and makes me cry. You can hear a pin drop in that church when he speaks. I think I'm going to volunteer to be a lector. It's time to integrate myself into the community and show my gratitude for finding this place.

I am thankful for so many things, including feeling closer to God. I felt the sacred energy on the Big Island from the first time we visited. And I have more time to think about God here; Her work is so close. For example, weather in Waimea is usually different from Honoka'a, 1500 feet lower. Waimea is not often sunny but, when it is, sunshine can coexist with a sideways mist flying in on the ever-present trades. As a result, Waimea has many rainbows, often doubles.

Recently I drove through a gloomy rain into sunshine and witnessed the most intense double rainbow I'd ever seen. It was right on the upper school grounds. The lower rainbow hung in front of me, brilliantly vivid, so saturated with color that I felt I could touch it. When I drove through it, the rainbow disappeared. Coming back down the school's driveway, Jade and I broke through it from the other side, and looking back, saw it again, still intensely drenched with color. I felt like I'd passed through something miraculous. The intensity of the light and the colors made me joyful. My heart was bursting. It sounds corny but the feelings were real and I thanked God for the gift of that moment.

Other examples materialized at the Waikoloa Marriott this weekend when we celebrated the girls' birthdays. On Friday afternoon we discovered five Hawaiian Green Sea Turtles basking on the beach – such large lovely old spirits. I also watched the sun set. It's special for me to see the sun go over the horizon. Even when I'm on the west side of the island and the day starts out sunny, by evening clouds often cover the skyline. This can be the result of "vog" (volcanic fog) blowing off our active volcano Kilauea during the afternoon and settling on the Kona side. So it was a real treat yesterday to actually see the sun setting. I have a beautiful memory of that large orange ball slowly sinking. Wind rustled nearby palms. Then, calm and quiet – another moment with God.

The Span of Spam.

November 30. I was at a church supper enjoying the potluck when I took a forkful of spaghetti with sauce. As I bit down into the ground beef, I stopped abruptly. The texture was wrong, softer than it should be. I cautiously explored the meat chunk with my tongue. I felt regular squared-off corners. Wait, it's a cube. This can't be hamburger. Then it dawned on me – Spam!

Spam is practically the State Food. This is a local custom I can't adopt because nitrites in bacon, sausage, Spam and other processed meats are a migraine trigger. The only time I ever ate it was in college when I went camping, long before I knew about headache triggers. It was easy to transport and I couldn't ruin it on a campfire. Locals here eat it regularly: Native Hawaiians,

Portuguese, Filipinos, Okinawans, Japanese, Chinese – everyone eats Spam with gusto. The custom dates back to WWII when soldiers traded their K-rations, including Spam, to locals for fresh fruit, fish and vegetables. Locals found the canned meat a change and a convenience because people didn't have refrigerators to prevent spoilage back then. But they may have taken this love affair too far.

Last week Father Bob asked the parish keiki how many had turkey for Thanksgiving. A few kids shyly raised their hands. Then he asked how many would rather have Spam. About two-thirds of them enthusiastically waved. If this is any indication, then the maker of Spam, Hormel, has no need to worry about future sales.

We have a custom at our church to welcome all visitors. When people identify themselves as Minnesotans, we chuckle because we know what's coming next. Deacon Larry will make a big deal about thanking them and their state for being the home of Hormel, and can even work it into his sermon at times.

People eat Spam fried, with the obligatory scoops of rice or potato salad, *and* macaroni salad on the side for a plate lunch. Breakfast is fried Spam with fried eggs and hash browns. People cook with it as a natural substitute for ham. But many locals also use it in place of ground beef, which I discovered at the church supper. Spam enjoys such a central place in people's lives that the Country Fair in Hawi, a village on the north end of the island, had a carved Spam exhibit. I kid you not! While I didn't see it myself, someone I know verified that she saw and smelled the carved specimens. She said it's lucky we don't have many flies.

And varieties! I didn't know there were so many! Of course, there's original Spam, now called Spam Classic. But I'm guessing that our local stores carry every kind of Spam that Hormel makes. A cursory look at the Spam section at KTA showed Turkey Spam, Hot & Spicy, Hickory Smoked, Spam with Bacon, Jalapeno, Black Pepper, Spam with Cheese, less sodium Spam, Spam Lite (what's that?) and, of course, Spam Classic. Besides a complete shelf of Classic, another full shelf was reserved for less sodium Spam. I guess people who eat Spam are concerned about their blood pressure. Then there's Spam Singles in Classic and Lite pouch varieties. Finally, on the top shelf, I spied Spam Spread. I also saw Hormel pickled pig feet in jars, not technically Spam, but far more interesting to scrutinize.

One Spam product that may only be available in Hawai'i is Spam Classic-flavored macadamia nuts. Yes, believe it. It's not a Hormel product, but the nut company uses the Spam name. It has to be a niche product but, then again, this is Hawai'i. We even have a yearly Spam Festival on O'ahu, the Waikīkī Spam Jam. Proceeds from the event benefit the Hawai'i Food Bank.

Because of my migraines, I never served Spam, so the girls never had it growing up. But now Faye loves it, especially on musubi. Jade tried it once. "No, thank you." BG experiments now and again. I found a can of Spam with Cheese on the kitchen counter the other day. As a Wisconsin Cheesehead, I was almost intrigued enough to try it. Almost.

Spam A Lot - Broadway

Girl time.

December 5. I had a great weekend with the girls. I took Faye, Jade, and two of Jade's friends to the Marriott in Waikoloa on Saturday night. This was our second mini-vacation there in two weeks, and basically free with my Marriott points. We had such a great time the night we spent there over Thanksgiving break that we decided to go again, mostly so I wouldn't have to drive Jade home after her high school's Winter Ball held at the Waikoloa Hilton.

We arrived in the afternoon and headed straight for the many pools, relaxing there for a couple of hours. Then Jade and her friends prepped for the dance. Jade never acquired a habit of using makeup, so she needed assistance with dark eyeliner, blue eye shadow and a pale shade of lip gloss. All the girls had great dresses. The final touch was high heels. (I remember those days, but not with fondness. I haven't worn heels in many years. Now all I wear is sandals.) They looked fabulous, like young women ready to go out clubbing. Jade was so beautiful. She'll be off to college next year and I'll miss her.

Faye and I dropped the older girls at the dance and then went for some quality mother-daughter time. She wanted sushi. I trust things will appear when I ask the Universe so, of course, we found a sushi restaurant near our hotel. Sensei has since become Faye's favorite place to eat.

We talked about how I'd like her and Jade to gain a broader palate and that I was proud that she loved poke, sushi and other Japanese food. But otherwise she's a very picky eater. She almost never eats dinner, though I do insist she sit with us. I'm worried about the nutritional value of what she eats. She replied that, with all the changes going on (the move, making new friends, moving up to eighth grade instead of seventh) she needed to stay in her comfort zone with food. I took a good look across the table and saw a mature poised young lady. Where is my baby? It went so fast. She'll be grown in the blink of an eye, too. I resolved to spend more time with both of them over the Christmas break.

Diane M. Scheurell

Putting things in God's Hands. *take up journaling*

December 12. I wish the girls would take up journaling. It's been one of the key tools for my personal transformation. Sometimes it's the fastest way to learn something about myself. When I just think about things, the ideas don't solidify as fast as when I write them down. The act of writing does the crystallizing. Once it's on paper, it becomes real. I can deny a fleeting thought, but not a sentence on paper. I don't typically go back and read what I wrote because it's not about capturing moments for history. It's about capturing something to make it clear to me right now and for the future. I build on what I learn.

My journaling is also part of my daily prayers, putting things in God's hands. It's my request for help. I start every entry with "Dear God." The act of writing causes neurons in our brain to connect. As the writing flows, it helps solve our problems, or at least quiets our anxiety in the act of turning it over to God. I end every entry with "Dear Holy Spirit, grant me a day of grace, and fill me with Your spiritual energy." I'm not greedy. I don't ask for a lifetime of grace, but I'm persistent. Every day I ask for a day of grace and I'm not disappointed.

I don't know what I would've done without that spiritual energy during those six weeks when I packed up the house in Wisconsin. It kept me healthy when others caught colds and it kept me relatively migraine free. I actually had the energy needed to put in a full day at work and then come home and work for several more hours! It's a miracle I made it through all that! But why should I be surprised? Trust – Ask – Accept with Gratitude.

The holidays are upon us. I may bake cookies for the first time in years. Who knows, maybe I'll even tackle a vánočka, my family's

Trust – Ask – Accept with Gratitude

traditional Czech Christmas bread. Whoa, that was a new thought. The act of writing *does* create statements one didn't know were coming! I'd better stop writing or I'll have myself committed to several new projects that I shouldn't start until I've organized the carport, arranged my closet, and alphabetized the spices.

Translating yoga into surfing.

December 22. This year we popped over to Maui for a few days during the girls' holiday break. It's just one island over – inexpensive as Hawai'i vacations go. The girls wanted surfing lessons as their Christmas gift, but were hesitant unless BG or I went along. Much like the horseback riding adventure last year, I "won the toss." Paying $25 extra, we bought a private lesson, and got lucky with our instructor Johnny, a young surfer with a patient, "you can do it" attitude. With his blond hair sticking out of his red cap, broad smile and confidence, he easily won us over. We were excited to start. Well, the girls were excited. I was apprehensive until I saw I could use my yoga training.

We started practicing with a board on dry land. As Johnny demonstrated the moves, I translated each one into yoga. First, assume *Plank* position to situate yourself onto the back end of the board. Lie down, paddle, turn around and face shore. When the wave feels right, paddle hard, then follow through with an *Up-dog*. Pull your knees forward and plant your foot forward firmly, as if you were about to do a *Warrior Lunge*. Quickly plant your back foot at a 45° angle and rise up into *Warrior Two*. Now ride the wave to shore! If you begin to fall assume the *Shavasana* position to create a big surface area and break the fall on the water's surface, rather than on the coral beneath. With that tutorial and the confidence I gained from relating surfing to yoga, I was ready to surf.

Faye went first. She was a natural. Having danced ballet for many years, she has good form and excellent balance. She scrambled up and coasted to shore. Jade went next. With the confidence of her natural athletic abilities, she nimbly stood and rode her wave. While I waited for my turn, I pondered what the hell I was doing, and cursed my hubris. What's an almost 60-year-old doing on a surf board? I was tired just paddling out there! Thankfully, Johnny chose a fat, old, stable board for a fat, old, unstable broad. I said a quick prayer to God that I wouldn't break any bones, then readied myself. Johnny talked to me calmly and confidently as we waited for the right wave. When it came, he shoved my board and I was off. I paddled, did the Up-dog, pulled myself into a kneeling position . . . and froze. But I rode my wave to shore, smiling all the way. I didn't even get my hair wet, for which Johnny congratulated me when I paddled back out.

Next time, I again pulled into the kneeling position, but saw a child *directly* in my path. I quickly executed the technique Johnny taught us; look away and your board will follow you in that direction. It worked! I didn't collide with the boy and made it to shore without wetting my hair or my pants! No Shavasana needed. Johnny congratulated me on avoiding the collision. With my third wave, I planted my front foot in the lunge position. But that took me so long, I landed on shore before I could do any more.

Paddling back out, I felt exhausted. It dawned on me that this would have to be my last wave. When I told Johnny, he said we'd try something different. He instructed me to start in the kneeling position to give me more time to stand before I reached shore. He gave me a strong shove, and with the resolve that came from knowing this was my last chance, I pulled my front foot forward, planted my back foot and stood up. Yeah, I was surfing!! Look at me! I'm surfing! It was exhilarating: the wind in my face, the approaching shoreline, and my family cheering me. I was grateful when the wave petered out near shore and I stepped off the board, dizzy and disoriented, but hair dry to the very end!

Triumphantly, I dragged my board up the beach, where I collapsed near BG and put my glasses on. Now I could see the girls more clearly as they gracefully cruised into shore. When the lesson ended we had high fives all around. It's a sweet, proud memory, and I've crossed one more thing off my bucket list. But I would not have made it without the yoga I learned from my dear teachers. The muscle memory was there. And my teachers were there, too, cheering me on inside my head.

Yoga has taught me breathing, meditation, balance, core strength, flexibility and patience. Well, I'm still working on patience. But now I can say it taught me surfing, too. Call me Surfer Girl.

Home for the holidays.

December 24. It was nice to spend a few days in Maui last week, finally seeing a different island. Life is so different living on one island in a group of islands. While Oahu and Maui may have more department stores and chain restaurants, that does us no good on Hawai'i. Of course, they get hurricanes when we don't. Local lore has it that major storms pass us by, veering away from the mass of Mauna Kea and Mauna Loa.

Surfing was fun. The girls went a couple of times. They looked so graceful on their boards gliding in toward shore – real island girls.

Well, there was that moment when Faye fell onto the board of the guy next to her and then nimbly stepped back onto her own. She just continued her ride toward shore. Is that clumsiness or superior agility? Except for that, I could hardly tell them from all the other beautiful Hawaiian and Asian girls on their boards.

Still, it's good to be at home for the holidays. It'll be the first time in many years. We've always taken a Christmas vacation, scouting possible retirement locations. With that decision behind us, we can enjoy a family Christmas here. As for decorations, I'm scaling back and simplifying. I'm even waiting until the day after Christmas to get a bargain on an artificial tree.

Meanwhile, we have the sad little Charlie Brown tree with its one red ball, sitting on the living room cabinet. I put up the patchwork Christmas stockings in time for St. Nick's feast day visit. I can never remember if it's on December 6 or 7, so I just go with Pearl Harbor Day. There's always a news story to help me remember to fill the stockings, especially here. That's it, except for the crèche we leave out all year and one large wreath that had been buried in the Racine garage and moved with all the other detritus. I'll hang it outside today.

I'm already accustomed to seeing Christmas lights strung up on palm trees and depictions of Santa in aloha shirts or on a surf board. On the other end of the spectrum, the crèches look far more authentic without snow. And the large poinsettia hedges and bushes in people's yards are spectacular. I have poinsettia envy. Maybe I'll plant one.

We're roasting a turkey today, perfect for Christmas Eve. We took it out of the freezer before we left for Maui. I'm looking forward to homemade turkey with the usual Czech fixings, including sauerkraut. For dessert we're enjoying the apple pie Jade made last night. She's been baking it for holidays and no-special-reason days for years and even changed the recipe to eliminate sugar so her diabetic grandparents could eat it. We'll munch turkey sandwiches while watching the Packer-Bears game tomorrow. It's kind of weird; people here don't seem to relish football, except for the Pro Bowl, which is good for our economy.

As for gifts, I'm hoping for warm fuzzy socks. We are freezing our coconut balls off. Since the house has no heat, it's quite chilly in the morning up here at 1000 feet. I recently bought an area rug for the dining room so I could enjoy warm feet while I eat.

I've also pulled out the small heater we brought. I was sure we'd never use it, but the laugh's on me. There's no heat at the school, either, so Jade bought herself mittens that fold back to expose her fingers. Still, it's better than fighting the real cold and snow in Wisconsin. Mele Kalikimaka.

Circle of women.

December 29. Last month my yoga teacher, Anita, invited me to a Women's Circle. She'd just had her third chemo treatment and the circle was honoring her that evening. I can only hope I'd be as upbeat as she is if I were in her place. She's even still doing a bit of gardening. This week Anita gave me a pumpkin. Now I have to figure out how to prepare it because I've never tackled an eating pumpkin. At the circle, we chanted a healing prayer for her, but it worked its magic on us, too, and put me into a meditative state. After 108 rounds of this chant, we sat there, calm, quiet and contemplating. This group is awesome. The women are all different, each one strong, creative and powerful in their own way.

I've never been part of a women's circle before but I now go as often as possible.

It's called the Women's Empowerment Circle and every week one of the women volunteers to be Queen. She organizes the evening, often at her home, though we could go to other places like the studio where I take yoga. Activities are as varied as the women who organize them. Sometimes we ponder a question like "Who inspired you as a young woman?" or, at Thanksgiving, "What are you grateful for this year?" Sometimes we watch a documentary and then discuss it, or play a game and laugh. Sometimes we just pass the talking stick, share what's going on in our lives, maybe cry a little and eat a few pupus. Tonight we will observe New Year's Eve a bit early to share and celebrate our blessings from this year. I have so many.

BG makes out like it's all so mysterious and calls it the "Tom-Tom Club" because he's sure we beat drums. I'm not going to burst his bubble. This circle is a wonderful way to network and meet new women. I'm gradually fitting into my community.

4. CREATING A NEW LIFE IN A NEW YEAR

Water aerobics.

January 9. Dianne from the Women's Circle told me about the water aerobics class at the Honokaʻa pool held on Monday, Wednesday and Friday at 10 a.m. The pool and showers are solar-heated. What a deal, for only $15 per month! So I joined. It's all women, except for Ben, who usually winds up in the middle of the group. I enjoy the people in the class, especially Dianne. We have a young, perky instructor who enthusiastically shouts out the choreographed actions while the ladies talk; she doesn't seem to mind our chattering. The important thing is that we keep moving for an hour.

Some of us hang out after class drifting around the pool, talking about movies, sharing recipes and comparing notes on books we've read. They told me about a great beach for swimming called Hapuna, and another for snorkeling called Spencer. These women are an inspiration. Some are in their seventies and move with more ease than I do. Feisty Connie is a retired nurse, born on the island in one of the plantation camps. When she found out where I came from, she immediately peppered me with questions about Wisconsin politics. Apparently when she's not swimming, she's following politics.

Then there's Lois, who had cancer at 60 and a stroke at 70. She's in great shape, tall and lithe. She and her husband have a business in Honoka'a, though they're trying to sell it. Today she told me about a way to jazz up scones: add lilikoi – pulp, juice and the seeds, which add a nice crunch. I'm going to try it. There's an old gent who swims laps just before the water aerobics class. He's 98 and often swims as many as 20 laps! Apparently he walked with a cane when he started swimming a year ago. No more. That motivates me to stick with this. I need this workout routine in my toolbox or I won't live long enough to enjoy the fruits from the rest of my practices.

The last grandchild.

January 11. I find that with the sameness of the weather, and having no job to ground me, I lose track of days and weeks. If it wasn't for the Christmas decorations I just put away, I'd hardly know it was January. I have to make a conscious effort to look at the calendar. Today, as I did so, a flood of memories came back.

Today is the twelfth anniversary of when we travelled to get Faye in China. We were excited that other families were also bringing siblings, so Jade wouldn't be the only child in the travel group. We were even more excited to learn that half the families would receive babies from the same orphanage where we adopted Jade. Our adoption agency rep was investigating whether we'd be allowed to go into the orphanage with the other families. That was iffy. Because of bad press about "dying rooms," the Chinese government had closed orphanages to visitors.

We'd waited a long time for Faye. With Jade, the whole process from filling out the first form to having her in our arms was 10 months. Heck, it takes that long to have a baby the normal way! Jade was one of the first children adopted out of that country.

But a second child took more time. The popularity of adopting from China had increased exponentially and Chinese institutions were swamped. On top of that, we were fast approaching Y2K and the US government didn't want Americans in China when the clock rolled over to the year 2000. There was so much worry that computer-operated equipment like airplanes and elevators would stop functioning. So they closed the US Embassy for a couple of weeks just as we were matched with Faye, around Thanksgiving. We gave thanks that year for a new baby, and anxiously waited for news on when we could travel to get her.

It was actually a good thing we had a bit more time to prepare for the trip. In those days, I found it challenging to pack lean enough to fit a 17-day trip into three suitcases, especially with a five-year-old and a 13-month-old who would be in diapers. We also needed extra vaccinations. I grimly remember chasing a screaming Jade around an exam table to catch her while the impatient nurse looked on. Jade did not like shots – still doesn't. We also started our antimalarial drugs and Jade learned to swallow pills whole.

Finally, it was time to go. We were leaving early the next morning. That night, as we settled down to sleep, the telephone rang. It was my sister, Grace. Dad was in the hospital on a ventilator. On top of his diabetes, emphysema, high blood pressure and high cholesterol, he came down with pneumonia and congestive heart failure. He wasn't conscious. Were we coming to say goodbye?

Diane M. Scheurell

A lifetime of memories flashed before me: singing with him; dancing with him; cuddling with him; and later arguing with him over college, politics, Vietnam and the Church, to the point where one of us would have to leave the room. But we had long ago resolved our differences, and I was once again his adoring daughter. I loved my dad. How could I not be with him? But I also knew we wouldn't get a second chance to adopt Faye, who I'd called daughter since November. I had to choose between the dying and the living.

A quick discussion with BG sealed our decision. We would get Faye. "Take care of him, Grace." I knew she would. She was a seasoned nurse and a dear sister. She'd either pull him through or say goodbye for me. This was the year 2000. You didn't just call the US from China. We didn't even own a cell phone. I had to put Dad out of my mind. I could not afford to lose focus.

The experience of adopting Faye was so different from adopting her older sister. Jade was just under six months old when we got her, still drinking mostly formula and gumming a bit of Chinese rice gruel. She'd been in an orphanage, one of many babies looked after by caretakers there. She adapted to us almost instantly, two people lavishing attention and love on her from day one.

On the other hand, Faye at 13 months had been with a foster family. When her Amah, her caregiver, handed her to me in the hotel lobby, Faye cried inconsolably. As we walked back to our room, I wondered if we had done the right thing, pulling her away from the only family she'd known. She had to be thirsty with all her crying, so we tried to give her a bottle. First we offered her formula, then water, but she refused both. The adoption agency rep told us to try a cup. We had a sippy cup along, but she refused that too. Finally, in desperation, we took the top off the cup and

62

tentatively offered it to her. She grabbed it unsteadily and drank it all. She hadn't known what to do with a bottle or sippy cup, which was only one of many missteps we made based on assumptions! But at least she wasn't thirsty anymore.

We let her cruise along the hotel bed and she backed herself into a corner to continue her cry, face down on the bedspread. It was torture for all of us. But Jade came to the rescue. She crawled on the bed towards Faye and held out a Cheerio. Setting a couple in front of her, she ate a few herself. Slowly Faye's hand reached out and grasped one. She put it in her mouth and we could see her moving it around to explore it. She stopped crying and began to eat them as fast as Jade could pull them out of the bag. Faster and faster, she ate every one. We weren't seeing smiles, and she wasn't making eye contact, but she wasn't crying, either.

Soon it was time for supper. We went down to the hotel restaurant and placed Faye in a high chair. Within seconds she cried again, raising her arms to the waitresses to rescue her from these strange-looking people. But, as we fed her she stopped crying and even pointed to the food on the table. Poor little thing fell asleep as soon as we got back to the room, tuckered out. We were too.

Breakfast was the same story. She cried and held her arms out to waitresses until we started feeding her. Her Amah had told us that Faye only pooped every other day. She ate half an apple a day scraped with a spoon plus her formula and rice cereal. That morning, we just let her eat, starting with scrambled eggs. She ate two servings. Then she ate three bananas. She finished with rice cereal. She'd been starved! No wonder she only pooped every other day! We're sure that her caregivers did the best they could with what they had, but it wasn't enough.

By noon of the second day, she ignored the waitresses and demanded food. She and Jade communicated in their own way and we began to bond as a family. She smiled and cooed and giggled, and so did we. There was only one moment in that long trip that I received a strong image of Dad. It caused me anxiety at that moment, but my attention quickly returned to the mundane tasks of changing diapers, dressing an unwilling toddler, giving my five-year-old "equal" attention and otherwise participating in the magic of becoming a family.

Meanwhile, we travelled with the other families getting their babies from the orphanage. We received word that, because Jade had come from there, we'd be allowed in! The director singled her out during the welcoming comments to the families in the greeting room. I don't know how much she understood, but she saw the orphanage, the room she'd been in and even the bed she once occupied. To this day I can see her taking a picture of that bed with her little disposable camera. The onsite clinic doctor showed her around and gave her an orange, a pencil and some paper. Jade even met a woman who had taken care of her as a baby and remembered her. She was a star! The whole wonderful experience gave me chicken skin. Still does.

When we arrived home, I immediately called Grace. Dad was still in the hospital in serious condition, but off the ventilator. There had been a moment when he lamented that he had no reason to live. Grace sternly told him, "God isn't done with you yet. You have a brand new grandbaby to meet, to hold and cuddle and sing to while she snuggles on your chest." He looked at her with tears in his eyes, nodded "Okay," and drifted off to sleep.

A funny feeling ran up the back of my neck and I shivered. "When was that?" It turned out to be the moment my memory of him flashed before me while in China. He and she, the last grandchild, were now linked. I had made the right decision, choosing the living over the dying. In fact, he lived another three years, perhaps because of her. Nothing that happens is an accident. Today is a good day to thank God for both of them.

Hold on my child — Joy comes in the morning your weeping only last for the night. The darkest hour means dawn is just in sight.

New thoughts on sustainability.

January 14. I told my Women's Circle last week that I'm grateful for my first Hawai'i winter. But I'm having doubts about the yard. I had no idea how quickly this lovely botanical garden would grow wild. No wonder the Property Manager insisted I hire a landscaping service while I rented this place out. I thought I was being robbed at $150 per month, but now I'm not so sure.

Our first step in trying to regain botanical control is trying our hand at partially sustaining ourselves with a garden. This weekend the girls and I tackled an overgrown flower bed off the back lanai and took it down to bare ground. The only things we salvaged were the oregano, basil and rosemary that Jade planted in the fall. What struck me is that the soil looks so poor here with none of the rich black-brown topsoil we had in Wisconsin. At least it's porous, unlike the clay we had in Georgia. Yet plants grow like crazy, so I hope our eating garden will take off. I have strawberry and tomato plants, and cucumber and bush bean seeds I'll plant after breaking up the soil and adding nutrients. Luckily we've been composting since August, so we have some nice rotting vegetable matter ripe for "planting."

We hear much about sustainability here on the islands because we import 85% of our food. That leaves us vulnerable to the high cost of shipping fuel or a potential world crisis. It's especially worrisome to our ranchers. The business model here is to raise calves with their grass-eating moms for two years. But then they fly the calves to the mainland for a switch from mother's milk and grass to a corn diet, where they fatten up for slaughter. Some of that beef ships back to us at an exorbitant markup. Editorials urge more state government action to encourage local food production. But the best sustainable action we can each take is to have an eating garden and buy from local farmers. On Saturday, we have a small market in Honokaʻa and two larger ones in Waimea. There's also a smaller market on Wednesday in Waimea, so we really have no excuse not to support local farmers.

The idea of buying local is not new. But here it takes on a real urgency. The northern part of the island, North Kohala, has a goal of 50% sustainability by 2050 in their Community Development Plan. Living out on a rock in the middle of the Pacific we realize that, in a world crisis, no one will take care of us but us.

This message of buying local is not limited to food. During the holidays we saw articles asking us to buy local gifts, especially services: gift certificates to local restaurants, massage, nail services, and hair salons, pet grooming, landscaping, you name it. Our unemployment and under-employment rates are high, especially in rural areas. Small shops and services are going under, still feeling the effects of the Great Recession. We need to understand that when we buy gifts from big box stores most of the money goes off island. When we buy locally, that vendor can also buy locally and so on. My money spent here can benefit a whole chain of islanders. That's also sustainable action.

Sustainability has a much broader meaning for me now. I thank God for a winter warm enough to start a garden, and pray I'm part of a larger trend that sees us growing, acting and buying locally.

Paintbrush meditation.

January 21. The past two weeks I've been working my butt off on the house with my new handymen. Kim and Thomas divided the passage between the pantry and bathroom, installing pantry shelves on one side and a linen closet on the other. We had a curious conversation about whether I wanted double-wall or single-wall construction. I hadn't noticed, but the inside walls of my house and most of the exterior portions are traditional plantation style, single wall. There are no studs and no interior spaces where mold can grow unchecked. It's a less material-intensive way to build, which is a good thing on an island where we import lumber. A horizontal board like wainscoting holds the vertical boards together. This also means a whole different way of installing power and plumbing. With single-walls, noise travels easily from room to room (this must be what all those novels mean by paper-thin walls), and we have to be careful not to use nails that are longer than the paneling is thick because they'll punch through to the other side. Who knew?!

I'm always busy while they're here, making decisions on the fly, walking to the hardware store for supplies and painting new pieces after the guys leave. Next week I have to take everything out of my closet. It seems I just put it all in there – oh yeah, I did! This weekend I'm painting three sets of louvered doors. It's exceptionally mind-numbing, so I try to make a meditation out of it. Paint brush up, paint brush down, paint brush up, paint brush down, all done to the rhythm of my breath. The Karate Kid gained muscle memory with this exercise; I gain spiritual serenity.

As I practiced this paintbrush meditation I mentally chanted my mantra, and my mind wandered to the connection of my mantra with my life. For years my mantra has been *peace* (said on the inhale), *serenity* (on the exhale), *peace* (inhale), *tranquility* (exhale). Mechanically, this mantra does two things. First, it causes a longer exhale than inhale, because the words have different syllable lengths (one versus four). This produces a deeper relaxation. Second, it focuses my mind because one time I'm saying *serenity* on the exhale, and the next time *tranquility*. So I have to pay attention.

[handwritten: It's not what you think you are, But what you think, you are]

Mechanics aside, continual thoughts of peace, serenity and tranquility have produced that in me. They say that you are what you eat. But it's even truer that you are what you think. Back in the corporate world, I experienced substantial pressure for long periods of time. Oozing stress from every pore, I almost vibrated, first with energy, then with angst. During earlier good years, I thrived on action, passion, doing. That pressure was self-induced. The pressure of latter years was driven by things outside my control: my boss, corporate politics, the economy. Either way, self-induced or circumstance-induced, my thoughts weren't about peace, serenity and tranquility. I needed a big change.

[handwritten margin note: Practice self care]

My coaching sessions with Rita, yoga, journaling and my experiences with the two Dr. Barbara's taught me to practice self-care. My rituals nourish me, helping create the person I am and will become. One of the most important daily rituals is taking time for quiet reflection, using the meditation mantra. Anyone can do this. But make sure to pick words that mean something to you. Choose wisely; you are (or will become) what you think.

Of course it's easy to be peaceful in paradise. But meditation and other self-care practices are what got me here. Everyone's paradise is different, and their route and the transformation tools they use will be different. Just know that when you practice self-care, you'll reach yours.

[handwritten: Walking & thinking works for me.]

Rural life on the Big Island.

January 26. When I tell people I live on the Big Island, I can tell they immediately envision beaches and palm trees. I'm happy to tell them all about rural Hawai'i. Waimea is home to Parker Ranch, the largest privately owned cattle ranch in the whole US. This is a cowboy town, there's no mistaking it. KTA's shopping center has one statue of a paniolo (cowboy) and another of a seven foot cowboy boot. Parker Ranch Shopping Center across the street has a statue of a paniolo roping a steer. It also sports stop signs that say WHOA instead of STOP. There's a well-trafficked feed store and a shop for horse riding equipment right across from the Police Station.

People often ask me why we didn't move to Waimea, since it's such a pain to drive the girls there every day. My answer remains the same. "What's the point of moving to Hawai'i and then living in Wyoming?" The pastures around Waimea are barren compared to the exuberant foliage of Honoka'a, especially those on the dry side. I prefer the warmer weather in Honoka'a at 1000 feet versus blustery Waimea at 2500 feet. The altitude difference is substantial. It's still a surprise every day to have my ears pop as I drive through the uplands between Waimea and home.

This week the rural nature of the Big Island really hit me. Our route to Waimea is a state highway and the only way to get around the island. On Tuesday, I rounded a curve and suddenly saw cars and trucks ahead pulled over or stopped dead in the road, and a police car with its light on. I assumed an accident. I was wrong. It was a steer loping down the road! The steer seemed nonplussed about the commotion as it wandered from one side of the center line to the other. The police car followed it slowly, then deftly pulled alongside the steer. He nudged it first onto the shoulder, then into the ditch. It finally dawned on me that he was herding the steer with his vehicle! With his car between the steer and the highway, he left enough room for two lanes of traffic to resume slowly. And resume they did, as if this kind of event happened all the time.

In all the years I lived in Wisconsin with its vast cow population, I never saw a cow on the road. (In Hawai'i they call them steers and cattle instead of cows.) Maybe it's because I didn't live in rural Wisconsin. Maybe Wisconsin farmers keep closer tabs on their cows because they milk them twice a day. Here, cattle seem to be on their own in pastures, just ambling around eating grass. I never see paniolos riding herd on them, yet they seem to be in different pastures every day.

My retired neighbor was born and raised here, a cowgirl in her youth. She told me about helping her cousins and uncles move vast herds of cattle from one pasture to another to give pastures recovery time. They used horses in the old days. She says that today you're just as likely to see a cowboy on an ATV as on a horse. I haven't seen either, but there's plenty of time to learn through observation on the drive every day.

I did have my first encounter with a paniolo a couple of weeks ago in the hardware store. I kept hearing a jingling noise and, as I rounded the corner to the checkout counter, there he stood, a real cowboy with spurs on his boots. This was no tourist in new cowboy gear setting out to ride horses for the afternoon. He was the real deal. His boots were mud caked, his jeans dusty and his cowboy hat well worn. Lean and tanned, his face had that leathery outside-all-the-time look. I could imagine him on a horse all day. He made his purchase and then jingled his way out the door. In that instant, Bonanza and Gunsmoke came alive for me.

Actually, lots of people here have horses. On the way into Waimea, you can see small hobby ranches with two or three horses in corrals or pastures. Faye and I counted them once. We saw 33 horses in an eight-mile stretch of highway. Early this month, when my friend Amy visited, we saw two teens mosey into a small village on their horses. They dismounted in the middle of the main street, tied their horses to a stop sign, strolled over to a sandwich shop across the road, and came back with lunch for themselves and apples for their horses. This is a side of Hawai'i that most visitors don't see.

Horses aren't the only hobby animals around. I see lots of properties with a few sheep or goats, even donkeys. These groups of animals are way too small to be herds, so what do people do with them? I think they're pets. Even some of the ladies in water aerobics have a goat or two. One of them found three baby goats out on the lava, hungry and bleating pitifully. A hunter probably took their mother. She brought them home, nursed them back to health in her house and gradually moved them outside. I asked her if she milks them. "No, I'd have to get them pregnant and then take away their kid in order to milk them. I couldn't do that to my goats. But they do keep the grass short."

That's not what Dianne says. She has two goats named Coffee and Cappuccino. She says they're browsers and when she first got them, they went straight for her best flowers, vegetables and small trees. Now she keeps them in a pen. She says they're pets but they also produce good fertilizer. Their poop can go straight onto the garden; no composting needed.

When I first looked at my property, my real estate agent made a point of telling me that I could have a goat. But I've never even owned a dog or cat, so I'm not about to keep a goat. Besides, I have neighborhood chickens to keep me company. I don't mind them coming into to my yard. They eat bugs and coqui frogs. But BG still hears and hates the round-the-clock crowing. He's constantly yelling at them to be quiet.

Well, it's time to take the girls to school. Maybe I'll see another steer on the road. On a recent trip to Kona, driving along the upper highway, I did see a wild goat and a big tom turkey with his feathers spread out. Both were close enough to touch. Unlike Wisconsin, Hawai'i has no rules to call the Department of Land and Natural Resources to report when you hit something, and I hear goat meat is tasty. Or maybe a wild pig; we have a butcher in town who could cut it up for us. Pulled pork anyone?

January weather bliss.

January 29. It rained much of November and part of December. But January has been gorgeous: sunny skies, warm temperatures and a nice breeze. Last week we had a couple of days of vog across all the islands when wind patterns switched from the normal east/northeast trades to "Kona" winds from the southeast. That takes the wind up the volcano where it catches the vog and carries it as far as Kauai, more than 350 miles away. But the trades came back quickly. Last night it rained all night, perfect sleeping music. The Honoka'a pool temperature has been a consistently warm 79° for a couple of weeks.

Last week, BG willingly helped me in the yard, a sure sign of spring. I wanted the vista to the ocean opened so that we could look for whales. Of course he has to do it his way, with multiple tools that match the exact specification of each job. And my friends think *I'm* the one with OCD. He used a massive pruning tool for banana leaves, his machete for the stalks and a pruning saw on a six-foot extension for smaller avocado branches. Then he brought out one of his three bow saws for the larger branches. Propping a ladder against the tree, he gingerly climbed into the lower limbs for a proper examination. He teetered back and forth in the tree as he used the bow saw. It made me very nervous. I was happy when he switched to the chainsaw and even happier when he finally climbed down. And I'm thankful for the beautiful view to the ocean. Now I need to find time to sit on my lanai and watch for whales. If only the mosquitos weren't quite so prolific. There's a myth that we don't have mosquitos in Hawai'i. Perhaps the resorts spray for insects so tourists don't experience them. But I can verify that we have the little buggers.

I love being a stay-at-home Mom. I can do things on a whim. Jade's been working hard studying for college entrance exams. So when she asked if I could take her and two friends to the beach right after her exam ended, I said, "Absolutely!" We grabbed sandwiches and drinks at the organic food store, and headed to Hapuna Beach. Travel books report this is the best beach on the Big Island.

I brought a stadium seat, a blanket and a library book, and camped out under a shady tree, marveling that I'm at this beautiful beach in January. The girls timidly tested the water, concluded that the water was a bit cool, and marched up and down the beach talking. I'm glad they decided against swimming. The waves were rather large and, despite the presence of lifeguards, I would have felt the need to watch them in the water.

My location was blissful: nice breeze, no vog, the rhythmic sound of waves and the distant murmur of voices too indistinct to make out words. Three hours later I pulled myself out of my novel, found the girls lying on the beach still gabbing, and reluctantly tugged them back to real life. Time to go. For me, the best part of the day was listening to them talk on the way home. They act as if I'm not there, just a chauffeur. It's not that Jade doesn't want to talk. It's that she has no time for chitchat. She's always studying.

On the other hand, Faye just doesn't *want* to talk these days. She went on a two-day field trip with her class to Volcanoes National Park, staying in military camp cabins. She's not much of a camping person and she came back crabby, having walked or run about 13 miles during the two days. Maybe it's better that she doesn't want to talk when she's in that kind of mood. She recently dropped the bomb that she wants to attend college in England or Scotland. It seems that Stanford, her more recent choice, isn't far enough away from Mom and Dad. Where does she get this stuff? She just turned 13! Well, I hope she plans on getting a scholarship. The retirement plan covered college for the girls, but not anything as exotic as that, or Stanford for that matter.

Cherry Blossom Festival.

February 8. The cherry trees in Waimea are in full bloom with dark pink blossoms. The town is organizing a Cherry Blossom Heritage Festival this weekend, "showcasing the blooming of Church Row Park's historic cherry trees and the Japanese tradition of viewing them" (from the *Hamakua Times*). Activities will be held all over town, with Japanese cultural demonstrations such as a tea ceremony, origami, mochi pounding and bonsai, as well as performances like the bon dance and taiko drumming. Even the wine store participates, offering free sake tastings. It all culminates in planting additional cherry tree seedlings sent from the Japanese Embassy. I love all the ethnic foods, traditions and festivals here.

I'm just beginning to understand all the back stories of various local groups. The Japanese were the largest wave brought over to work the plantations: 200,000 out of 337,000 immigrants. Plantation owners purposefully brought in different ethnicities and housed them in separate camps to hamper labor-organizing efforts. When the Japanese workers' labor contracts were up, 55% returned to Japan. The rest settled permanently in the islands. They suffered discrimination and distrust. They, like other non-European or non-American immigrants, were denied the vote under the Provisional Government that overthrew the sovereign nation of Hawai'i and its monarch, Queen Lili'uokalani.

On the other hand, they fared better than their brethren on the mainland during WWII. The US government interred many Japanese, 62% of whom were US citizens! But in Hawai'i, only 2000 of 157,000 Japanese suffered that injustice. The islands could not afford to have a third of their workforce locked up, especially when many were employed in banking and commerce.

The Japanese are currently about 13% of the population here. Many serve in Hawaiian government and civil service jobs and they've become a strong part of the political establishment. In this diverse state we see their influence everywhere, from street signs (Japanese tourists are a vital part of our economy) to favorite foods and festivals. One of the ladies in water aerobics told us about her brother hiring a roofer in Hilo. The guy was listed under a Japanese name. Her brother was surprised when a blond transplant from the mainland showed up. The roofer confessed that he purposely used the Japanese business name because Hilo has such a large Japanese population.

I'm looking for someone to attend the Cherry Blossom Festival with me. BG and the girls don't see interested, so I'll go with one of my new girlfriends.

Honoka'a People's Theatre.

March 16. One of the cool things I want my visitors to experience is our local movie theater, an easy walk from my house. One of the women in water aerobics said, "It's the heart of the town." It was built in 1930 during Honoka'a's hey-day as a sugar plantation town. At the time, Honoka'a was the second biggest town on the island, after Hilo, and much bigger than Kailua-Kona or Waimea. In fact, at one time, when sugar was king, Honoka'a was the third largest settlement in the state.

The Tanimoto family built the theater. Mrs. Tanimoto continued to run it until 1988, living in a little apartment upstairs. By then she was frail, and a local plantation doctor, Dr. Keeney, started to help her. He bought the theater from her and restored it, living in the dressing rooms behind the stage. It now has the biggest screen on the island (50 feet) and the sound system is superb, better than any I heard in Wisconsin. Dr. Keeney and his family have set prices low: $6 for adults, $4 for seniors and $3 for keiki 12 and under. This is in keeping with the original intent of the theater to provide entertainment for the paniolos and plantation workers.

I'm on an email distribution list for the movie and event schedule. They present an eclectic mix of movies and live performances. Last week they hosted Luminous Ragas, three Indian music masters. This week they're playing Oscar-nominated films from the "best short films" category, both animated and documentary. Current movies arrive here a couple weeks later than in the first-run theaters. For example, Faye and I saw the second Sherlock Holmes movie, *A Game of Shadows*, three weeks ago, and *War Horse* last weekend, movies that played in Kona last month. I also saw *The Descendants* with Stacy. But because this really is the people's theater, Dr. Keeney asked those of us on the distribution list if he should bring *The Descendants* back. Enough people voted yes, so he'll show it again next week.

Maybe the most endearing thing about the Honoka'a People's Theatre is that they post people's notices in their big windows. There I can find out who lost a cat or parrot, who I can hire to cut my lawn, where to go for a Sheep & Goat Clinic, a Soil Health Workshop, Doula or Yoga Teacher certification, who is holding a bazaar and when, and who offers piano and ukulele tutoring, yoga classes, babysitting, reiki sessions, massage, tango lessons, intuitive readings, Traditional Chinese Medicine and a host of other interesting things. The postings are part of what makes this the people's theater.

On a side note, I see many Japanese tourists in town and, curiously, they all take pictures of the building. I asked a local about this and she explained that a Japanese movie, *Honoka'a Boy*, was filmed here. The main character, a Japanese immigrant, works there as a projectionist. Economically, it was a big deal for Honoka'a and they even used locals as extras. I'll have to see if I can find it on DVD.

April Fool's Day.

April 1. I always think of Dad on April first. No one pulled a better April Fool's joke. I'm sure he died that night, though Mom found him the next morning, so his death certificate says April 2,

2003. After spending all that time in the hospital three years before, he died peacefully in his sleep at home. It's what we all wanted for him. When Mom called with the news, we packed up and headed home.

Driving was treacherous that day. A freak ice storm blanketed the state's eastern section, like the numbness that blanketed my feelings. We all figured Dad had talked St. Peter into sending one more joke to us for his funeral: the awful weather. I remained numb for several days until the visitation at the church just before his funeral Mass. It had been years since I'd been in a church, maybe Mae's wedding.

Greeting all the people who came to pay last respects, seeing old familiar faces that brought up memories of family, friends and good times . . . that was when I finally broke down. My childhood friend, Vicki, and her mom came. My first mentor, Dr. Chuck, came with his wife Marilyn. I hadn't seen them in two decades. After big tearful hugs, I introduced them to Jade, now 8, and Faye, 4. Did they even know I had kids? I couldn't remember. I'd lost touch with them somewhere along the way. We've since reconnected. My cousins turned up in force, as well as remaining siblings, spouses and cousins of my dad's generation, there to comfort Mom. He was the patriarch of the family, yet all but two of his siblings had preceded him in death. He never got over that. He felt he should've gone first, at least before his little brother, Uncle Billy.

All the grandkids were crying except Faye. She sat on my lap, not fully understanding what happened to Grandpa. But I could see her listening and observing everything. She startled me, shamed me, with an innocent question: "Who is God?" Deep breath. "Well, God takes care of us. God's all-knowing, all-seeing, all-powerful . . ." She interrupted me before I could go on. "Oh, sort of like Jafar!" (If you haven't seen the Disney movie *Aladdin*, you won't get the joke.) That broke the tension and everyone laughed for the first time that morning. But while they laughed, I examined the execution of my duties as a mom to raise moral children. Was I failing them?

My grade-school music teacher, Sister Cecelia, and Gary, a former classmate, were up in the choir loft, just like old times. She was bent over with osteoporosis, but still as bright-eyed as ever. I knew I'd have the chance to visit with her during the funeral lunch. She played all my favorite songs: *Wind Beneath My Wings*, *Amazing Grace*, *How Great Thou Art* and finished with *An Irish Blessing*. My girls instantly recognized it as the prayer I sang to them every night at bedtime. My family isn't Irish but BG's is and the song meant much to me because Sister Cecelia had taught it to me. She hadn't lost her beautiful voice, or her ability to bring me to tears with her powerful organ playing.

Mom held the lunch at the Eagles Club. I can't tell you how many Friday nights we spent there as a family enjoying a typical Wisconsin fish fry. Dad and Mom would sit at the bar for one Old Fashioned, and then we'd troop downstairs for Lake Perch with fries, coleslaw and buttered rye bread. In those days Catholics refrained from meat every Friday, not the reduced schedule the Church practices today during Lent. All dressed up, we'd sometimes sit at the bar with Mom and Dad and have a kiddie cocktail or, as I got older, a little wine in some Seven-Up. That was the culture back then.

It was the early '60s in a safe city, so we could be out of our parents' eyesight at the Eagles Club. How many times had we played hide and seek in the long drapes? How many times had we performed mini-plays or sung songs on the little stage in the darkened room off the bar? It was a magical place where our parents let us run free to use our imaginations.

Now I could see the threadbare carpets and dusty velvet drapes. The finish was worn off the stair bannister from decades of children and elders clutching it for balance. My sisters and I snuck into the bar just to see it again. The stale smell of cigarettes filled our nostrils. Still, it was fitting that we took this last meal in honor of Dad here.

Downstairs everyone found a seat. Mae with her family and I with mine wound up at the table with Sister Cecelia. My heart was full to bursting with love for this old woman. I first saw her in second grade at St. Boniface School when we moved to the south side of town and changed parishes. All nuns wore severe habits back then – severe habits and severe faces. But not Sister Cecelia. She was a smiling, loving and joyful music teacher at the nearby conservatory. We were lucky to have her teach us music two or three times a week. Over the six years at St. Boniface School, I learned proper breathing techniques, voice projection and singing with throat open and on key even without accompaniment.

Once I moved to high school I stayed close to her; the era of the guitar Mass was upon us. She pulled five of us together, Nancy (alto), my best friend Vicki (soprano), Gary (tenor), Jeff (base) and me. I sang alto and soprano. The six of us played and sang for Mass every Saturday evening, an innovation of the second Vatican Council. We didn't need the range of voices for the simple songs of Mass, but Sister Cecelia always thought and taught bigger. Soon we were performing madrigals at nursing homes. She even encouraged us to publicly sing songs we composed ourselves. I owe my love of singing to her influence.

I hadn't seen her since leaving town for college 30 years before, and I was nervous about talking to her. What would she think about my not practicing Catholicism? The news came out in a way I could not have predicted. My niece, Alice, told Sister about her First Communion last spring and Jade innocently asked when she'd have her First Communion. I was dumbstruck.

Soon after, I began to pray earnestly to God. While I avoided organized religion, I still talked to Her. My daughters seemed to be missing something in their lives. We talked about God at home. We prayed as a family and alone. Both BG and I were spiritual, just not religious. We were certainly teaching them the Golden Rule and the Commandments. But it wasn't enough. I began to feel I should take them to church, that we needed to belong to a community of worshippers. BG understood. He'd been raised Catholic, too, with all of the cultural richness of that life, and all the mental anguish of severing ourselves from it. That was something my first husband never understood. And that was the current stumbling block: I was divorced and remarried.

For a while I tried other religious services in Racine. But they didn't feel right. Meanwhile, I walked past St. Richard's Church every day on my way to work. I still wrestled with the same issues that had taken me away from the Church three decades before. I disapproved of the Church's stand on birth control and gay rights, on priests marrying and on women serving as priests. The sex scandal had just broken in the media. Yet so many things were pulling me back. Could I return to the Church despite all of that?

Finally I took the plunge and started to attend Mass with my family. Jade was fine. Faye did what four-year-olds do when confined for an hour. But since she was cute, people around us just smiled. This parish was largely third and fourth generation

German, Polish, Irish, Lithuanian and Slavic immigrants, an amalgamation of several smaller churches. Most parishioners were elderly; the congregation did not have many young families. So they were tolerant and even welcomed our girls.

After about two months I got up the nerve to speak to Father Jack. BG and I genuinely liked him. He spoke to our hearts and never made us feel uncomfortable with his sermons. I asked him point blank if there was room in the Church for a divorced woman. He said yes and urged us to continue coming.

"What about Communion? Can I receive Communion?"

"Yes, please do. It's food for the journey." I left crying with relief.

Four months later Father Jack baptized the girls with their aunts and uncle as Godparents. My Mother beamed. She revealed that she'd said a rosary every day for 35 years, praying that I'd return to the Church, and now her prayers had been answered. I never knew. Jade studied her religious education lessons and finally received First Communion. I volunteered to teach Sunday School to Faye's kindergarten class and continued that for four years. And I was cantor at Saturday evening Mass.

Six months after Father Jack baptized the girls, he told the congregation that he was moving to a Milwaukee parish to be closer to his aging parents. BG and I looked at each other, distressed. He quipped wryly, "Who says God doesn't have a sense of humor?" A year followed with temporary priests, one of whom confessed in a sermon to being attracted to men and lamenting the Church's stand on gays. That took courage, but drove away many parishioners. Another priest assigned to St. Richard closed the elementary school. The few young families we had moved to other parishes.

But we hung tight. We'd just arrived. We weren't going to let these mishaps drive us away . . . again. God rewarded our patience with Father Ron, a soft-spoken, loving man who preached from the heart and spoke the healing words we needed to hear. He healed a whole parish. It was hard to leave him behind when we moved to Hawai'i.

In the space of two years, I transitioned from anti-church to fully engaged worshipper. And I rediscovered a related set of tools for my transformation process: being grateful for my blessings, honoring traditions, and prayer. To think it all started with Dad's death on April Fool's Day and a chance meeting with a special nun at his funeral. If he were still here, I'd have to tell him, "Good one, Dad."

5. RETHINKING THE CHICKEN AND THE EGG AND OTHER MEATY MATTERS

We got an egg!

April 2. After listening to the rooster racket for nine months, the chickens finally did something nice for us. A hen laid an egg by the side of our carport. There were three "nests" side by side (rounded out grass shapes) with an egg in the last one. We don't have any idea how long it sat there, but I think something would have taken or broken it if it sat too long. BG wants to lure more hens to lay eggs. I don't understand that at all. He's been swearing at them (mostly the roosters) every day. Now he's building a chicken palace with soft fluffy dryer lint.

Just when we have an exciting development here, I have to travel back to Wisconsin for a week. But that's exciting news, too. After months of having our Racine house on the market in this lousy economy, we've found a renter who's also taking an option to buy in three years. It will be a big relief to have someone in the house. An empty place is just an invitation for vandals. I'll be finalizing paperwork and meeting the new tenant. I'm also looking forward to visiting family and seeing Wisconsin with fresh eyes. But I'm not going to enjoy wearing shoes, or worse, boots again. I've been barefoot or wearing sandals since I arrived in Hawai'i.

Spring in Hawai'i.

April 12. I'm back in Hawai'i after spending a week in Wisconsin. While there I was struck by the relative starkness of their landscape. Stark isn't quite right; it's "not lush." I'm now used to rolling hills, winding roads, skies obstructed by trees and lush vegetation, not flat empty fields, vast expanses of lawn, and roads laid out on a grid.

When I returned to Hawai'i it was a bit warmer than when I left. Now I can sleep with my windows open again. Trees are in bloom and there's a type of tree, the Jacaranda, in the higher elevations that's just gorgeous. It's tall, with a large canopy full of purple flowers that bloom before the leaves emerge. It rained hard last night, so this morning a carpet of purple petals surrounded each tree. There are also trees with strangely shaped flowers, some red, others orange, yellow or white and all exotic to my untrained eye.

I harvested tomatoes from the garden, but the plants look like they won't recover from their push to produce. I see only five pea plants coming up, but that may be enough for a good crop. Last week BG took down the biggest bunch of apple bananas I've ever seen. He needed a wheelbarrow to move it, and it took two of us to hoist it up to the hook on the front lanai where it's ripening. I love these local apple bananas, smaller and sweeter than the store-bought kind from South America and a perfect size for smoothies.

I also noticed calves along the road. They're frisky, galloping away from their mothers, stopping, then charging back. I saw two of them pushing each other back and forth, little heads low to the ground, forehead to forehead. They also chase the white cattle egrets that eat the bugs the cattle rustle up. When Faye saw two brown calves running, she thought they were dogs because they were so agile, unlike the plodding adults. At some point the calves will be flown to the mainland and fattened up for an eventual place of honor on the country's dinner tables.

I've also seen little foals sticking close to their moms. In one scene played out this morning, a mare galloped in a field with the family dog in hot pursuit while a skittish foal watched with legs splayed for balance, then bolted past the dog to its mom.

Last week one of the Honoka'a dress shops was selling little Easter ducklings and rabbits in tubs outside. Faye asked if she could have a duck. We said, "Yes, but you'll be responsible for housing, feeding, watering and cleaning their nesting area." She decided against it.

One thing that hasn't changed is the roosters crowing. They've become blasé about BG's ire. Even I can ignore his frequent outbursts of "Bloody chickens!" They regularly strut through our yard with their hens in tow. Personally, I like them in the yard. They eat bugs. Jade found another egg on our back lanai while I was gone. That was one brave hen to come so close to the house. She must have flown since the lanai is six feet off the ground. As with the last egg we found, we don't know how long it sat there. But if I understand correctly from my brother-in-law, a fertilized egg is good for a month at room temperature. Vitmer said you can even take an egg that has been sitting out that long, stick it back under the hen and hatch a chick! I'm sure this egg was fertilized because the roosters are jumping the hens all the time, horrifying the girls. So the next time we find an egg we may eat it.

magic of discovery

Manifesting Paradise

Reviewing these thoughts, I realize I've slowed down enough to notice all kinds of things. That's a major shift. I'm far more present than I ever was before I retired. Some call it stopping to smell the roses. I think of it as slowing down to see what's beyond the surface, understanding the meaning of what I'm seeing. There's a quote by Marcel Proust that we often used in my department. "The real magic of discovery lies not in seeing new landscapes, but in having new eyes." Having new eyes, being present, lets me live larger. It's a great tool for the toolbox.

food for thought

my Hawthorn tree is beautiful this fall

Garden party, Hawaiian style.

April 18. My yard continues to grow wild. I had to do something. So, yesterday, I hosted a "garden party." Five women, mostly new friends from the Women's Circle, descended on my yard and helped me weed, rake and thin my east garden. Stacy had been telling me for months that she would help me figure out the difference between a weed and a keeper. Yesterday was the day.

She brought Rebecca, a new homeowner, and I gladly gave her plants to fill her own yard. Rebecca brought Lori. They were both members of the Women's Circle (small island!). Judy and Julia overheard me talking to them about the garden party at a circle gathering and asked if they could come. Judy needs plants for her yard. And because I'd helped Julia clean her apartment when she moved, she wanted to help. Then Thomas, my handyman, showed up unexpectedly. I'd promised him some unusual bromeliads in exchange for cleaning out the hot tub I'm putting on Craigslist. He just joined in the cleanup, doing most of the bush chopping.

side note I have ferns in my yard that Diana gave me 6 years ago - I need to take some with me when I move

After four hours of work, I discovered some interesting boulders that had been hidden by unkempt flora. Stacy taught me that the

New discoveries - been there all the time

87

Diane M. Scheurell

Elephant Ear in my yard is so common as to be a nuisance. When we took it out, we found it had been hiding some beautiful ginger plants. We also transplanted the Anthurium out of their crowded space and into the shade where they can thrive. We thinned the dwarf ginger, a nonflowering multicolored foliage. And we cut back the leggy purple Mexican petunias so they can bloom again. I found out that the African tulip tree growing near the lanai is an invasive plant – too bad, the orange flower is very pretty – and that a certain large bush is actually a type of basil. We even found a path I didn't know existed.

I now know the difference between a weed and a keeper, and I've cemented my friendship with five beautiful women and Thomas. We celebrated with a meal of huli chicken, basmati rice and a big salad washed down with Japanese beer. It was satisfying to cook for them.

This is a garden party Hawai'i style – giving and sharing, with no expectation of something in return. This sharing is characteristic of all Pacific Islanders. Stacy told me the story of how descendants of missionaries and other newcomers took advantage of the Native Hawaiians' tradition of giving. They took and took – mostly land. It was the time of the Great Mahele (1845), when King Kamehameha III gave each Hawaiian a piece of land. They had to file for it within a two-year period. Many didn't file, and those who did often gave away or sold their piece for practically nothing. They didn't understand this new form of land ownership. By 1893 foreigners controlled 90% of the land. In that exchange, native peoples lost their right to gather food, hunt, farm and use the land the way they'd done for generations.

Stacy told me that local Hawaiians and Japanese, who have the same giving tradition, might bring me fruit, veggies, whatever they think I might need. Indeed, one day I found a big bunch of bananas on the front lanai and no note. I never found out who brought them.

sustainability + giving

Everyone seems to share Hawaiian style. It's part of how we define sustainability. We gladly help one another, and the receivers reciprocate when and how they can. We also barter, trading labor and goods. I did some of that back home, but the sustainability movement here is taking root within me in a different, stronger way. It's about sustaining each other as well. Maybe this is the physical manifestation of unconditional love, a new way to view one of my favorite tools.

Going vegetarian-ish.

Look up on Youtube!

April 20. I recently watched two scary documentaries about food. One was *Forks over Knives*, about the ills of eating animal protein (cancer, diabetes and more). It must be a popular video, because I'm twenty-eighth on a waiting list at the Honoka'a Library. I'll wait. I want my family to see it. Grace turned me on to it during my visit this month. She and Vitmer had viewed it and immediately made the decision to eat vegetarian. Grace has always been fanatically careful about cooking and eating healthy. But this change surprised me, because Vitmer is a big meat-and-potatoes guy. Their decision made me curious, so I watched the film with them.

That was four weeks ago. I'm now eating vegetarian about three-quarters of the time and experimenting with vegetarian main dishes. I've even had tofu in burritos! When making casseroles, I use ground turkey instead of hamburger. I can't say I solely eat an animal-free diet. We had three hams and a lamb in the freezer when I started. We served the lamb for Easter. I had bought it at the Saturday market from the farmer who raised it and likely treated it humanely. The lamb probably didn't have to stand knee deep in its own excrement day after day as our farm-factories do with cattle today. *[handwritten: I wonder if this is true, Dear Lord I Hope not!!!]*

My family does not practice vegetarianism with me, so I have to be artful about my cooking. They all liked the new quiche recipe I made. No need to point out that there was no meat in it. I'm serious about this dietary change. My convictions were reinforced by watching another documentary, *Food, Inc.*, reporting on the food industry and those who control it with our politicians' help. It encourages viewers to get involved in changing how our government supports these food/chemical giants who put profit ahead of food safety, farmer welfare and environmental stewardship. What our nation is doing with our food supply is not sustainable. We've reduced biodiversity to such an extreme that if something harmed a specific crop, it would seriously increase world hunger. As the film says, we vote with our mouths every day. I'm voting for sustainability.

So now I'm trying to eat organic as well as local or vegetarian. I'd been on the "buy local" kick for some time. Local food purchases increase my chance that the seed stock is more diverse than standard crops and is not genetically modified. It increases the probability that the farmer raised the animal humanely, without hormones and antibiotics. And it also increases what I pay for food. Our government has set corn subsidies below the cost to produce it, which lowers the cost to produce corn-fed meat. No wonder a fast-food hamburger costs less than veggies and other healthy food. No wonder people who live below the poverty line are more likely to be obese and suffer from diabetes and heart

[handwritten margin note: Food Inc. — Look up on Youtube]

disease. It's cheaper to eat fast food than to cook at home. Our country's farm policy is having unintended consequences for our nation's health.

I see I'm on the verge of ranting, so I'll stop. I admit that this diet is not easy for me. I guess I'll have to watch these films regularly to firm my resolve.

We almost got chickens.

May 8. My vegetarian-ish diet is going okay. BG is not happy about what I've been cooking but I'm not making him eat it. I'm still making meat dishes for the family. Yet something bugs him about my change in diet. He growls, "You're going to live until you die."

I'm reading *The Omnivore's Dilemma* by Michael Pollan. Between that and the films, I'm thinking that eating organic is even more important than eating vegetarian. I'm still eating wild-caught fish and free-range poultry and organic produce whenever I can find it.

Pollan's book points out that not all foods labeled organic are alike. There is a large system in place to provide grocery chains with produce and other foods that can be called organic because they aren't grown with pesticides, hormones and antibiotics. But these foods are otherwise grown, prepared and slaughtered using conventional methods and shipped all over using lots of petroleum. Cattle are still raised in CAFOs (Concentrated Animal Feeding Operations) where they eat corn instead of grass (albeit organic corn) and still stand knee-deep in their own excrement.

Even packages that say free-range chickens are misleading. The law says that to use that phrase chickens must have "access" to a run yard. Chickens spend the first five weeks of their lives indoors after which the farmer opens a little door between the inside and the yard. Unfortunately, they only live another two weeks before slaughter and, by then, they're trained to be inside. Few chickens take that stroll, so it's best to buy local organic and free range; know what you're eating. *Damn Government!!*

Thinking about this makes me crazy. Two weekends ago, I almost bought a dog kennel to raise my own chickens for organic eggs! Dianne offered me twelve newly hatched chicks. The girls and I went to her house on Friday evening and learned "Chickens 101" from her husband Mitch. The routine he pitched sounds so easy and healthy. You keep only females who produce up to one egg per day. You give them kitchen scraps and clean water daily. In Hawai'i, they don't even need a coop, and the pen (a dog kennel) is only about $100 at Home Depot. If you let the chickens out, they eat bugs and slugs in the yard. They run back to the kennel at night when they hear you shake organic grain from a container into the pen. Mitch says they're surprisingly easy to train. Then you use the chicken droppings to fertilize your garden by putting the poop in a bucket, filling it with water and serving the steeped liqueur to the plants. How wonderful; it's an ecological system!

Faye caught and held a chick. Jade petted its soft little head. They both crooned over the sweet little things. Mitch suggested we "take the chicks now. I'll give you the mother too. She'll teach the chicks all about being chickens, and you get eggs right away. But you have to take all twelve. When you figure out which ones are males, you kill them and proceed with egg harvesting." Apparently, chickens don't need sex to produce eggs. We were almost pulled in. The only thing that saved us at that moment was not having a place to put them.

We came home excited to tell BG about the plan we'd hatched and right away cracks developed. BG was unwilling to help at all, including killing the male chickens. Hmm, I'll have to think about that. Saturday the girls and I piled into the CRV and drove to Home Depot in Hilo. More cracks. They no longer carried the smaller $100 kennel. What they stock now cost $289, weighs 267 pounds and is too big to fit in the car without folding down the back seat. We were bummed. I tried to justify buying it anyway, but first I needed assurance that the girls would help. Ah, more cracks. Jade flat out said no. She's too busy and she's going to college soon. (Next year is soon?!) Faye, ever the lawyer, wanted me to define my terms. She offered to water the chickens once a week. This wasn't looking good at all. I decided to sleep on it. We drove home in silence.

[margin note: Too funny!]

Sunday I woke up to the realization that I loved the *idea* of raising chickens, eating organic eggs and fertilizing my garden with chicken poop. I could buy a lot of organic eggs with $289. The break-even point was about a decade down the road! That was a close call but I came to my senses in time. Still, they were cute. And the whole economic analysis I just developed, devoid of other considerations is what fuels *Food, Inc.* in the first place. See how crazy-circular this can be? Faye now tells me she's willing to water the chicks every day. Maybe I can hold out until she's willing to do the whole thing. Most likely I'll chicken out again.

Meanwhile, I found a source for free-range duck eggs. I go to a community organization once a month called Third Thursday Thrive where I encounter lots of new and interesting people. I met a woman there who sells duck eggs for $6/dozen. The eggs are fresh, delicious and big, so big that I'll have to adjust my recipes. The shells are hard; I have to crack them with vigor. The first one I tried to crack with my usual effort just bounced. And they're pretty: pale blue, pink, light beige, white and green. The other day I opened one with two yolks in it. That's a sign of luck.

I've also found places to buy organic food besides the farmer's markets. We have a great natural food store in Waimea. And one farmer from the market sells his vegetables at his farm on Tuesdays, so I don't have to drive to Waimea on Saturdays and burn another $7.00 in gas just to buy his veggies there. It's just a small detour on the way from picking up the girls from school. There's something comforting about buying vegetables from him at his farm. On the fields, I see neat rows of baby greens in different colors like a patchwork quilt. I smell the earth, wet from Waimea's mists. I see the care he takes with his property. It's a good feeling to have a relationship with the farmer that supplies me with my food. The Saturday market bread vendor also set up a tent at the farmer's stand so I can purchase fresh bread and frozen pizza dough for Jade's homemade pizzas on the grill.

I suppose that if I wanted to go back even further than farming to hunter-gatherer days, I could encourage BG to hunt. It's a tradition in Hawai'i. Last week I saw a big banner at the grounds of the Farmer's Market advertising the Annual Wild Pig Hunting Tournament, raising money for charity, maybe feeding the poor who might otherwise eat fast food. Hunting and eating wild pigs solves another problem. They're a nuisance, overrunning the island and digging up ecologically sensitive areas. It's a win-win for the 'āina! There's a common theme that links organic eating, sustainability, and practicing the Aloha mindset. It's doing the right thing.

I can't manifest for someone else.

May 11. Jade's been dealing with painful knees since her Volleyball Team Manager role ended in October. She's seeing a specialist in arthritis, taking lab tests (nothing detected), and physical therapy (no improvement in pain level). Although she said she won't manage the team again next year, it was a useful experience, because she can now add "slave" to her resumé.

Last week she was Confirmed. Grace flew in from Wisconsin to be her sponsor. I have to say the Catholic Church knows how to do a ceremony right, including the impressive Knights of Columbus Honor Guard. Kids from parishes all over the island gathered at our church. The bishop flew in from Oʻahu. He and the local parish priests wore red to symbolize the Holy Spirit and the Tongues of Fire. Almost a dozen men celebrated Mass together with the Bishop leading, an inspiring sight. Jade looked so excited and happy. She studied until the night before, picking out her Confirmation name. For months, she went through books on baby names, saints and angels. Nothing clicked. She finally chose Gabriella. I half expected her to change her mind as she walked up to the Bishop. But Gabriella it is. Now she'll have an archangel watching over her.

On the other hand, she's still incensed because, while she'd been driving with her regular license for nine months "at home," she had to go back to a learner's permit here. Hell hath no fury like a teen deprived of driving. Refusing to drive at all for the first five months, she's decided to beat Hawaiʻi's rules by waiting until her eighteenth birthday and then taking the test for the regular license. That way she doesn't have to retake driving school. She hated it the first time ("BORING!") and she wasn't about to go through it again. But this is a daily irritation to her and, frankly, to me. I can't wait until she gets her license. Then she can drive Faye and herself to school and back, saving us one daily round trip to Waimea and saving me two hours of time. But that won't be until the end of the year.

Faye's life is very different from Jade's at the moment. She's almost finished with her trimester elective. The first two trimesters she took pottery, then yearbook editing. This time she decided to try track because she remembered enjoying sprinting on her Racine School's team. Mistake. She's one of a handful of girls, while the guys are all the eighth grade jocks. She's slow on longer events, but that happens to be their focus. She hates it, but will soon put it behind her. Now her mind is on this Saturday's eighth grade dance at Kahua Ranch. She wants to ask a boy in her class to go with her, actually, meet her there, since neither drive. And she's coming to me for advice. Wow!

Both girls still occasionally give me grief about moving them here when they find something else in Hawai'i that doesn't suit them, like driving permit regulations. I hope we can get past all that this summer when we spend more time together at the beach. But, with the exception of praying, I've found that trying to help them manifest something like less knee pain or winning a sporting event doesn't work very well. It has to come from inside them. And trying to convince them to use the tools for themselves isn't working either. Why are teens so resistant to learning from their parents? You can lead a horse to water . . .

I'm thankful to celebrate Mother's Day.

May 13. Today I will receive cards and coupons for little treats from my daughters. I almost missed it all. There was a time when

I thought the whole motherhood thing wasn't for me. This notion had its inception in the heady days of early college. So many new ideas: Earth Day, civil rights, women's rights, protests over the Vietnam War – all of it swirling around me as I made my first tentative steps into independent adulthood.

My peers and I felt so much idealism back then yet, at the same time, felt betrayed by The Man. Government lied to us; Big Business turned our earth into a garbage dump; the Church couldn't see the importance of allowing birth control even with the world's population exploding; socialism as practiced by Russia, China and others failed. The world was falling apart. Our parents didn't see it, the government acted as if they didn't care, the Church chose not to reform. Change had to come from within us. That's where the excited idealism lived if it didn't get snuffed out by the cynicism of those around us.

Dr. Chuck taught us about Zero Population Growth, ZPG, in freshman biology. This powerful concept seemed to fix so many of the world's problems. I wonder why the idea seems to have disappeared. When couples have no more than two babies, they replace themselves and the population doesn't grow, maybe even shrinks eventually. With a smaller population, fewer children starve, we place fewer burdens on our planet and produce less waste. Women could contribute more to society by not spending their most productive years caring for lots of babies. Everyone has a better shot at reaching their potential, a fantastic win-win.

But the Church remained an intractable roadblock. Instead of changing their stand on birth control, they urged Catholic children to save pennies for pagan babies during Lent. Dad and I had countless arguments, in fact fights, about the Church's stand on this and other issues. I felt myself losing respect for the bedrock of my upbringing, a sorrowful process. As I slowly freed myself of the notion that I had to listen to the Church on this matter, it became easier to dismiss their stand on other things.

I decided ZPG was for me. In fact, as I began to make decisions for myself, I resolved to go one step better than limiting myself to two children. I'd not have any, a radical idea in 1972. The world was polluted, our political and social systems were going to pot, even a big war felt possible. Why would I want to bring a baby into this mess? Besides, I had important things to do. I didn't know what they were yet, but I felt that children would hold me back. I believed I could not have it all, career *and* kids. One had to go. I was a realist, or so I thought.

At 21, I married Alex, partly because he felt as I did – no kids. I was thrilled to discover that I wasn't a freak, that another felt the same way. This new way of living was made possible by the Pill. It liberated a whole generation of women. But it wasn't foolproof.

I remember the terrifying day I thought I was pregnant. I couldn't have a baby now. I just started graduate school! Alex would freak. He was not the daddy type; a genius, but not a dad. I didn't even tell him I was going for a pregnancy test. It was a cold, gray February day, as bleak outside as I felt inside. Much to my relief, I wasn't pregnant. But I couldn't risk it again. The next month I went to the hospital for a tubal ligation. A simple snip-snip solved my problem. The hospital happily took my money with no interrogation. I was all of 23 and sticking to my convictions. No one knew except Alex. This was really *too* radical.

All through my adult life, I never questioned what I did. When I divorced Alex, moved south for a new job and placed an ad in Atlanta Single's Magazine, I clearly stated that I didn't want babies. "If you do, don't call." BG willingly accepted this, though he said if I changed my mind, he wanted to go for it. No, thank you. At age 35, I had important things to do, though now that I knew what those things were, I wasn't sure I'd achieve them.

It wasn't until my little sister Mae had Maggie that I welcomed the chance to be with a baby, hold a baby, play with a baby. I was 40 and dumbstruck with love for this tiny being in my arms and the idea of having a baby of my own. I was no longer sure that I could leave a legacy through my work. By that time I was a manager, but it wasn't likely I'd get much further. Still, I could leave a legacy through a child. Even then, I didn't mourn for the child I might have had because I still believed in ZPG.

At 42, I set off for China with BG to start a new adventure in our lives. I so appreciated my sisters cheering us on all the way. Mom and Dad thought I was crazy. Some girls from my high school class were already grandmothers. What was I thinking? But I wasn't thinking. I was loving. The moment Jade came into my arms, I knew she was my baby. Five years later the three of us traveled to China for Faye, and again, instant love. By then I was almost 48. Now I look back at these as some of the best years of my life. I often said the girls would keep me young or kill me. I'm not dead yet, so I must be young.

Yes, today they'll give me Mother's Day cards and homemade coupons for back rubs, cleaning the bathroom, doing dishes and the like. But it's not Mother's Day that's important. It's every other day of the year that I get to be Mom and still live by my convictions that ZPG is a good thing. After all, it brought me Jade and Faye. And I'm living proof that people can change their minds and manifest anew. I still have important things to do and I can make them happen.

Diane M. Scheurell

Banana slugs and other critters.

May 15. My sister Grace was here last week for Jade's confirmation. She was surprised to see that I tolerate geckos in the carport, on the lanai, even in the house now and then, though we do shoo them outside. They're cute and they eat bugs. We who live in the subtropics have an interesting relationship with critters. It's best not to be too squeamish. You have to know when to live and let live, and when to kill.

Our kitchen ant problem completely cleared up after my short daughters went under the house and placed an ant spike near each post in the pillar-and-post construction, a perfect house design for this product. I'd also brought copious roach products when we moved, but I've hardly seen a roach in the house since we arrived. Large cockroaches that live outside are another matter. They're big enough to outfit with a saddle. I swear one of them wore a bandana as he galloped across the top of the hot tub. But as long as they stay outside (and they do), I don't care.

Plant pests are a totally different animal. I finally harvested enough green beans for a good meal. Then something ate the leaves and they were pau, done. The leaves had more holes than leaf. But I didn't see any bugs, so their demise is a mystery. If I do find them, respect for all species and sustainability be damned. This is my garden we're talking about. My peas are coming, but I only have two producing vines. The neighbor's chickens ate most of the pea seeds and scratched up the rest of the young pea plants as they sprouted. Bloody chickens.

The strawberry plants have taken hold and are growing. Now they just need to produce some berries, though locals warn me to guard against banana slugs. One of the women in the Women's Circle told me "try corn gluten meal . . . It's best if you lace it with crushed up egg shells to cut up the little buggers when they gobble it." I thought that was a bit harsh until I saw my first banana slug the other day, actually a herd of them. They were huge, light tan on one side, yellow on the other. As I expanded my front walkway and lined it with large rocks from the yard to make a border, I uncovered nests of these slugs. Ack! But armed with my salt, I waged war.

Finally, a note on the egg situation. Yesterday, BG noticed a hen sitting inside our carport on our Christmas boxes. She appeared to be dozing. That afternoon BG went to investigate. The hen was gone, but he found four small eggs. Now that's a Mother's Day effort. To honor her, we ate them for breakfast this morning. The shells were hard and the yolks a beautiful orange color, probably from eating my pea seeds! Of course we had to supplement them, and what a contrast between her small eggs and big duck eggs. Altogether, it was tasty and economical when you get half of them for free. Well, free if you don't count the aggravation from enduring the roosters and BG bellowing back and forth.

I saved the shells for the slugs. No tools to talk about here, unless you count "selective tolerance." Sometimes a story is just a story.

6. RELISHING AN AUSPICIOUS BIRTHDAY

On turning 60.

May 1. It's a jungle in my yard! Last week Kim and Thomas beat back the heliconia trees, one of which leaned precariously toward the house, and cleared out some post-fruiting banana stalks. They took three pickup truck loads to the trash transfer station and they're coming again tomorrow to continue the cleanup. I want the yard to look good for my 60th birthday party on Sunday. I can't believe I've made five trips around the zodiac. The Chinese consider 60 to be an auspicious birthday. And I'm a *Dragon* at 60. Now that's auspicious! I'm hosting an ice cream social to celebrate my Wisconsin roots. This is a great milestone – I'll get senior discounts at more places.

Last week in Women's Circle we did drumming. Our Queen owned a couple of large drums and we brought our smaller ones, so there were enough for all. BG always calls the Circle the Tom-Tom Club – now it is! It felt so good to wail away on that drum. During check-in, one younger woman talked about her mom turning 60 that week and how physically difficult it is for her to travel here. I was all sympathetic for her elderly mom's plight until it hit me – she's my age! Sixty sounds so much older on someone else.

This week I was struck by an essay Bill Moyers wrote for the AARP Bulletin, a favorite source for news lately. His thesis is that one should not retire, but keep working instead. He's probably right that we need an outlet for our passion. But I know retirement from the corporate world was good for me. I no longer have the heart-clutching anger that my old boss or some new company policy regularly triggered in me. I am peaceful, serene, tranquil (well, sometimes). Is that dying? I don't think so. But even if it is, I'll have had some time in paradise. As Barbara C. asked recently, "When did just living become not enough?"

I admit I could pick up the pace a bit, but do I really want to do that? It's not like I'm a couch potato. I'm active with water aerobics, yoga and gardening. I'm an avid reader. I'm also secretary for the weekly Women's Circle – not sure how that happened, but Dianne told me she manifested me so she wouldn't have to do it anymore. I've also joined a new grassroots nonpolitical organization in town, Third Thursday Thrive, or TTT. We meet, potluck style, every third Thursday of the month and listen to local musicians and invited speakers. We're focused on community networking and sustainability. We host talks on reforesting indigenous trees on the slopes of Mauna Kea, community gardening, Sustainability4free (making free stuff from trash), and other issues of bountiful living on the Hāmākua Coast, roughly Honoka'a to Hilo. People bring their seeds or extra produce to share. We've been meeting for about four months now and, somehow, I find myself on the organizing committee. (I can see my Wisconsin friends rolling their eyes and laughing when I tell them.)

I'm also putting out feelers for freelance editing work. I already have a regular client who writes a monthly article for a local newspaper. She's a French doctor of Oriental Medicine. Her English can use a bit of help, so I edit her articles. In exchange, she treats me with free acupuncture; more of that bartering economy. This weekend the editor of one of the monthly island publications sent me his own article as a trial for my editing. Wish me luck. Unfortunately, I couldn't hold back. I edited the hell out of it. I pray that he's a big enough man to swallow all the edits. I pray that he'll see the article is now tighter, better, and that he'll hire me for occasional editing. It would be nice to have some income instead of relying only on my savings.

The other thing I'll explore is teaching college. That was what I originally wanted to do with my Ph.D. My bachelor's degree was Home Economics Education but, during my interning experience, I found I couldn't stand working with high school kids. Most were disrespectful because they didn't want to be there. I didn't have to put up with that. So I went on to graduate school planning to teach college where, I was sure, students had a better attitude. But first, I took a corporate job to give me some experience and to satisfy my own consumer wants before going back to academia and a lower-paying job. I never made it; that slippery slope stuff.

Now I could go back to that old dream. The University of Hawai'i has both a four-year campus in Hilo and the North Hawai'i Education and Research Center (NHERC) right here in Honoka'a where I could teach. But I just can't seem to dredge up enthusiasm for developing a class syllabus and putting myself in front of students. It feels too structured. I'll think about it some more.

Meanwhile, the girls end school this week. Praise God! I'm looking forward to NOT driving to Waimea two or more times a day. Of course, they have other plans: the beach (other side of the island), shopping (other side of the island), new movie releases (other side of the island), visiting friends (other side of the island). Here's to the start of summer.

Life is greener on the other side of the island!!!

A ping from the past. Or is it a pang?

May 25. I received a patent! Yes! I can hardly believe it. I just found out, after all these years . . .

At one time in my corporate career I had three goals:

1. To have a job that required a hardhat: mill engineers would respect me.

2. To get a patent: research scientists would respect me.

3. To become a Vice President of Research: everyone would respect me.

By the time I wrote these goals, I had my Ph.D. and was already productive in my corporate research and documentation. I was presenting papers at conferences, some internationally. These were important credentials for a corporate research manager.

I achieved my first goal. At the Georgia job, I was the product developer for a new kind of paper hand towel. When we built the mill, I was part of the launch team and wore my own hardhat. I was there for almost a year, driving home on weekends. It was a blast, the most fun I'd had at work up to that point. I still feel pride when I walk into a public washroom and find they're using my hand towel. The hardhat sits on the top shelf of my bedroom bookcase. It could be handy in an earthquake. I never thought it might have future uses but the Universe works in strange ways.

Same for me with formulating colors for Glade products! my handywork is global :)

Diane M. Scheurell

I never should have had that third goal. My new friends can hardly believe I ever *worked* in a corporation, much less aspired to be a vice president. They say I'm not the corporate type. I feel the same way. I never did fit in. For example, I always made a point of wearing jeans on the day I received my performance review. This was during the '80s and early '90s when the expected attire was a skirted suit, pantyhose and heels. I claimed I wanted them judging me only on my merits. But deep in my heart I know I was daring them to give me a bad review. When the company allowed business casual attire, I stopped wearing jeans. It lost its thrill.

Then, my second year working in Racine, the Finance Manager cut our department budget by 25 percent. That was almost our entire discretionary budget: no skill improvement workshops, no new equipment, and no travel that year. When we needed a new camera, I decided enough was enough. My team made baked goods, I dressed up as an elf (it was near the holidays) and took my cart of goodies around the research building to raise money – a corporate bake sale!.

Higher-ups were not amused, but they forked over the cash and treated their research departments to cookies, maybe to make me go away quickly. One of the research directors took me aside and said that if we needed a camera, he would have paid for it. But that wasn't the point. The point of the bake sale was to shame Finance into restoring our budget. And when I didn't sell all the goodies in the research building, I jingled over to the halls of Marketing and Administration, padding around in my curly-toed elf shoes. We made $1247, enough to buy a really good camera. The next year Finance reinstated our original budget. Yes!

All things considered, I didn't do too badly. At both corporations I rose to a position of research manager with teams of 25 people reporting to me, including three managers. While the titles of Director and above eluded me, I was happy having the respect of the people who really counted – *my* people.

Still, that second goal, the elusive patent always bugged me. I'd put in a few Invention Disclosures at both companies, but found myself being pulled farther and farther from the research end. I did have the privilege of announcing my team members' patents, congratulating them with heartfelt praise. But the question still nagged me, why hadn't I done more to receive that distinction myself? I tried to let it go.

Today I lurched back into the corporate rat race. I was perusing a Google search of my name, taking stock in honor of my impending birthday. It was all familiar stuff: the seminar papers, chairing sections of conferences, starting chapters of professional organizations and some new things like my work with Third Thursday Thrive. Suddenly, I came across the entry that I had earned a patent! While at my Georgia job, one of my engineers and I were brainstorming on a problem. We came up with a novel way to solve it and submitted an Invention Disclosure.

Soon after, I left that company and went to work in Racine. Since I never heard anything more about it, I assumed that they'd decided not to pursue a patent. But they did. There it was in black and white: Patent 6170698, "Adapter for dispensing stacked interfolded sheets from a rolled product dispenser," issued January 8, 2001; Inventors Stephen Phelps and Diane Scheurell. And they never contacted me, or gave me the token dollar that companies give to employees in exchange for a patentable idea.

Gee, all these years I could've had that on my résumé. All these years I could've been satisfied that I'd met one of my three key goals. All these years it could've helped my trajectory; it would've checked an important box for some decision-makers . . . Nah, who am I kidding? The bake sale removed any brownie (or elf) points I might've made by having a patent. Still, I think I'll put it on my resumé now, a celebration of sorts. That, and write to the company to ask them for my dollar. Then I can put this behind me and get back to real life. After all, any change in my past might have changed my course and prevented me from living in paradise. Still, the news was a nice 60th birthday present.

Boomers rule; 60 is cool!

May 27. My birthday party was a big success. I could actually see the community roots I've put down in the faces of all my new friends. It's wonderful to already be part of the fabric of life here.

Lois and Connie from the water aerobics class came. They've shared chicken enticement strategies, information on 911 services in town, recipes and a surprisingly avid interest in the Wisconsin recall election for governor. My cowgirl neighbor came. We had become friendly when she broke her arm and I chauffeured her for a week. Through her I found a family doctor, important because the shortage of MDs on the island means many are no longer taking new patients.

My tattooed handymen came. I've probably spent more time with Kim and Thomas than with anyone else here and they've become friends. I remember seeing them for the first time: a tall lanky guy with a nose ring and long hair (later a buzz cut), and a short bald guy with a foot-long gray beard. Both sported wide tribal tattoos around arms and legs. They seemed downright scary, but no longer. They brought me a vine native to the islands called "shooting star hoya" as a gift, and then planted it for me. Real sweeties, despite their unnerving appearance.

My yoga teacher and her husband welcomed me to the club of old-timers. I was honored. She hasn't gone too many places since her cancer, not to the Women's Circle, and only recently to yoga class. At one time, Anita and Bob had a couple hundred yoga students in California, and he even had a yoga TV show. In this tiny community with its small population they inspire a much smaller circle of students. I am blessed to have them teach me yoga, patience, love, self-care, healthy eating and so much more. *Self care* She is among my oldest friends here; I went to her class whenever I was on the island, a couple years *before* we moved here.

Faye's best friend Ivy came with her mom, Lillian, all the way from the other side of the island. I explore my visual arts creativity with Lillian. I just know she's going to expand my horizons. The Women's Circle came in force, including Judy and Julia, who'd helped me clear out the east garden during my spring garden party, and Dianne, of chicken fame, and others. These new sisters taught me the meaning of sustainability as it relates to supporting each other. I realize now that I didn't cultivate enough deep friendships on the mainland; too busy with work and family.

Stacy came. She knew most of the people in the room and had helped several of us buy or sell homes. I don't see her often enough so this was a treat. Among her many jobs, she worked her way through college by delivering singing telegrams. She displayed that dormant talent at my party with clean versions of birthday songs.

Thirteen new friends, nine kinds of ice cream, my loving family, the good wishes and blessings of my extended family and old friends and 60 fabulous years or five trips around the zodiac cycle. You know, we Boomers are giving 60 a new prestige. It's the new 40, because most of us aren't going out without a fight. We're staying active, taking our health into our own hands, and having plastic surgery. I look forward to my next two or three Dragon Birthdays, living in Hawai'i on my terms.

Small eggs for nothing and chicks for free.

June 2. I've figured out my own angle on the egg question. One of my neighbor's chickens has been laying eggs in our carport for the last couple weeks. Unfortunately we never know where or when we're going to find the little delicacies. But I'm still in love with the *idea* of having chickens. So the chicken-savvy women at the pool told me to make a spot for her using a box with straw. They advised putting it up high, where she'd feel safe that no mongoose could steal her eggs. BG found a wooden box among the carport detritus, a Johnnie Walker Scotch Whisky crate his parents received when Poppa was stationed in Bogotá in the 1960s. It still has the shipping label stenciled on it directing the crate to the US Embassy in Columbia. After BG cleaned it, I lined it with paper and grass and placed it where we'd found the most eggs, on top of the Christmas boxes. That's appropriate – free eggs are like Christmas presents though, at this time of year, I'm still thinking of birthday gifts. Sure enough, the next morning we found an egg in the guest box.

Then my chicken advisors said I should replace the egg with a fake one, so that *Hen*rietta didn't think we were ripping her off. Yes, BG named her. That should've set off warning bells. I put a translucent egg-shaped stone in the nest and a wooden egg, neither of which is the right color or size. Her eggs are quite small. So I consulted a Ph.D. in Ornithology. Dr. Chuck was my first mentor, my biology professor in college and my first employer. I recently rekindled the friendship with him and his wife. Now, all these decades later, I can actually ask him a bird question. "Should I try to find an egg replacement closer to the size of her eggs and should I paint the wooden one white? We've been gathering an egg a day for five days." His response:

> Hi, Farmer Di,
>
> Not sure how many more eggs you think the chick can put out. Seems Henrietta is doing a great job with the stone and wooden egg! An interesting study was done long ago where a researcher put an oversized egg in a nest. It was so big the bird had to straddle the egg, and she accepted it as her own. So, size doesn't matter. But, why not play around and see if color is a factor (paint the egg black, blue or even red), or try some other variable. Have fun! You might find something very interesting.

I like science and I've been doing research most of my life. But I don't really want to start a research project at the moment. Heck, my whole life is an experiment right now. So I just left well enough alone. I guess that was fine with Henrietta, because she started to spend more and more time here. In the early days, we'd just find an egg. If we saw her beady little eyes peering at us over the side of the box, we'd avert our eyes and slink out of the carport like teenagers caught doing something elicit. She began to stay a couple of hours every day and all we'd see was the top of her tail. She faithfully laid an egg a day. We collected free eggs with none of the work of feeding, watering, or otherwise taking care of a chicken. That's having chickens my way.

Yesterday we ran into a complication. Henrietta stayed all night. She's still there this morning. BG did check to see that she was still alive. Yes, beady little eyes rose up like a periscope when he approached. I'm not going to move her to pull out the egg. And, worse, BG started feeding her. He's arguing that we should let her keep the eggs to raise chicks (though she'll be disappointed in the stone and wooden one). He even wants to keep her, saying that she's changed allegiance, has permanently crossed the road.

Maybe I should be happy about this. After all now it's his chicken, not mine, and I still get eggs without the work. Hmm. This could be a great birthday present. Yes, I'm still celebrating. I only turn 60 once!

Weather, diet and ice cream guilt.

June 9. Summer is almost upon us and I'm still using a down comforter at night and wearing a sweatshirt in the morning. Summer humidity hasn't settled in, despite the fact that it's been overcast and raining on and off for a week. But you wouldn't know that from the TV weather forecast which reports sunny skies across the islands. While Hawai'i is the second smallest state, it's spread across 360 miles of ocean. All our TV stations broadcast from Honolulu on O'ahu, and the meteorologist who focuses on the weather there is never correct for us.

The other forecasting problem is that, because of the terrain, we have many different microclimates. Hilo, at sea level, is always 5 to 8 degrees warmer than Honoka'a at 1000 feet. The Big Island boasts 11 out of 13 of the world's climate zones. It can be totally different one mile to the next. Sometimes the weather map doesn't show a rain system within a thousand miles of us, yet it's raining in Waimea. Along Lake Michigan in Wisconsin we used to say "if you don't like the weather, wait five minutes." Here, it's "drive five miles." Frankly, I think they design the weather report for our tourists – always sunny.

It's a hoot to watch the weather report anyway. It includes wave heights for surfers, dangerous situations for swimmers ("the box jellyfish tide will rise until Thursday and then subside for the rest of the month"), and the traffic report for Honolulu. Otherwise, our meteorologists would have nothing much to say. For the first couple of months, I could barely detect a difference in the weather story from one day to the next. Ah, the perils of being a weatherman in paradise.

Henrietta still sits on her nest. She hasn't left since Saturday. Mitch told us about broody chickens. He said they were in a docile, drugged-like state and that you could pick them up and walk around with them like a puppy. That must refer to chickens who know you. When BG tried to put some food and water up near the nest he nearly lost his eyebrows. According to my brother-in-law Vitmer, it'll take about 21 days for eggs to hatch. BG hasn't figured out what he's going to do then. But it's not my problem. They'll be his chickens.

I finally received the *Forks over Knives* documentary from the library. It was just as scary viewing it now as when I saw it two months ago and started modifying my diet. Only now I'm also feeling guilty. It reports on a researcher who ran an experiment with mice showing he could turn cancer on and off by feeding them different levels of animal protein. He used casein, the protein in milk. What a bad choice it was to have an ice cream social for my birthday party. Maybe I'll have to switch to beer next year, another fine Wisconsin tradition. Worse, of the nine kinds of ice cream, we finished only one quart at the party (maybe they knew!). I wound up eating the other three gallons, having some every night since then, and doing my part to rid the planet of the evil stuff.

Outside of ice cream, the choice to reduce animal protein in my diet is going fairly well. Notice I said reduce, not eliminate. This is a work in progress. I've even discovered that I love tofu and cooked beets. Yes, the plant-based diet is pretty good. Maybe I'll earn a few more birthdays over the course of my life by making the switch.

Lessons through Mom.

June 11. Yesterday a friend called me about her mother's sudden death. We talked for a long time, and I relived my own mom's passing only a year and a half ago. She had been diagnosed with Alzheimer's, living first in an assisted living facility and then a nursing home. At the end, she still knew all of us, but it looked like we were in for a long protracted journey as her mind, her personhood, slowly dissolved right in front of us. So it was a shock and a guilty relief when Grace called with the news that Mom died of a heart attack while walking back to her room from dinner. The doctor said it killed her before she hit the floor, so she didn't suffer.

I always felt bad that I wasn't closer to her. She was born in 1931, a first generation Czech, and grew up knowing nothing beyond the Depression and then WWII, no references to a happier time. She was just 14 when the fighting ended. When she finished high school, she met an attentive older man, my dad, and they married two years later. That was the dream in 1951 – find a husband and settle down to the new post-World War II prosperity. They moved into the apartment above her parents and I came along 11 months later. Now she was both a young bride and a young mother.

I heard a story from one of my aunts that Dad married Mom because, after living with three sisters, he liked her quiet manner. But she was also quite the shapely babe. I could always see people mentally adding years to her age when they found out I was her daughter. She loved to dance. She could take off across the dance floor like she was running the 440 with a polka partner, rarely my dad. He preferred a slow two-step while crooning into her ear.

Dad overshadowed her and she became quieter with every passing year. Her mom also challenged her on how to take care of me and provided direction on all things domestic. That may be why Mom decided to become a bookkeeper at a local hardware store while Dad, who worked second shift, and Grandma looked after me during the day. It took her out of the house and gave her some power in the form of money to contribute towards their dream of owning a home. We moved into that home when I was seven.

When I think back on it now, her job ensured that I would work, too. It wasn't the big decision many young women faced back in the 1970s, whether or not to work outside the home. Of course I would work – my mom worked all her life. She had been liberated through necessity. But I would work on my own terms. I would have a career. Mom didn't understand my desire for a master's degree and Ph.D., nor could I explain it sufficiently back then. Maybe, in my gut, I knew I didn't want to be like her – a person without a voice. Wow, I only realized that when I wrote it.

My sisters and I often wondered if something horrible befell her as a girl to make her almost mute, some other explanation besides

Diane M. Scheurell

being somewhat deaf. She suffered a bout of rheumatic fever as a child which scarred one of her ears. Later she discovered that she also had otosclerosis, a genetic disease that progressively took her hearing away. A friend once told me she liked that my mom was so attentive when she talked with her. "That's because she's lip reading," I explained. I remember she went to Madison to have an ear operation when I was about six. It helped for a few years, but she eventually needed a hearing aid. She had so much scarring in the other ear that, combined with the otosclerosis, she became totally deaf on that side.

As her hearing diminished, she grew quieter and more detached. Dad was hard of hearing too; ear protection wasn't required in the shipyard back then. So our household became the Loud Family, everyone shouting and the TV blaring. To this day, I speak quite loudly, especially when I get excited. *Kind of funny, I can relate to this very well!*

About the time that I was old enough to have an adult relationship with Mom, she became almost one-dimensional. There was no depth to her personality, and what remained were her strong beliefs in the Church and her attentiveness to her own mother, who was by then living with us. I loved Mom, but I could not relate to her in any way. We had nothing in common, except that she was my mom. In my 20's, I was still working to become independent of my parents' influence, choosing my own path. In my 30's, Mom focused on Grace and her kids, enjoying her new status as Grandma. Again, I could not relate.

They can't give us what they don't have!

The year I turned 38, I finally saw her bloom, if only for a week. We girls decided to accompany her to Czechoslovakia (later called the Czech Republic) the year after the Velvet Revolution, visiting her mother's family, with whom she'd been corresponding all her life. She'd sent money across the Iron Curtain for decades. Now

She was powerful in her own way, making life better for her family still in the homeland — that was her voice!

we had the opportunity to meet Teta (Aunty) and the rest of the family. Within an hour of landing at the airport in Prague, they whisked us to my grandmother's hometown, the medieval walled town of Louny and we were drinking the local brew at a picnic table in a real beer garden, complete with children on a nearby swing-set and goats wandering through.

It was another world and they treated Mom like royalty. Her Czech came back to her and she translated across the divide, lip-reading and straining to hear people when the English-speaking friend they included in all the activities wasn't around. For a week, she was the center of attention, maybe the only week of her life, and Mom looked happier than I've ever seen her. It was a shared experience that we sisters treasure to this day.

In my 40's, when we adopted the girls, she opened her heart to them but, being 1000 miles away, we didn't interact much. Phone calls were excruciating, because she didn't say anything. I mean literally. She was mostly silent on the other end of the line giving only one-word answers. It wasn't disinterest on her part. She enthusiastically said "Yes" and "No" or even "Wonderful," but the conversations were totally one-sided and exhausting. Then we moved from Georgia to Wisconsin and we visited more frequently. In this environment, she was able to participate in her own way, because we sisters chatted loudly to include her.

In my mid-50s we received the horrible news that Mom had Alzheimer's. It's not an exaggeration to say that this struck me with terror. I knew Alzheimer's was hereditary. That was my worst nightmare because I've always relied on my intellect. In the corporate environment, if you don't have your mind, you have nothing, you are useless, you cease to have meaning.

so very true!

As if to confirm my fear, I began to notice that I forgot things. I immediately jumped to the conclusion that I had Alzheimer's, or some sort of dementia, too. My friends said it was common for menopausal women to have these symptoms, that this was normal, and they had them, too. Others said that the high stress in my life was likely contributing to the mental lapses. I understood that these could be contributing factors but I was still terrified. My fear became almost crippling, a painful detour on my journey to becoming authentic and living my life to the fullest.

Then, one day, I was writing a PowerPoint about my department. I started to type out the four word name: Consumer and Product . . . I blanked. "Focus, Diane," I scolded myself. I started again. Consumer and Product . . . Nothing came. I became flustered. "What the hell? Diane, you know this." Consumer and Product . . . With each repeat of the first part of the name and the inability to remember the last word, my feelings changed from annoyed to agitated and finally to frightened. I even knew the first letter of the last word but, for the life of me, I could not remember it, though I had instituted the name change nine years earlier! Finally, I panicked and froze in front of my computer. I began to cry helplessly. Tears rolled down my cheeks and created big blotches on my dress. "Diane, you have to get a grip!" I told myself. "Someone could come in here any minute!" I immediately began meditating. *Peace* on the deep inhale, *serenity* on the extended exhale. *Peace* on the inhale, *tranquility* on the exhale.

Finally calm, I called my doctor for an appointment. I knew from reading that medications could slow the progression of Alzheimer's. I wanted to start them while I was still a highly functioning executive, not later when my mind was already impaired. Two days later I was in my doctor's office asking her to prescribe them for me. She'd been treating me for almost a decade and I trusted her. But she gave me a sideways look and said, "Yes, I could do that. But why don't you see a psychiatrist first. He can order an MRI to see if there's anything else that could explain your memory loss. We need to rule out other causes." She gave me the name of the psychiatrist in my health plan and five days later I was sitting in his office explaining my situation again.

It was clear that Dr. Smith mostly talked with a patient's caring relatives, not the patient herself. He addressed me as he would a seven-year-old: eyes wide, broad empty smile, short words, slow pace and even that singsong lilt that adults use with children. I threw a few 50-cent words at him and he slowed down a bit with a puzzled look on his face, but then picked up where he left off, recommending neuropsychological testing with yet a third health care professional. I pushed him further. "I understand that you could test my blood for certain markers that identify people with Alzheimer's. Will you run the tests on me? I want to know."

"No, I won't, because these markers have not proven to be conclusive, nor are all the markers identified. So you could get a false positive or negative." Well at least he was now talking to me like an adult. But as soon as he wrote out the order for the MRI, I grabbed the card he gave me for the neuropsychologist and ran out of there. I began to have an inkling of what it might feel like to live in a nursing home with no one believing you could think. It was so creepy it made my skin crawl. And it was so possible. Fear struck again but, this time, I felt I was somewhat in control because I was *doing* something. The following week I had the MRI. It was quite interesting – lots of irregular banging sounds and the equipment vibrated a bit at times, but really no big deal unless you're claustrophobic, which I'm not.

At the end of that week, I was participating in the assessment with the neuropsychologist. Unlike Dr. Smith, she treated me like an intelligent adult and, at once, I felt at ease. I explained that I knew I was smart enough to compensate for memory loss by using alternate ways to arrive at solutions to problems. So my brain may have been hiding this for some time. She agreed and said that the MRI in combination with the testing could show any irregularities. I liked that word. It was much safer than the phrases I was saying to myself.

We spent the next eight hours going through a battery of tests measuring intellectual ability, memory, language, visuospatial proficiency, attention, concentration, processing speed, executive function, motor examination, mood and personality. It was everything from "What is this?" (a comb, a lamb, a truck), to math problems and picture puzzles (which of these five pieces, in a variety of positions, fits the empty hole?) to name as many flowers as you can. Some of the tests were timed, others were not. The whole experience was actually fun, but exhausting. I left feeling tired, yet good, even confident, and appreciating that I would know something at the end of three weeks.

The MRI came back showing no issues. One down. Then I went back to see the neuropsychologist. She smiled as she gave me her report. "You knew you would come through with flying colors, didn't you, Diane?"

"No, I didn't," I insisted.

She looked at me kindly. "You have a very high IQ."

"Really? I guessed that, but no one ever told me my IQ before. Besides, isn't it exactly a high IQ that could hide Alzheimer's?"

"Yes, but you are a long way from needing to worry. If it's your IQ that's hiding dementia, then your intellectual capacity will continue to assist you for many years to come."

"Then why did I forget the name of my own department?"

She shrugged. "Self-fulfilling prophecy? Likely it was stress, combined with panic that blocked the answer." I left the office, her eight page report in hand, feeling relieved.

[margin note: Blocking out — ways I used to survive my own childhood abuse!]

Soon after that my mom died, bringing that guilty relief. I wish we had requested an autopsy to look at her brain, but we didn't think of it. I cried for her passing and I cried because I hadn't tried harder to bond with her. My heart aches knowing that I had a lifetime of opportunities and I didn't take them. Now it's too late.

[margin note: I tried for 60 years — to have a relationship with my Dad. now, I refuse to take one more second of abuse from him — no longer will I be his scapegoat]

Some weeks after that, my thoughts took a different track. Mom was only 21 years older than me and she was dead. I was damned if I was going to spend another year in the corporate world with that kind of potential deadline haunting me. I might not have Alzheimer's, but anything could kill me. I had genetic and personal risk factors for heart disease. I passed through a dangerous neighborhood frequently. I walked to work and could be hit by a car. Anything could snuff me before I had the chance to manifest my paradise. The whole internal conversation firmed my resolve to escape and bolstered my courage to find my new life. It was time to choose and execute.

[margin note: Time to choose & execute!]

These thoughts also swirled with my desire to bond with the girls. I hadn't bonded with my mom. I felt it was my fault for abandoning her just because she couldn't reach out to me. I miss her, but I miss what could have been even more. I'm not going to repeat it with my daughters. So here I am, living my new life and reaching out to them, and wondering what unintended lessons

Unintended lessons

Diane M. Scheurell

they've already absorbed from me. Those unintended lessons may make it harder for us to connect, but I won't stop trying. With unconditional love and an attempt to be present, I hope to report that our relationships are much improved, even rich, by the time I'm 61.

Was this goal met?

7. CHOOSING YOUR ATTITUDE

Connecting with my girls.

June 13. The girls have been home for summer break for three weeks. We're all trying to adjust to so many people in this small house all the time. Part of my rationale for leaving the corporate world early was to bond with them, renew our more intimate connection before they go off to college. That gives me one more year with Jade, four with Faye. Unfortunately, neither was happy about this move and, at first, I felt like I was going backwards. But as they settled in, made friends and did well in school, they softened their stand a bit, except for Jade's driver's license anger. But regain intimacy? That's going to take longer.

When we first adopted the girls from China, we lived in the Atlanta area. I was the primary caregiver, responsible for waking and dressing them, taking them to the doctor and daycare and attending to boo-boos and lost blankets. But we moved to Wisconsin to pursue a job for me and create stronger bonds between the girls and my extended family in Manitowoc, who'd now be two hours away by car instead of a thousand miles by air.

In Racine, BG worked from home as an engineering consultant for the company he left in Georgia, and also took on the primary caregiver role. The girls were six and two. For the next 10 years Daddy was there for them, taking them to school and appointments, doing homework with them and teaching them how to use tools and solve problems, while I went to bed early with a <u>headache or exhaustion</u>. I did plan great family vacations, took them clothes shopping, made costumes, took them to ballet and basket ball practice and had "the talk" (several times). But I missed out on the daily details of life. This was an advantage only once, when I escaped the trauma of Faye <u>catching lice</u> during summer day camp. I was in England on a business trip when I received the email from a distressed Jade that <u>Daddy was cutting off all of Faye's long hair</u>. I could mentally hear Faye wailing. He did the whole lice treatment that week. They didn't talk to him for a month, Jade in solidarity with her sister. Glad I dodged that one. Still, they're definitely Daddy's girls. Can I regain lost ground?

Jade and I are planning our July trip to the mainland to research colleges, so we're talking regularly. She's not the usual teen. She didn't go through that stormy I-hate-my-parents stage of noncommunication and noncooperation. Sure, she has her moods, but they aren't continuous and she remains sweet and willing to help out, even voluntarily cleaning when she sees a job that needs doing. But she's always been quiet, more like BG. This year they had even more bonding time because they signed up together for a church project. Almost every Saturday since March they've worked with Habitat for Humanity building a house for three elderly sisters.

Recently Jade begrudgingly admitted that her new school has some cool aspects, like the graduation ceremony. We went to the senior graduation in May just to watch. They filled the gym with beautiful flowers, every surface covered with lush tropical greens and blooms. The grads all wore white, the girls in long aloha-attire gowns with yellow flowers in their hair, the boys in white shirts and trousers with a red cummerbund. The ceremony started with Hawaiian blessings and music and ended with the graduates performing three hulas: one girls-only, one boys-only, and the third with both boys and girls. It was beautiful and fun, with lots of hooting and hollering from the audience. Afterward everyone met out on the school lawn where family members and friends laid lei after lei on the grads until some were up to their eyes in flowers. Even Jade concedes there's no way her old school could match that.

My relationship with Faye is in some ways harder and in some ways easier. These days she hides in her room with a book, her iPad and her phone. She's far more rebellious than Jade on what she eats (only junk food and sushi) and general communication (nonexistent since turning 13). When she's in the mood, we still talk about personal things. From the time she figured out there were two genders, she's asked me how to deal with boys.

We understand each other because her personality is more like mine, though not our diurnal clocks. Her idea of a great summer day is to sleep until 1 p.m., emerge to watch TV in the afternoon just as I'm going down for my nap, hunker down in her room with her iPad and phone in early evening then, after we've gone to bed, she emerges to watch more TV until the wee hours. So, basically, we don't see her. I have to ask her several times and, finally, yell at her (several times) to get her to do anything, even come to the table for meals. I want to have normal chats with her, but she drives me crazy and I wind up scolding instead of conversing.

The thing you don't want to happen happens

Diane M. Scheurell

Reconnecting has been slow and tentative with both. I expected that. They are their own persons now, no longer malleable, if they ever were. It's time for a midcourse correction. I can't control them, but I can control me. I've decided to try one of the tools I learned at work, a program developed by a fresh fish company in Seattle to help employees connect with customers. This program is explained in the book *Fish! A Remarkable Way to Boost Morale and Improve Results* (Lundin, 2000).

The company had four simple rules for their employees:

1. Choose your attitude. Any job or task can be boring, even depressing. Likewise, any job can be challenging, even fun, if you choose to look at it that way. You can choose to be happy or grumpy. Even if you feel grumpy, research shows that if you fake a smile you're likely to start feeling happier. Choose to be happy at work and in life.

2. Play. Parts of any job or task can be done in a playful manner. If you can play while working, you'll be more energized.

3. Make their day. Create great memories by respectfully including others in what you do. When you focus on other people, do things for them, they feel the positive energy you bring to them.

4. Be there. Tune in to the other person. Listen carefully, intently, with your eyes and intuition as well as your ears.

For years, I had these rules posted on my file cabinet at work to remind me how best to treat the people around me. They've been on my refrigerator since October, right in front of my nose. If they work with customers and colleagues, they might work with my teens. I can choose to have a fun, helpful attitude. We can play. I can focus positive energy on them to make their day and make memories. And I can be there for them. No more absent-mindedly answering a question without looking up from my laptop. I hope this approach goes well. If it doesn't work, I'll try something else.

Don't give up... try, try again... make the change

Playing while I work

June 18. I woke at 4:30 this morning and watched dawn break. It was perfectly still: no trade winds, no bird songs, no coquis. The coconut palms in my yard stood absolutely motionless, stark black against the sky lighting behind them. The silence must be what woke me, that and the sweet smell of my puakenikeni bush. It's an old Hawaiian flower used for white and yellow lei. But when the wind blows and carries the fragrance west, I can't smell it. I call it a bush but, like many other things in my yard, it got away from me. By the time Kim and Thomas tackled it, they urged me to stop the trimming process halfway up, so that it looks like a tree. That was fine with me. They left some branch stumps along the lower part of the trunk to hold orchids and bromeliads.

Henrietta is still on her nest. Assuming 21 days to hatch, she's in her third trimester. During one of the few times she left, BG removed the wooden egg and rock. He didn't want her trying to hatch them forever. That left one solitary egg. He considered adding a few fertilized eggs from the grocery store to the nest, but by the time he thought of it she was pretty far along. Faye suggested adding fertilized duck eggs. I think she's still moping over the ducks she wanted at Easter.

My editing career did not take off after I "edited the hell out of the Editor's article," striking out close to a fourth of it. He liked my work and agreed with my suggestions, but told me he had to fill the space the paper gave him. I wish he'd said that before he gave me the assignment. I guess I didn't Make His Day. Meanwhile I still edit for the doctor who trades me for acupuncture, and I manifested another editing opportunity.

Mitch and Dianne (of free chicken fame) and their daughter are starting a web-based business. They want me to write and edit content for them in exchange for a piece of the business. No thanks. As a contractor, I'm second after the website developer to receive money if it flies. As part owner, it might take years. Besides, I know that if I was part owner I'd fight for my point of view and, frankly, I'm not that passionate about the business or the business model. Besides, I'd like to keep these friends. But they insist that they want my input.

So to Be There for them, I've made a different deal. I'm deferring payment for writing and editing, and attending their meetings for free just because it's interesting. I can express my opinion, bring my business background to bear, and then let them decide what to do. I also have the freedom to punt when my editing business picks up. That was three weeks ago and I've been having fun ever since. Yes, I'm editing a few things. But I'm also facilitating their business meetings. With 20 years of experience, I just took over and they let me. I run the meetings, take notes, issue minutes and propose the agenda for the next meeting. This is such a kick! I totally satisfy my management yayas and Mitch and Dianne are happy that I keep them focused and even mediate family quarrels.

It reminds me a bit of my childhood when I was the leader of the neighborhood kids. We put on plays (with me as director), created clubs (I was President and made the badges), played Kit Carson pioneer days (following the script in my head), made tents outside from blankets (under my direction), and even slept in them at night (I kept the kitchen knife under my pillow). You get the idea. I always tell my younger sisters that they were the best training I could've ever had for a job in management. And now I'm playing at management again with my friends. I can't help myself. This must be why BG and the girls took me aside early in my retirement and flat out stated that I could not expect to manage *them*; they are not my employees. While I feigned surprise and hurt, something in their words rang true.

Yesterday the girls and I went shopping for new swimsuits. I had hoped it would Make Their Day and even qualify as Play. But it didn't turn out like I thought. In my effort to Be There and Choose My Attitude, I went overboard. On the drive to the shopping center, I noticed that Faye was sullen.

"Sweetheart, what's the problem?"

"*You* are Mom. You're a morning person. You're chatty. You're cheerful. You get your best work done before I even get up. I don't *want* to talk in the morning. I just want to sleep as you drive. Your cheerfulness makes me mad. I'm a night person. By the time I'm energized enough to have a conversation, you're thinking about bed. We don't mesh."

Rats . . . not enough Be There. We're off to the beach today, and I get to try this new approach all over again.

Life's a beach.

June 23. I'm glad Faye decided to take the Junior Lifeguarding course this summer. It's a two-week program offered by the

Hawai'i Fire Department lifeguards. She's attending with her best friend Ivy, a competitive swimmer who's qualified for four events at State next month. Ivy's participated in this program every year since she was eight. Monday the girls had to prove they could swim 200 meters. Unfortunately, the usual lifeguard wasn't there; the Fire Marshall substituted. When he drew the line at 25 kids, Ivy and Faye didn't get to register. Lillian said not to worry. The usual teacher was cool and would let both in.

We kept a positive attitude and showed up at Hapuna Beach on Tuesday. Sure enough, the regular lifeguard said yes, mostly because he knew Ivy. Relationships are so important on the islands, especially among Native Hawaiians. He's been running this program for 16 years, "Longer than most of you been on earth," he tells the kids. He comes across real tough at first. "No throwing sand. You throw sand, you do ten pushups. You throw sand again, it's twenty."

He was all business at the beginning. "The buddy system is required at all times . . . If you leave the beach for any reason, you must tell me . . . This program is about good sportsmanship. No negative talk about anybody . . . No swearing. Stay positive in everything you do. Failure to comply will result in disciplinary action . . . No slacking. If you take it easy and I know you have more in you, I *will* push you . . . We check the beach every morning for Portuguese man o' war. If they there, we won't go in." After 30 minutes, he started to soften up. "Let me know if you're having a girl day . . . Let me know if you need sunscreen. I get it from the guys at the airport who get it from the tourists trying to board with too much liquid."

The program doesn't claim to make these kids lifeguards, but to provide them with ocean awareness, first aid instruction and safety lessons. I can see by his remarks that he also considers it a leadership program. After talking, he got down to business: calisthenics on the beach, followed by a long swim and a longer beach run. Faye was the last to drag out of the water and she didn't look happy about hard charging down the beach. But, even pooped, she's competitive.

Wednesday we're back. The beach is about 40 minutes away, so we rise early to arrive at 9 a.m. Faye sleeps on the road while I drive. I'm learning to Be There the way she wants it, not the way I imagine it.

Most people imagine that the islands must have fabulous beaches. While that may be true of islands within the continental shelf, the Hawaiian Islands are different. They come straight up from the ocean floor in the middle of the Pacific Ocean. The older islands developed nice beaches over time, but Hawai'i is just too new. Our shoreline is mostly rocky lava that once flowed to the ocean, and coral in the shallow water. Hapuna Beach is one of the exceptions with a long sandy beach and a sandy bottom all the way out. The one main rock is a landmark ("swim from the end of the beach to the rock"). Today's waves are small and frothy, like narrow ribbons of white lace edging up to shore.

Kiawe trees edge the interface between the grassy areas and the beach. They're part of the mesquite family and drop very large thorns, so prudent swimmers wear slippers out to the sand. Island folklore says the missionaries planted this tree to make the Native Hawaiians learn to wear shoes. But I learned from the Internet that ranchers introduced it for cattle feed in 1905.

Besides kiawe, shady trees and palms, picnic tables and a few pavilions dot the long gentle slope from the sizzling parking lot to the sand. The beach leads a double life all year. Tourists use it during the day but, as they leave, tired and sunburned, the locals show up after work and swim or surf until sunset. Every time I've been on the beach it's been breezy and comfortable, no matter how hot the sun.

Today, as I walked up and down the beach with Lillian, I noticed hills of sand, some almost a foot high. Near each was a hole ranging in size from a macadamia nut to an orange. Lillian explained that each hole contains a sand crab. So far, I haven't seen any. I hadn't seen these hills before, but it's low tide and maybe I haven't been here at low tide. Every day is a learning day. At the same time, I can start discarding information, like what clouds look like when they contain snow, and how to stay safe in a tornado. I no longer have to stay alert for deer running across the highway, or worry about bloodsucking leeches in the water.

At the beginning of today's training, our lifeguard showed more of his personal side. "I'll start each day with a prayer for our learning and safety." There are many places on the mainland where he couldn't do that. But this is Hawai'i and we enjoy exemptions to mainland rules. For example, we have two official languages, English and Hawaiian. And we're the only state in the nation with a royal palace. Hawaii enjoys many exceptions to help preserve the native culture. The Pope even granted a special dispensation that allows Catholics to dance a hula to the Our Father during Mass, "because we are on sacred ground." It's part of what makes Hawai'i a fascinating place to live.

The teacher also talked to the kids about protecting the ocean as well as enjoying it. "Always clean up the beach, especially plastic bags," he told them. "They should outlaw them on the islands. Offshore breezes push bags into the water and it chokes and kills coral. And turtles and other marine life eat the plastic." Later he talked about fish farms with permits in island waters. "The offshore fish farms draw sharks, so they should only put them where people don't swim, snorkel, surf and canoe." These kids are going to acquire a good dose of this guy's personal philosophy. Luckily I agree with him so far.

I notice more every time I come. On Thursday, I see the "lands" that cradle the beach on both ends. They're actually giant lava formations from the 1859 flow, extending into the water about 400 feet. Rising 30 to 40 feet, they provide some shade. Lillian took me to a lava cave reachable only at low tide. We skirted the waves and stepped inside. As I tentatively crossed into the darkness, I shivered with the damp chilliness of the air. It was quiet and still inside, a muffled eeriness. We stopped in our tracks, eyes searching the dark spaces. The ceiling towered above us and we found ourselves surrounded on four sides by lava frozen in space. I could feel the lava's power, its mana. The hair on the back of my neck stood up and I shivered. Lillian must've felt the same and we quickly left the dark space, splashing through the shallow waves instead of waiting for a lull.

By the time we wandered back to the main pavilion, the class had already warmed up, and completed their daily run and swim segments. The lifeguard was back on leadership training. "The motto of this class is *never give up*," he said, arms folded across his broad chest. "I'm not impressed with how good you are, how fast you swim or run. But when you improve yourself, then I'm impressed." He looked at Faye, standing in her damp black suit. "The one who's improved the most so far is Faye. On the first day she was last in swimming. Today she's in the middle of the pack. That impresses me more than the rest of you who don't put out your best effort every minute of every day." Faye was beaming and so was I. He definitely Made My Day!

Today's first aid lesson focused on moving wounded people. But before starting, they listened to a guest, Aunty Sue. All elders here take on the respectful title of Aunty or Uncle. She talked about her son who died two years ago in a car crash. His death might've been prevented if his companions had known some safety training. As she showed his picture, she urged the kids to take these lessons into every aspect of their lives, not just swimming. It was all the more moving to us because the teen was from Honoka'a.

The teacher reinforced Aunty Sue's message and added his leadership twist. He told the kids that they need to have the guts to stop others who are doing the wrong thing, like driving under the influence. "If you can't stop them, then leave. It's betta' to be embarrassed by walking home than going to the morgue in an ambulance." Tough talk, but everyone listened intently. I love this guy and so do the kids.

Friday, as we exit the car, I hear the surf before I see the water. The waves must be up today. The slow rhythmic pounding of water on the beach is already affecting me as profoundly as the meditation we do in yoga, so calming and soothing, Mother Earth's heartbeat. I automatically start breathing deeply, filling my lungs with salt air. As I stroll over the rise in the hill between the parking lot and beach, I study the stunning colors of the water in this bay and beyond. Hawaiian waters are especially blue because they're deep and contain few nutrients to cloud and muddy the color. That's why whales leave after giving birth to their babies – no food. I offer up a quick thank you to God for the intense aqua color stippled with white foam waves, shading to the deepest blue-black on the horizon, and enjoy this moment fully.

By the end of the week, Faye was dragging because she chose to Be There, and it's hard work. She hasn't been this physical since running track. Her mantra's been, "I can sleep in on Saturday. Don't wake me up!" So here it is, Saturday morning and she's sleeping. Only one more week of this, I began to crab to myself, missing water aerobics and yoga while being Taxi Mom. On the other hand I've spent a week of blissful early mornings at the beach. How can that possibly be wasted time? Beach as therapy; I'm Choosing My Attitude.

Life's still a beach, or is it?

June 27. It's Monday of the second week of class and we arrived at the beach early. As Faye and I got out of the car, a bunch of guys leaving the beach with their long boards surprised me. They were locals heading off to work after surfing early in the morning! It turns out this beach does triple duty: locals in early morning, tourists during the day and locals again after work.

Heading toward the beach, we heard happy shrieking. It turned out to be an entire family on their boogie boards. Grandpa, in shallow water, teased the kids, splashing them as they roared past him. Dad raced the eldest son and mom took action pictures from shore, watching the littlest kid out of the corner of her eye. They were clearly having a blast. This was the first morning I wished I'd brought my swimsuit.

As the teacher began his opening remarks for this second week, I watched families arrive with their loads of gear. While there's almost always a nice breeze, the sand turns blistering hot later in the morning and there's lots of beach between the shaded lawn area and the water. So people learn to bring chairs to get them up off the sand if they're going to spend the day. This beach is full of colorful umbrellas and even small tents by midday in summer.

Soon the kids in the class gathered on the beach to do calisthenics. The teacher expects respect and discipline in the ranks, so he doesn't need to say anything. The kids lined up in neat rows and measured themselves off to provide proper spacing. After stretching, arm circles and jumping jacks, the teacher gave the signal, and the kids took off sprinting to the other end of the beach. They pushed past waves into the water and swam the length of the beach back to the teacher. I have a hard time understanding why Faye signed up for this voluntarily. It must be Ivy's good influence.

Ivy and her family live only a few minutes from Hapuna, so Lillian suggested that Faye stay with them for the week. What a deal! I don't have to drive to Hapuna three out of five days and Faye can sleep an extra 40 minutes each morning.

I talked with Faye last night. She's determined to do well, especially after the teacher's comment on how much she improved last week. So, afternoons and evenings, Ivy helps Faye improve her stroke, coaching her while she swims 650 meters in their condo pool. I can only imagine the internal dialog between Faye's couch potato and her competitive ego. I'm sure this isn't what Faye thought she was signing up to do. But I kept my mouth shut. Why spoil our chat? Be There, Make Her Day.

Odds and ends.

June 30. *Odds:* Henrietta still sits on that egg. She's now a week overdue. I told BG that he should do what Vitmer suggested when we first started this endeavor; gently shake the egg to see if it sloshes. If so, odds are it's rotten. Do not crack it open. Just discard it.

BG says he'll wait until it starts to stink because he doesn't want to risk having the irate mother tear off his eyebrows again. She's been particularly testy of late. Who wouldn't be, sitting on a hard lump day and night for four weeks! The two of them (BG and the chicken) have been going at it for a while now. I made the mistake of putting her box near his tools. Every time he goes out there for something, she raises hell with him, and he gives it right back to her, like a pair of squabbling siblings. As for the rotten egg, it's his. He'll have to deal with it.

Ends: I picked Faye up from junior lifeguard class yesterday. They had a farewell picnic and the lifeguard's wife came with their preschooler and two-week-old baby. That explained why he wasn't there on the first day of class. It was so sweet to see the big tough guy who could silence a lippy punk with one fierce look, also tenderly hold his little ones.

I stepped over to thank him for letting Faye into the class.

"No worries," he grinned. "She did really well. Improved her stroke over last week!" It sounds like the additional pool practice paid off.

Faye went up to him as we were leaving and stuck out her hand to thank him. "No, Girl, we do it island style," he said as he gave her a fatherly hug. "You be back next summer?"

Absolutely!

Finally free.

July 1. A friend of mine recently quit her job and, in an upbeat way, described herself as "finally free." She's Choosing Her Attitude. It had been a long slog with a bad boss who constantly played political games. Gloria actually quit before having another job in hand. That takes courage. I admire her faith that a new job will show up. The Law of Attraction says you obtain what you think about, so when Gloria was focusing on what she hated about her job, she attracted more of it. Now that she can concentrate on what she does want, I hope something will shift inside her. She seems to be happier and that should put her in a better frame of mind to claim a new job.

I found the Law of Attraction has worked for me time and again. To keep attracting good into my life, I write a gratitude journal. It keeps me grounded in all the good that's in my life. Thanking God is the best start that I can give to myself each day. Some days I struggle with what to say, but then I just look out the window at the view, smile and write, "I'm grateful to live in Hawaii. Thanks for this beautiful yard." The rest just starts flowing.

Meanwhile, I'm praying that Gloria remains happy with her decision to leave her job. I pray that she finds the money on the first of next month, and every month, to pay her bills. I pray that she looks forward, never back. I pray that she's finally found peace. I asked her to hold onto this lovely feeling of being free, to cement it in her mind and heart. Better yet, write it out in her journal. And if the day comes when she questions her actions, I hope she pulls out the journal, recaptures her joyous feelings and lives them all over again. It's what I would want for anyone. Meanwhile, I'll try to Be There for her.

8. LOOKING BACK

Family traditions.

July 2. Honoka'a, HI. We have many important family traditions. The strongest one by far is the annual trip to Boulder Junction, Wisconsin, 12 miles from the Upper Peninsula of Michigan. My family's been going to the same bay on the same lake every year since I was two years old. The trip's original pull was the good fishing that Dad and Grandpa enjoyed and cooler weather "Up Nort" in summer. But, over time (58 years), it became the fun and importance of strengthening family ties and teaching Scheurell values to the next generation. We older Scheurells also feel a nostalgic tug for a simpler time, probably the same reason Honoka'a had such a draw for me.

Now, living in Hawai'i, it's even more important for me to honor this tradition. And there's no better time to visit with family than the week when everyone's on vacation. So the girls and I will travel this month. BG hasn't joined us Up North in many years. His idea of a good time is reliable electricity and plumbing, which are not always available. Blustery summer storms sometimes take out the power, shutting off both.

We'll combine the trip with some visits to colleges for Jade. It's a complicated trip of four full weeks and has taken me the better part of three weeks just to plan it. Dianne says the multicolor trip schedule I made is evidence I have OCD. I don't care. At least I'll know when I'm supposed to be where.

The trip highlight is the week with my sisters and their families, each of us at a different cottage. We can escape to our own places when we feel the need, yet be together at a moment's notice. In the old days before cell phones, I'd send a kid down the hill in the morning to see if Grace was awake, or up to the fish-cleaning shack to tell Mae's husband Emmet that supper was ready. While the kids are happier to phone instead of run, the charm is slipping away. Still, there was the time three years ago when Vitmer's pontoon boat had engine trouble and he, Grace and I were stranded in the middle of the lake. Grace was able to call her kids to come rescue us.

It used to be my grandparents, parents, aunts, uncles and cousins who invaded the resort every year on the same week. I remember our family of five plus Grandma and Grandpa piling into Dad's big aqua Mercury at 3 a.m. on the day of the trip. That car had a trunk as big as Baltimore, plenty of room for suitcases. But the Merc could also drag Dad's trailer carrying a modest aluminum boat that served as a second trunk, stowing boxes of food, a heavy metal chest with its ice block and frozen meats, towels, games, box fans, lifejackets and various fishing accoutrements including the motor. In fact, the boat's primary purpose may have been its storage capacity in transit.

We always grumbled about leaving early, but I realize now that it wasn't just that Dad wanted to avoid heavy traffic in the big metropolis of Green Bay. No, he wanted to drive in the cool of predawn because cars didn't have AC back then. The road song lulled us back to sleep so that he didn't have to listen to us bicker ("Quit looking at me! Move over!"). The longer we girls slept, the easier the six-hour trip was for all of us.

Once there, we cousins ran wild, though we were always within sight of someone who'd yell at us. It was grand: swimming, digging in the sand, croquet and beanbags, and the occasional trip into town for ice cream. Dad was a safety nut, so we'd have to wait one full hour after eating before we could venture into the lake. His swimming rules were a production. First the anxious wait: "Is it time yet? How about now? Can we go now?" Then we'd hurriedly put on our swimsuits, grab towels and a salt shaker to remove any bloodsuckers that might attach and run down to the lake – with an adult. Sunscreen wasn't on the radar yet.

Finally, we had to strap into the big orange boobies, the lifejackets of the day. Stored in our boat down at the dock, they always felt damp and cold from the last swim and, phew, they always smelled of fish. As we grew older, we realized they were quite the fashion statement. How we loathed them! But no life jacket, no swimming, even though we had adult supervision and we only played in shallow water. That was Dad's rule, so we dutifully strapped in.

The week's highlight was always the trip to the dump at night to watch the bears eat. We'd change into PJs, pile into the Merc and drive to the dump right around dusk. (But no snacks; they might draw bears to our car!) We and other vacationers surrounded the active part of the dump, turned off lights and waited. When the bears ambled up to feast, some people put headlights on so we could see them more easily. The bears were pretty nonchalant about the observers, digging into what could've been the remains of our lunch from the day before. The law doesn't allow open dumps any longer, so my kids missed out on this tradition.

Now it's my generation bringing our kids Up North. It's a special place, all the more so because my girls led sheltered lives in Racine. They weren't even allowed to walk or ride their bikes around the block without an adult along. (Holy cow! I sound like Dad!) But at the lake they played in the sand, fed the ducklings, explored the nearby woods, learned to pump on the swing-set, stayed up past bedtime at the bonfire and otherwise ran wild with Mae's kids, Maggie and Alice.

Jade was only 21 months younger than Maggie and three months younger than Alice. They were and still are quite the cohort. And when brave, bully little Faye came along, she pushed her way into the group. I never had to plead with them to take her along. Together they learned to catch toads and, years later, create hairdos and paint toenails with Grace's daughter Norah, now 26. They all adore her. They used to propel around on Grace's paddleboat and caught hell one time when she found them on it without lifejackets. That only happened once. When Grace chews you out, you don't forget.

Vitmer taught them to fish, casting first off the dock, then from his boat, and even refurbished a rod and reel from Goodwill for my girls. I had their first catches – Faye's miniscule sunfish and Jade's tiny bluegill – mounted at Al's Taxidermy in Boulder Junction. Al looked at me as if I had two heads. "Ya know, I'll have ta charge you da base setup fee on each a dose." I was okay with that, $94 each, but he dropped the per-inch fee. We picked them up the following summer on the annual trip and they're now swimming on the walls of our dining room.

The girls didn't fear playing in the lake, despite its tannin-stained water and the bloodsuckers lurking in the muck under the dock, as long as we remembered to bring the salt shaker along. For the last seven or eight years we also drove to Crystal Lake where the water is clear all the way out and there are no bloodsuckers. I told them that if they took Red Cross swimming classes through Level 6 (something I wanted), they could swim out to the rock pile at Crystal Lake without a lifejacket (something they wanted). That strategy worked splendidly and propelled them quickly through the swimming classes offered at home in Racine year after year.

This is a special year. We welcome Rachel, the first of the fifth generation, to Fishtrap Lake. Grace is all gaga about being a Nana. I'd be, too. Babies are magnets and Rachel is adorable. The girls can't wait to play with her. She's already a camera ham and has learned to crawl since I saw her in March. However, she'll be in prime teething season. Thank you, Lord, for separate cottages. As Mae used to say, "God made 'em cute so you wouldn't kill 'em."

Aloha driving.

July 8. Portland, OR. For our mainland trip, we managed to stuff everything into one very large suitcase, the "pink pig," plus a carry-on for each of us. I have a vendetta against extra airline fees so, with personal satisfaction, we checked only the one bag. We flew out the evening of July 4th and saw fireworks on takeoff from Kona and again as we flew over Honolulu. At the Portland airport the next morning we piled into a rental car and headed south to a couple of Oregon's universities.

I used to be a teeth-baring aggressive highway driver, especially on long distances like the yearly trip Up North. I was the obsessed executive with multiple deadlines and an internal clock wound tighter than a two-dollar watch, both at work and at home. It took the whole week at the lake to unwind, only to coil up again during the six-hour drive home. I commonly drove 85 to 90 mph while on a divided highway, sitting on people's bumpers and cursing them for driving slowly (the speed limit). Praise God that I never caused an accident and never received a speeding ticket.

Odd that I hardly noticed my shift to aloha driving in Hawai'i. Gradually I came to drive the speed limit, even *under* it at times. Now people sit on *my* bumper! Perhaps the frequent fog warped my sense of how long specific trips should take. With few divided highways and no Interstates, the hills and curves make it difficult to pass. So traffic moves at the pace of the slowest vehicle, usually heavy trucks lumbering their way up the mountain.

Aloha driving is not just patience with traffic flow. It's also stopping traffic behind you to allow a car to make a left turn in front of you. In Waimea, at the height of rush-minute, that kindness may help you make a left turn a mile down the road. Kindness and thoughtful driving promote the same in others, especially when you look them in the eye, smile and wave. More importantly, it prevents gridlock, something one does not associate with rural villages unless you're driving in Waimea at 7:30 in the morning.

This change in my driving frustrates the girls, especially Faye. "Go faster, we have to get there. What happened to sitting on someone's bumper?" I pontificate about the virtues of aloha driving but, truth be told, I like going slowly and being polite. Maybe it's the yoga and the meditation. Maybe I'm adopting island time. Maybe I'm even afraid of driving faster, schooled by fog and curves. I'm ashamed to admit that I discouraged Jade from exploring colleges in or near Los Angeles simply because I didn't want to drive there for visits. Don't tell her.

Fast forward to renting a car in Portland. I didn't like it one bit; too many things to think of, especially in a strange car. I used to laugh at Dad when he worried about driving in a new place where he might come upon an "only" lane. Now I *am* my father! But about two hours outside the city, the land flattened into a broad plain. I relaxed on the clear stretches of Interstate 5 and slowly picked up speed. Suddenly, I found myself cursing a slowpoke driving in the fast lane and clasped a hand over my mouth. The girls exchanged knowing looks and burst into laughter.

While in Oregon, we received some sad news about Henrietta. BG faced the fact that his chicken's egg was a dud, disposing of it when she left the nest for food. When she found the egg gone, Henrietta flew the coop for good. But she left a nice crop of chicken lice behind. They spread to BG's upstairs office where they've been biting him ever since. He's tried various insect-killing products without success. In tonight's terse and grim telephone briefing, BG informed me that we will not have any chickens of any kind in any portion of the property. I bit my tongue, deciding it best not to point out that Henrietta was his chicken. Maybe this is the beginning of a new behavior for me – aloha listening.

No phone, no TV, no interruptions.

July 15. Boulder Junction, WI. Yesterday we settled into a new cottage. Cottages here are like seats at Lambeau Field Packer Stadium; people put them in their wills for their children. At the resort, families come back year after year to the same cottage during the same week. But every once in a while, someone decides to punt. Then it's a mad scramble to move into a better cottage. Good luck to the punter getting his old cottage the following year; the schedule is set to the new order.

This summer we lucked out and scored the primo cottage right on the lake, with our own bench on our own pier, a large kitchen, a fireplace and air conditioning! Last summer was stinkin' hot and humid. If you've never experienced that, count yourself lucky. So, when the only air-conditioned cottage became available, I seized it. Then Mae grabbed our old cottage. That moved them right on the lake, with their own pier and the best deck of anyone here. And the two cottages are right next to each other, perfect for eating together as one family. Emmet grills and Mae and I cook. Grace and her extended family are farther away from us but, as predicted, Rachel is teething and fussy so the distance is fine with us this year. Their cottage has two bathrooms, four bedrooms, a screened-in porch, and a dishwasher. I have four dishwashers – Jade, Faye, Maggie and Alice. Still, air conditioning trumps all. If we have another hot week, everyone will be at our place.

This morning I slept in, gradually waking to the sound of birds in the pines. I recognized the songs of the chickadee, cardinal and mourning dove. I smiled listening to the bullfrogs, the bass of the amphibian world. They're such a contrast to our tiny but very loud soprano invaders in Hawaii, the coqui frogs. I rose, made coffee, and sat outside on my deck, listening to distant loons and watching an eagle hunting for breakfast, gliding in wide arcs over the lake. It's so quiet here. We're at the end of a small blacktop road that winds out from a small village far away from anywhere. There's no road noise except for the rare car arriving at the resort. We hear boats as fishermen and women motor out early in the morning and pleasure boaters strike out during the day, but it's not excessive and our end of the lake is too narrow for water skiing. I love the quiet. There are so few places that ordinary people can go to escape from man-made noise.

When we were young the resort didn't have TV. Today we rarely hear them in anyone's cabin. I forbid it in our little haven. We're supposed to get away and I don't even follow news when I travel; never did. The girls are okay with this because they can quietly play movies on their computers in their room if they wish. But they're having too much fun with Maggie, Alice and Norah to waste time with that. The cottages still don't have phones and cell phone reception is exceptionally poor. But you won't hear me complaining. When I worked, I took vacations seriously. I never brought my computer and I didn't have a cell phone. My out-message at work said "on vacation – no cottage phones, no cell phone, no email." I set a good example for my people on work-life balance, if not highway driving.

As I meditated with my coffee, I noticed the lake was like glass with a perfect reflection of the far shore floating like a twin woods on the surface. A muskrat swam to the lily pads, pulled out a fresh blossom and dragged it home. The ducks were still asleep, floating under the dock with their heads tucked under their wings.

We decided to celebrate Christmas in July this year, since it's unlikely we'll be back in Wisconsin for the holidays. Grace stopped by to tell me she'd brought a vánočka over for breakfast on Mae's deck. Vánočka is the Czech Christmas bread that Grandma and Mom made every year. We all love it: braided yeast bread with slivered almonds, mace and blond raisins. Add a light layer of butter, nothing else. Early in Grace's marriage, Vitmer added mayonnaise to it, an incredible effrontery! He's never eaten it since. I'm not sure if that is his choice or Grace's and it's better not to ask. As we girls grew older we had an unspoken competition every year to see who baked the best vánočka of our generation. But when I got caught up in my job I didn't have time to bake, especially during the holidays. Too bad, because I liked mine best. Don't tell Grace and Mae.

After breakfast, Mae and I brought out the Scrabble board for our second game of the week. We played last night with Emmet. They were both beating the stuffing out of me, but I pulled ahead on the last play. This morning Emmet punted and went fishing instead, rowing his boat out to his favorite spot while Mae and I went at it. I started by using all my letters on the game's first play and my good luck continued. I had a 403 point game, which I'll write down on my list of 400-plus games in the Scrabble box back home. Of course we play by our own rules, using an official Scrabble dictionary freely.

This afternoon I took a nap. Mae and the girls swam and bounced on the raft moored out in the small bay. Rachel finally slept. All the girls then went into town with Norah and it became even quieter. Soon Emmet will start the grill for salmon. I'm making salad and pasta primavera to accompany it. I can't wait for a home-cooked meal. Even the girls are sick of the restaurant food we ate for a week, even though we rarely eat out at home. After supper we'll play Scrabble again, probably two games. Tomorrow Vitmer will take the ladies out for a pontoon ride so we can see the loons up close and inspect the eagle's nest from a vantage point in the lake. Or maybe Grace and I will take the paddleboat for a spin. We're all falling back into the wonderful rhythm of the week at the lake. No phone, no TV, no interruptions. Ahhh.

Can you spell competitive? How about obsessed?

July 17. Boulder Junction, WI.

Monday morning: I knew Mae was awake because she'd set the Scrabble board out on her deck, our signal that she's ready to play. I had to redeem myself. Yesterday she beat me by more than 50 points in the last game, though I won the other two. She was so happy. And I can't even blame it on having lousy luck in picking letters. She was just hot.

Monday night: We played three games today. I won all three, even scoring more than 400 points on one of them. But I grumped when I just missed passing my best-ever record of 444, scoring *only* 437 points. Mae declared, "Get over it!" The last game was close and we fixated on it even more than usual, straining our eyes as light left the sky, swatting Wisconsin's state bird, the mosquito, and slapping our legs as the mosquitoes scored. A sprinkle of rain hit the lake and a few drops even made it through the canopy of pine branches over the deck. We didn't move. We could have relocated inside, but our thoughts were focused on maximizing the next move. We didn't talk. We seldom do. I sighed. Mae took a cigarette break. We moved letter tiles around on our holders. We stared at the board. She had all consonants. I had all vowels. We sat there in the dark, cursing.

Tuesday: Same story. We played three games in the afternoon and evening after a morning at the Tuesday Flea Market. It's agony at the lake. What lake? I finally came in for the night and asked myself, "Is this even fun?" It must be, because I know we'll play another three games tomorrow.

Flea Market and remembered regrets.

July 18. Boulder Junction, WI. I didn't say enough about our trip to the Flea Market yesterday. Mae and Emmet don't go anymore, so I take all of the girls, even though some are old enough to drive. It's become a new tradition. The Flea Market brings back so many memories, most good, some bad. Every Tuesday during summer in the local library's parking lot you can find vendors selling bits of Wisconsin: fishing lures and the latest technology in knot-tying equipment or fish-filleting knives. Others sell handmade soap, soy candles, Up-North signs engraved on the spot with your family name, stained glass, honey, artisan breads, goat cheese, dried cherries, nuts and salsa. The salsa would have been out of place a few years ago, but Wisconsinites have broadened their palates like everyone else. My favorite vendor is an older couple offering jellies and jams, 29 kinds! I'm partial to the blackberry and gooseberry, but the girls want strawberry. What's the point of buying gourmet strawberry jam when they aren't going to savor it? This year the couple featured carrot-orange and jalapeno-raspberry. I passed on those.

I always buy blueberries, tomatoes and corn from the same farm vendor. Blueberries are everywhere up here and Emmet prefers to pick his own roadside. No thanks, I'll buy mine. I don't want the mosquitos to carry me away. I'd buy this farmer's kohlrabies too, but he sells the giant kind we saw growing in Czechoslovakia, and I prefer the small ones. Tonight we'll feast on corn.

The antique vendors (at least their stuff is priced that way) offer cast iron pots, enameled bowls with chips in them, colored Depression glass, blue canning jars, spoons and loads of other stuff. It reminds me of items passed down through generations in my family. I find the snowshoes, the pelts and the real bearskin rug novel, though not unknown to Wisconsinites. Another vendor makes deer antler key chains, lamp finials and pull chains, and turtle maracas. He also had buckets of buffalo teeth and deer hooves. I guess you have to come up with your own cool thing to make with those bits.

One of my worst vacation memories involved that library where the Flea Market takes place. I needed to talk with a hiring director at the Georgia company where I was employed. The resort had no phone service, so I borrowed a cell phone and settled myself in the library where I could get reception. The Manufacturing Director was to call at a specific time, though I waited 25 minutes, sweating out the thought that he had forgotten. I needed this job. My boss had recently told me that if I didn't move up, I would be blocking others from moving into my position as a natural progression. It was a scary message – move up or out. You could do everything perfectly for years, but if you got stuck for some reason, you could be served up as the next week's dinner sacrifice.

The open position was that of manager at one of the manufacturing plants in Mississippi, one that I had frequented regularly as a product developer for research trials. The people were welcoming and nice, but this was small-town Mississippi. I didn't exactly fit into their culture. But I was so desperate for the promotion that I was willing to learn both the culture and the whole manufacturing side of the business. Looking back, I cannot believe that I was willing to alter my path so drastically. What was I thinking? How would my Chinese daughter fare in a small Mississippi town? But I was hell-bent on getting to the next level.

And what about BG? I actually had the audacity to tell the Director that my taking the job was contingent on BG being offered a job there, too. I told him BG would be a good fit in

Quality Control. I had nerve, I had hope, and I had anxiety all during the vacation. But I didn't have the job. They gave it to a young man in Marketing! I was crushed and did a lot of soul searching after that debacle. I vacation to replenish myself and my family. I vacation to be with my sisters and parents. I vacation to commune with nature for at least one week a year. Yet I compromised all of that with the stupid job interview, fretting and focusing on it for nearly the whole week. I even begged off going to the Flea Market so I could prepare for my phone interview. No wonder my sisters called me a "suit." But they didn't understand the pressure I felt to get promoted. So Mae and my mom took little Jade to the Flea Market and I missed seeing her first proud purchase, made with a couple of dollars from Grandma.

Unfortunately, I didn't learn my lesson with that one botched vacation. A few years after I moved to another company, I had the chance to present some research to the committee that ran the North American consumer business. Unfortunately, they only met once a month and the meeting fell on a Tuesday during the week I was supposed to be Up North. This was a golden opportunity to shine as a new employee. So, instead of saying no, I talked my boss into flying me back to Racine for the meeting and returning me on the same day to Rhinelander, the nearest airport to Boulder Junction. My mom and sisters were appalled but forgiving, and they again took my girls to the Flea Market for me.

I was trying to live in two worlds, family and the corporation, but it wasn't working very well. I jumped too often when the corporation called, and didn't think of the effect on my husband and girls, except as it impacted my earning power. Thank God I finally began to see how far I had wandered off my original path. I stopped looking at the road right in front of me and took the long view, backwards and forward. By taking in the whole vista, I could see the changes I'd need to make to get my life back on track. They were scary but not insurmountable. One of the easiest changes was my out-message at work. To my usual "on vacation – no cottage phone, no cell phone, no email" I added "no way to reach me." And I meant it.

From then on, I took time to appreciate the simpler things of life, like wandering around the Flea Market with family members, buying gourmet jam, eating fresh local vegetables, finding a piece of depression glass to match something my mom gave me and spending time with my daughters and sisters. I can enjoy listening to the loons on the lake, trips to the ice cream shop in town and sharing meals with extended family. I can Be There. But what did I miss in the meantime? Why did it take so long? I can never get that time back, only vow to live life to the fullest now and thank God for Her help. I am so grateful.

My father's ghost is here.

July 20. Boulder Junction, WI. My dad is here at the lake with us. Grace brings his favorite cap and hangs it on her porch. It still smells like him, a mixture of Old Spice, Brylcreem, cigarettes and brow sweat, even though he's been dead for nine years. He was such a joker and storyteller. I see him everywhere: on the pier, on the cottage porch he and Mom shared, out on the lake in his boat, heading to the fish house with his catch. He loved to drive to the state forests, the Boulder Junction Flea Market and to town at dusk so we could spot deer along the way. On the road, he'd rev the Merc as we crested a hill so that we'd experience a moment of free-fall on the downhill side. He loved to hear us squeal.

Mom is here too, but her presence is not as strong because Dad completely overshadowed her. He was bigger than life. He worked in the Manitowoc shipyards and survived a tough early life. At age 14, when his father died of TB, he became head of the household to his five brothers and sisters. They and their mother lived through the Depression without the kind of social network we have today. They were poor.

All my friends loved Dad, the gregarious father who actually paid attention to kids, told corny stories and listened to us as if we mattered. But I always fell short of his expectations. I wasn't good enough. At least that's what I told myself. I think Dad was hard on me because I was the oldest. Grace, 2½ years younger, was "The Goodest One" – a moniker attached to her to this day – and Mae, 9 years younger, was the baby.

While we never talked about college until I was well into high school, Dad made it clear he wanted something better for his children than he had out of life. He was smart, but couldn't afford college even with the GI Bill. So I brought home the A's and B's, but still never felt good enough. I knew he loved me, but I felt I had to be perfect. Yet once I did excel in a life away from Manitowoc, once I became a corporate executive, I transformed into someone my parents no longer understood.

He taught me his important life lessons. I absorbed some and modified the rest to suit myself. Much of my reaction to his teachings was normal rebellion. But it also occurred during the upheaval of the late '60s, a double whammy.

- Save your money. I was the only second grader that knew about compound interest. This lesson stuck, but I didn't actually start saving for retirement until I turned 35. I was too cash-strapped before that, spending way too much time in college.

- Love and respect God. We regularly attended church, usually more often than required. One instance in particular began to shape me in a direction Dad didn't anticipate. At my Catholic grade school, we went to Stations of the Cross on Friday afternoons during Lent. On Sunday, Dad wanted to go again in the afternoon, after we'd already been to Mass. Only seven, I finally rebelled and said I wasn't going. It just happened that the Disney movie, "101 Dalmatians" was showing in theaters. So he came up with a challenge: "No Stations, no Dalmatians." I'm not sure he realized at that moment that he gave me a choice! I took it. I didn't see that movie until I had kids of my own. This was my first leap toward independence. As for the Church, I left at 19 and didn't return for 35 years.

- Obtain a good education that will provide you with a good job and security once you graduate. Why would you need a Master's degree or Ph.D.? He didn't understand my educational path.

- Love and respect your elders. We spent every Sunday with Grandma and Grandpa, eating supper, then settling down to The Ed Sullivan Show and Bonanza. Living so far away from my parents as an adult, I was not able to show my love in the same way.

- Be *safe*; don't take risks. Living through the Depression, he extended this lesson to every aspect of his life. Through osmosis, we girls became risk-averse too. Luckily, I learned to throw this off as I grew older, another way I thought I disappointed him.

He was a proud man and wanted to give us everything we asked for, but couldn't. Dad worked hard, taking second shift at the shipyards so he could be home with us during the day while Mom worked a day job as a bookkeeper. Dad also worked overtime as often as possible to bring in extra money. That allowed him to tackle many large-scale projects around the house, doing the work himself or bartering with others in order to provide a nice home for us. And one day every week he'd catch fish at the city pier, not for pleasure but to put food on the table.

Despite the demands of these projects, he spent time with us. I remember Sunday afternoon walks on the trails at Point Beach State Park, Dad listening to a football game on a transistor radio and Mom gathering mushrooms. He taught me the finer points of football as we cheered on the Green Bay Packers during the glory years. It's probably why I unconsciously sprinkle my vocabulary with football terms: tackle, score, punt. We swam at Harp's Lake and Lake Michigan and, of course, there was the trip Up North every year.

We hosted many barbecues in the backyard with extended family and friends. Dad was the Grand Master of Ceremonies. He'd splurge on a "Miami roll" – a large rolled beef roast – put it on the Weber in the morning, and watch the roast turn on the spit, dousing it with water when the fire roared on dripping fat. He brought out a case of Kingsbury Beer to share with his brothers and brothers-in-law, and declared the roast done when the case emptied, late in the afternoon. I can still see him proudly carving that roast, divvying it with his brothers and sisters and the kids.

I remember Dad dancing with me when I was little, singing to me, holding me close with my head on his shoulder and crooning a refrain that rumbled in his chest: "Ho-ho, ho-ho little Diney." He kissed us goodnight every night. It was clear Dad loved us and he often told us so. Even when we were adults, he always said we could turn to him for help. He promised us "a hamburger and a bus ticket home" from anywhere, no questions asked. That meant so much to me, especially as I started taking more risks in my life.

Yes, he expected much from me. His hopes shaped me to be the leader I became. But my neurosis about "not being good enough" was crookedly absorbed from his lessons of unconditional love, not from disdain. This misinterpretation of his message was *my* problem, not his. His intentions were always good. He always wanted the best for me. He believed in me. *I* was the one who decided I needed to be perfect. I only figured that out in the last few years.

It's great to see him again, here among the pine trees and on the lake. I miss him so much.

Stinkin' hot and humid.

July 23. Madison, WI. We're back to the college visit part of this trip and we took Maggie and Alice with us to Madison. Alas, we've had stinkin' hot and humid weather for the past two days. We did use the air conditioning one day at the lake, but that heat was nothing like this. Visiting colleges is bad enough. Madison was a killer; up and down Bascom Hill, tramping clear across campus and back, reliving my past. Then we took the 90-minute tour where we again tramped up and down Bascom Hill. I don't remember doing that for six years while working on my bachelors and masters degrees. I must've been in good shape, but not now. My calf muscles are screaming at me. And sweat! I always said I learned to sweat during my first summer in Madison. I did it all over again this week. It was the trickle-down-your-back-and-get-your-underwear-wet kind of sweat. Ugh! Even our much anticipated trip to Krispy Kreme was marred. It was so hot that the shop had shut down operations and shipped donuts in from elsewhere. They didn't even have a microwave, so we couldn't savor warm donuts.

On the good side, we scored Babcock Hall ice cream which brought back pleasant memories. The University makes and sells many more kinds of ice cream now than when I attended in the '70s. Ice cream is one of the great things about the big campus in the Dairy State but it doesn't make up for the sweat. People assume that we're accustomed to heat since we live in Hawai'i. What they don't understand is that we sit out in the middle of the world's largest refrigerator, the Pacific Ocean. Hawai'i is both warmer in winter and cooler in summer. Before I left on this trip, I still slept with a down comforter, the bedroom windows open to the breezes. So I find this continental heat and humidity unbearable. I've become a weather wimp.

Make it happen.

July 30. Milwaukee, WI. I trust that stuff will show up when I need it. It's part of manifesting. I have a large lap and things just fall into it. You can ask the girls. I always find a great parking space, more often than not in the shade. You could call me lucky. But I believe stuff shows up because I've asked the Universe and/or the Holy Spirit for what I need and They provide it. For the trip home, I needed something to read. And voila! One of my Wisconsin friends returned a book I'd loaned to her last year, Henriette Anne Klauser's *Write it Down, Make it Happen*

(Klauser, 2000). I've read it before and practiced it often, especially when I worked with Rita. I also preach it to anyone who will listen. It's another very effective way of asking the Universe for what you need.

Here's a clear example of the power of writing down what you want. Last month, while purging old computer files, I found a document on the financial retirement goals I wrote in 2008. I couldn't believe I'd written it four years ago. Downright spooky. Take a look.

> My financial goals and assumptions for retirement are:
>
> - To retire to the Big Island on July 15, 2011.
>
> - To sell our current house between now and then in preparation for the move. Once sold, we will rent in Racine.
>
> - To send Faye and Jade to the Hawai'i Preparatory Academy in Waimea for their remaining school years.
>
> - Given the need to be close to the school in Waimea, we have limited options. We're researching Honoka'a next spring, about 20 miles away.
>
> - To purchase a modest home on the Big Island with the proceeds from our house sale in Racine.
>
> - To utilize my IRAs and 401ks when I turn 59½. I will make withdrawals to hold me over until my pension and my social security kick in at age 62. BG plans to keep working all his life.
>
> - After age 62, to live off my social security, pension and interest earned on the remaining principal of my

IRAs/401ks. No further dipping into my principal should be necessary.

- To have enough money to take two trips to the mainland every year.

- To have enough money to take weekly classes: yoga (locally), aerobics (locally), and college classes (in Hilo).

- I assume we will not live in Hawai'i forever, maybe 15 years. Then move closer to grandkids!

I am SO on track, except for selling the Racine house, but it's rented which covers the expenses. These techniques work. I'm doing and living almost exactly as I wrote it.

As I peruse this gem of a book again on the flight home tomorrow, I can ponder my "current" big questions. If I think back to my journal entries over the past nine months (gestation period?) I see a recurring thought. Now that I'm retired, what do I want to be when I grow up? What's my passion? I think I must not be ready for the answer and that's why I haven't received one yet. I don't want to jump into anything right away. I don't want to shut down any options. And I'm not willing to risk making something happen that I might not like, so I've let the question hang there.

Anyway, I can't wait to go home after a month on the road. I need some mundane time, cooking, organizing, or even cleaning. Whoops, that was a written answer that I didn't want to see!

Downloading to BG.

August 2. Honoka'a, HI. BG greeted us at the airport with lei in our favorite colors. He also put flowers in our rooms. I don't think we realized how much we missed him until we saw him again, and the girls clung to their dad for several days. Taking stock at home, I find that the chicken lice have permanently exited the building, the sun is shining, the noon temperature is 78°F with mild trades and, for supper last night, I successfully nailed my first homemade pesto with our own basil. This morning I woke up with a smile on my face and realized I was listening to distant rooster music. The house seems large and I delight in the little things I'm rediscovering, like how much I love my coffee mug, my mattress and the weight of my down comforter. On the other hand, my herb garden is growing wild again, the grass is calf-high, and the mail bundle and laundry piles are daunting. I went to water aerobics yesterday and will participate in yoga this afternoon. I so need them! I was a slug on this trip.

I told BG that the best part of the lake visit was seeing the younger girls spend time with Norah. She and Jade cooked organic veggie and pasta dishes. She showed Maggie her fly ties. She imparted her 26-year-old wisdom to all. They already loved shopping at thrift stores, so when Norah took them antiquing, she revealed a whole new level of thrifting, especially to Alice who may have found a new passion. Norah hasn't spent this much time with them since they were little. In the recent past, she's had to work or attend classes. This year she was here all week and the girls monopolized her. She even eclipsed Rachel for their attention. Norah's such a great role model for them, cheerful, upbeat, curious, self-sufficient, a strong young woman. Her good example makes Mae and me happy, and Grace proud.

Even after so many years going up there, I still see new things. One morning as we sat outside on Mae's deck sharing breakfast, a deer ran out of the woods behind us and plunged into the bay. She swam all the way across and climbed out on the other side. I didn't even know deer could swim. Some years I'm lucky to see a deer at all. Grace reminded me that it's hard to see deer while driving 85 mph. Harrumph. This year, though, I saw one of the albino deer, again a first for me. This small family grouping has been roaming the area for probably 30 years. There never seem to be many, but one or two are born every year. When they sense danger they freeze in place just like other deer, but their white coats stand out so starkly. At least, that's what I'd heard. On Tuesday, driving to the Flea Market with all the girls, I saw one and stopped the car. We watched as she froze for a couple of minutes, looked at us, ears cocked forward, then slowly stepped her way into the woods.

BG enjoyed my cool new memories, though he was most interested in the college visits. I told him Jade narrowed her list from four to three schools based on the tours and her interviews. I had found it difficult to keep my mouth shut and my opinions to myself, but I managed it. I don't want to be a helicopter parent, always hovering. While on this trip I read a funny book about an obsessed Mom's journey to "help" her oldest child into college. It describes how she viewed her son's choice of college as a reflection on her. Ouch.

So I deliberately let Jade set up and conduct her own interviews with program directors and admissions personnel at the four colleges we visited. I didn't even go into the meeting rooms with her. She always emerged with the interviewee telling me she did a great job. It also didn't hurt that she presented each with a ribbon lei. That was her idea. As we drove to each college, she'd make a couple in the school's colors. Now, when she follows up with each person, she can refer to the lei and perhaps spark some recognition on who she is. They must see hundreds or even thousands of kids every year.

Final thoughts: I believe that the close quarters the girls and I shared for so long didn't keep us from having a good time. I tried to practice the *Fish* philosophy: Play, Be there, Make Their Day and Choose Your Attitude. Without these guiding principles and some judicious breaks, I think we might've killed each other.

9. EXPERIENCING HAWAIIAN POLITICS

Furlough Friday.

August 4. Hawai'i suffered when the global Great Recession began in 2008 because tourists are our lifeblood and they no longer had the money to travel. When I first arrived, I thought it strange to hear monthly reports on Hawai'i Public Radio of room occupancy rates on each island and statistics on arriving flights. Now I listen as avidly as everyone else.

Tourism affects me directly. My property taxes here are less than an eighth of what we paid in Wisconsin because the state picks up local school expenses, the library and other things that Racine County taxes covered including snow removal. Instead, the State of Hawai'i uses taxes on hotel rooms and rental cars to support government outlays. When visitors stopped coming, the state had to make the choice between cutting expenses and raising taxes. They cut expenses and instituted Furlough Friday. Once a month, all state government employees have a mandatory unpaid day off. This included teachers, so kids are out of school once a month too. Personally, I thought that went too far. I'd be happy to pay higher taxes if the increase went to education.

Yesterday was Furlough Friday, so our instructor wasn't at the pool. All the other community pools were closed. But because our other lifeguard works part-time, he keeps the pool open on furlough days. There's just one glitch; he won't teach water aerobics. No worries, that doesn't stop us. We have Connie. Yes, the oldest member of our class steps in and shouts out each part of the routine. We all give Connie more respect than the official instructor, by devoting our full attention to her and not chitchatting over her instructions. We just have so much admiration for her life experience and gumption.

She's a retired nurse and so much more. In rare cases when someone has an injury at the pool, she's right there, giving first aid instructions and helping. When the pool closed for renovation, she came every day, all day long, serving food to the volunteer workers, cleaning up and generally being helpful in any way she could. Sure, a few of us made food for the volunteers, but that was our kuleana, our civic duty. She was committed.

Connie is there for every class, driving down the mountain from her home. The only thing that stops her is sickness or a cruise. She still loves traveling and goes as often as her pension allows. She avidly follows politics. She has fun, but not at anyone else's expense, being much more likely to poke fun at herself. Lately she's been coming to class with a hat that has short blond hair that sticks up straight. Connie as a blond, now that's a sight. She's a hoot! She's my hero.

Today I'm a bit sore. I find I give my all at water aerobics when Connie teaches. Maybe it's that I'm paying more attention. Maybe it's because she quietly commands respect and, therefore, my best effort. Maybe it's because she's my inspiration for living a full life with gusto. Maybe it's because she is fully present. My Racine yoga teacher used to gently urge us to cultivate mindfulness, to be fully present for our practices. It's a great tool for living life to the max. That's what Connie models so well. I want to be Connie when I reach 79. Heck, I want to be Connie now.

All politics are local.

August 7. After a sermon on gratitude, Father Bob ended Sunday Mass with a reminder to vote in the primary this week and to be thankful for the freedom to do so. Amen. Voting placards and banners have popped up everywhere. The names reflect the great diversity of this state: Yagong, Kenoi, Kim, Hirono, Gabbard, D'Almeida, Case, Kia'aina, Gering, Ashida, Marx, Inouye, Lingle, Solomon, Poindexter. I recently learned that our mayor and County Council are voted on a nonpartisan basis: people don't declare a party when running. However, this is a moot point. Most people here are Democrats, our one spot of nondiversity.

Yesterday I received my polling place notification, the Honoka'a High School cafeteria. The form contained English, Japanese, Chinese and Portuguese languages, but not Hawaiian. Yet Hawaiian is one of the state's two official languages. I still don't understand everything I've learned about Hawaiian politics.

Government is organized differently here. There's no government below that of county level. The state controls the public schools, not a local school board. We have only five counties. Kauai County includes four islands. Maui County comprises Maui, Lanai, Molokai and two uninhabited islands. However, the Kalaupapa Peninsula on Molokai is its own county because it's a leper colony, population 90. Honolulu County is Oahu. That's a whole different story; we sometimes joke about the "State of

Honolulu" because the focus always seems to be there. The Big Island is a county all by itself, with Hilo as the county seat and one mayor for the whole island. It's split into nine districts whose representatives form the County Council. So if I want something done for Honokaʻa, I go to my council person for District 1, which is roughly the Hāmākua Coast.

Because I'm new to issues, I sit on the sidelines, though I don't know how long that will last. I'm active in the nonpolitical grassroots community organization focused on celebrating the Hāmākua Coast. A recent Third Thursday Thrive speaker urged us to respond to the state's decision to act without reasonable input. The state plans to lay pipe in the Lower Hāmākua Ditch, one of two irrigation ditches built in 1910, and bury the whole thing. "Ditch" makes it sound like a minor structure, but nothing could be farther from the truth. It's a peaceful waterway of chiseled rocks fitted together. After all these years, an ecosystem has developed around it, even supporting a rare local duck, the koloa maoli. Historians, archeologists, environmentalists and local farmers object to this project. A bunch of us (unrelated to TTT) now support a lawsuit that requires the state to leave the ditch alone to save this 100-year-old landmark and its ecosystem.

Here's where my local interest crossed over to politics. Last night the People's Theatre hosted a forum for the five candidates running for our District 1 council seat. I participated by salting the question box with queries about the ditch. Mitch, Dianne and I also handed out flyers outside the theater, highlighting the Ditch, my first activist endeavor here. I even met my state senator.

I never had time in Georgia or Wisconsin to involve myself in local politics, and often I arrived at the polling place not even aware of the candidates for the lower offices. So it was eye opening to meet and hear these candidates. One of the five was uninformed on local politics and another was unsuited for the role. I can support any of the other three, but the primary is Saturday so I'd better start researching them. It's much more difficult to vote with no party lines to follow. I see now that I used party voting as a crutch for "having no time" to do research. Shame on me, especially since I claimed to be Independent.

One of my friends urged me to go into politics, but I have a hard time seeing myself as a politician. I'm too straightforward in the way I talk. What you see and hear is what you get. There isn't a chance in hell I'd be elected. And I didn't grow up in Hawai'i, a handicap to anyone seeking political life here. But keeping politicians' feet to the fire is something I *can* do, and saving the Hāmākua Ditch is the cause that will finally drive me to do it. Nonetheless, I appreciated my friend's vote of confidence.

A place of contrasts.

August 12. Friday morning was cool and rainy, and I talked myself into exercising in the pool in the afternoon when it would be warmer instead of attending morning water aerobics. The county shares the pool with the Honoka'a middle and high schools that surround it. Teachers regularly bring classes over for Physical Education. This afternoon was no exception. Some kids jumped right in and did laps until time was up. Others fooled around in the shallow end. PE hasn't changed much in 45 years, except for the horrid swimsuits they provided the girls in the old days – one size fits nobody.

Watching the little kids arrive after school was more interesting. These are members of the Honoka'a Swim Team, mostly second-to fourth-graders. Immediately shedding coats and ducking into locker rooms to change, they emerged wearing swimsuits and goggles, plopped into the pool, and settled into a regular rhythm of laps. Such focus at eight years old! One pair in particular fascinated me. They walked in wearing padded winter coats, fur trimmed hoods up and little feet stuffed into fat furred boots! It's August! Yes, it was cool that morning, but this seemed extreme. I suppose they lived mauka (up the mountain) where it's cooler. Yet they emerged from the locker room with the smallest bikinis of anyone! From fur trimmed hoods and boots to itsy-bitsy teeny-weeny and bare feet.

I was reminded of contrasts again when BG and I went to vote in the Primary yesterday. First, we had a choice of paper or electronic ballot. It can't be efficient to manage both processes, though efficiency doesn't seem to be especially valued in Hawai'i. I chose paper. I want to have my hands on it.

County-level voting is nonpartisan and I acted on the knowledge gained at the candidate forum and later discussions with others. But, for Primary state-level voting, I had to declare a party and I could only vote for people within that party. Of course, there were Democrats and Republicans, but I could also choose Libertarian, Green Party, or nonpartisan. Unfortunately, there were no candidates under nonpartisan, so what's the point?

As we walked home, BG and I talked about the contrast between county- and state-level voting and the contrast in our votes. As usual, we cancelled each other out. Neither of us is middle of the road on anything, so I'm talking about zeroing out a huge political divide. Sometimes I wonder how we ever married, how we manifested each other. I guess that's just another contrast, so we should fit in well here. And I guess we do. I love it and he's a grump. But he'd be a grump anywhere, so he might as well be a grump in Hawai'i.

Energetic Eruption.

August 17. Last night we hosted another gathering of Third Thursday Thrive. Our goals are to facilitate local networking and initiate conversations on sustainability. This meeting definitely fit that description. We had a birthday party for the Hāmākua Ditch (102 years old) and, for the first time, attendees engaged in an energetic discussion representing many sides of an issue.

We started with a video produced by a local woman to spread the word that the state planned to pipe and bury the ditch. Then we heard an update from a lawyer who told us the state decided to use eminent domain against the few remaining landowners who won't sign onto the plan. Then the discussion churned as we ate the birthday cake. While the ditch is a cultural and historic treasure, vocal proponents revealed good reasons to consider shunting the irrigation water into a pipe rather than allowing it to continue as an open waterway.

A local farmer spoke on behalf of the pipe's ability to keep pigs and rats from defecating and dying in the water. Even cattle once wandered through it, though it's now fenced along the ranches that front the 25-mile stretch of ditch. It's the unfenced forested sections that concern the farmer, who wants to make sure his vegetable buyers aren't poisoned by E. coli. Then isn't one solution to fence off the remaining sections?

The other news that floored me was that there's no public access to the waterway. Proponents of saving the ditch mention future ecotourism, because its 2% grade makes for easy hiking. But how can it be a tourist attraction if the adjoining land is privately owned? There must be access points; my friend, Kristan, said her kids used to float in the ditch with the locals, like river tubing without the tube. Maybe they got in at points where it crosses under public roads.

More than 70 people lost their lives building that irrigation ditch 102 years ago, most of them plantation workers. Camp families prayed over the ditch workers every morning as they prepared to work, much like mining communities do. The ditch was the backbone of the sugar plantation life that it served and, as such, local people have a personal and emotional connection to it. The immigrants who built it carved their initials into the cut stones. Surely their descendants would want to know that the state is about to bury their ancestors' work. The state has not been transparent with this decision and they did not invite the public to express their concerns.

A few of us came away with a common goal: slow the state's implementation so we can do more fact-finding and expose more people to the issue while the legal process takes its course. We want citizens to make their concerns known to their elected officials, for or against the proposed action, but first they have to find out about it. Some of us want to host a public forum at the Honokaʻa People's Theatre. A TV producer requested $800 to create a TV show with a panel of concerned parties. And we will also take this issue to the County Council so they can weigh in with a resolution. They don't have legal jurisdiction, but that won't keep them from acting if enough of us let them know we're distressed about the lack of state transparency. Evidently, the council hates it when the state moves into their territory.

We'll see what happens. Regardless, I think I'll enjoy delving into community issues. And this one inspires me. It's a way for me to honor local history and all the traditions that surround it.

Mighty hunter.

August 19. Yesterday was one of the last mornings to sleep in before school chauffeuring starts again next week. I was in the delicious state between sleep and wakefulness, languidly drifting in and out of conscious thought. The sun peeked through the palms, enticing me to open my eyes. I could hear the music of distant songbirds and the gentle wind . . . when that damn big white rooster screeched right outside my open bedroom window! I nearly hit the ceiling! Now fully awake and in a foul mood, I ran out to the lanai and pitched a few rocks stockpiled there, but he and his girls scurried into the banana plants. We've played the rock game before.

A brown rooster comes around with his harem too, but he always takes a different route to our backyard and I don't hear him nearly as much. It's the white one I loathe. I've tried to live in peaceful coexistence with that bird but he's driving me to desperate action. I don't mind rooster music from a distance – their yard. In fact, I even like it. It's when it startles me close up, out of my afternoon nap or morning reverie, that I start plotting revenge. It was time to bring out my big gun, BG.

BG is a pretty good shot, even when he's only hoisting a BB gun. He used to kill squirrels in our yard because they chewed the house wiring in our attic. That was in Georgia, where they practiced the three S's: shoot, shovel and shut up. When we moved to Wisconsin, he realized his BB gun-toting days were over – too many rules, regulations and restrictions. He called it "the People's Republic of Wisconsin."

Now we're in Hawai'i, land of the pig hunt and individual rights. The roosters are violating my right to a peaceful nap. And they're damaging our crops, eating my peas before they sprout and scratching up the young plants. It's time for justifiable action.

BG is always ready to curse the roosters, even when they're crowing in their *own* yard. As the day wears on, his patience wears thin at the ever-present cock calls, and I expect at least one good round of "Bloody chickens!" shouted from the lanai. But I recently found out that the chickens' mistress claims she doesn't own them, just feeds them, or so she's told neighbors who have complained in the past. In my mind, that makes them fair game, literally. It's time to share that information with BG. Over coffee, he pondered the chicken caretaker's deniability of ownership. "You're sure?"

"Well, no, but we could go over and talk with her."

"Nah. We've suffered too long." It was time for some chicken-scaring tactics. A BB in the behind might keep them away for a while. We agreed that he should aim only for roosters, preferably the big white one. The hens that came along were generally not noisy, and besides, one of them might be Henrietta. While the roosters are colorful, the girls all look pretty much the same.

Amazingly, BG located his BB gun and ammunition in the labyrinth of stuff stacked upstairs. He loaded the BBs and strode out into the east garden where the roosters gathered. There he stood, calf-high rubber boots firmly planted in the tall wet grass, ragged work shorts, no shirt, long gray hair streaming out from under his colorful welder's cap. With a look of determination and focus, he took aim. *POP*. He missed and the roosters sauntered farther into the yard. BG advanced, pumping air back into the gun. Aim . . . *POP*. Nope. Advance, pump, aim . . . *POP*. No. This went on for about ten minutes. It had been 11 years since he fired it and the "scope needed recalibrating." At least the roosters left.

He gave one last shot into the air. "H&I," he said, "Harassment and Interdiction." No matter what anyone else may think, he's still my hero. I just hope this is legal here in Hawai'i.

Statehood Day.

August 23. The pool closed last week because Statehood Day is a holiday celebrated on the third Friday in August. In 1959 the US government finally admitted Hawai'i as a state. Congress debated Hawai'i back then as they do Puerto Rico today; conservatives didn't want another Democratic state added to the Union. If I read history correctly, Congress made a deal to bring in Alaska (conservative) and Hawai'i (liberal) more or less together so that Congress stayed balanced.

Of course, the controversy over making Hawai'i a state was also about race and culture. Even as of the 2010 census, Caucasians represent only 25% of the population. While Native Hawaiians constitute just 10%, the many waves of immigrants shipped in to work the sugar plantations were mainly nonwhite: Chinese (now 4%), Japanese (now 13%), Filipino (14%) and Korean (3%). The Portuguese (4%) were the only Europeans brought over in numbers to work the sugar fields.

These census figures don't do justice to the multicultural richness here. Many immigrants intermarried. That same census reports

Hawaiʻi as having 39% unspecified Asians and 24% having a mixed heritage of two or more races. It makes for interesting eating, customs, festivals and politics. Today it's cool to be from one of the original groups brought over, sort of like being able to say your family was on the Mayflower. Many politicians tout their heritage, even adding maiden names to campaign posters to ensure voters know they're part of the melting pot and that their family had paid their dues.

I asked about Statehood Day at the pool this week. Many of the women vividly remembered Hawaiʻi's admission to the union. Those in their late 60s recalled the excitement of the parades and fireworks. Older women recollected the injustice of having to wait so long for statehood. Connie practically spat out, "It was the end of taxation without representation." She vibrates with indignation even now.

As for Native Hawaiians, I imagine they do not celebrate Statehood Day. Many are still dismayed or angry at the US takeover of their kingdom. No wonder we continue to have a strong sovereignty movement. However, another state holiday, Kamehameha Day, on June 11, celebrates Kamehameha the Great. He was the first ruler to unite the islands and reigned from 1782 to 1819, dying just a year before the missionaries landed. This was one of the first state holidays the Hawaiʻi State Legislature passed after admission to the union, continuing a tradition that began 88 years earlier.

Hawaiʻi also celebrates Prince Kūhiō Day on March 26. Kūhiō was a prince in the royal line of David Kalākaua. When American and European businessmen overthrew the Hawaiian Kingdom in 1893, the Provisional Government of Hawaiʻi ended his opportunity to one day assume the throne. Five years later, the US annexed Hawai'i as a territory. Kūhiō later became the Hawai'i delegate to the US Congress and introduced the first Hawai'i Statehood Act in 1919. It took another forty years for Hawai'i to become a state.

These two days, Kamehameha Day and Prince Kūhiō Day, are the only holidays in the 50 states dedicated to royalty. Appeasement?

Community consensus – an oxymoron.

September 3. I've spent every spare minute of the last two weeks working to save the Lower Hāmākua Ditch. We have multiple programs moving forward, each with a deadline of September 14. These efforts have different players and we often find we're working at cross-purposes. We all have the same goal of slowing the State's action on eminent domain so that we can have an adult conversation about the future of the ditch. But we clearly have different ideas on how to accomplish that.

The forum's planning group believes that we need to present all facets of the issue, including the State's if we could actually figure out their angle. But landowners fighting the state oppose that. Then there's the video group. The producer just wants to shoot the video for mid-September TV airing, but the landowners want a say in the content. A third group presenting to the County Council needs help with their PowerPoint. I can do that. I also take notes at meetings then issue the task list. Clearly, no one else would do it. When I couldn't attend, only the coconut wireless (Hawaiian grapevine) passed the information along. It changed with each hand-off. This isn't quite the problem you might think, because the agenda, story and path change every day anyway. Decisions don't stick – too many people involved to achieve consensus.

I used to think corporate politics was messy, but that was nothing compared to this. In the end, the corporation had a hierarchy and some higher-up finally made a decision. In fact, much of corporate politics revolved around influencing that decision-maker. It might've been like herding cats but eventually everyone moved in the same direction, everyone purred the same tune and all tails swayed in unison. Influencing community politics is like trying to herd stampeding cattle running in different directions. There's no one decision-maker and part of the herd has scattered too far away to corral on any given day.

Friday we gained a reprieve. The state postponed the hearing on eminent domain, which means that the deadline for everything can relax. Presumably, we were now free to enjoy the Labor Day weekend. Well, at least I enjoyed it. I'm not sure I want to look at my email inbox tomorrow because people have had time to take a breath and begin a new stampede.

The long holiday weekend gave me time to reflect on my blessings. It was a day to pray for those who are unemployed or under-employed. This was my first Labor Day when I wasn't laboring at a paying job. I thank God often for the blessings in my life and the transformation tools that made retirement possible. I can honestly say that I have no regrets about retiring. No, I would not go back to corporate life or corporate politics for anything, not even consensus.

Facts for foodies.

September 7. People keep complaining that we didn't have much of a summer. It rained most of July, and August was cool. Personally, I'm quite content. It's still warm enough to climb into the pool for water aerobics without breaking out into chicken skin. Waimea also had more rain than normal and cooler weather, so the farmer I visit for a mid-week vegetable run doesn't have his usual array; his greens rotted in the wet fields. Yet, just west across the ridgeline, ranchers are suffering through their eighth year of drought. They're cutting back on cattle stock because the pastures have no grass and importing corn is expensive.

Last night Dianne and I went to the Waimea Community Association town meeting. They had a speaker I wanted to check for a future Third Thursday Thrive event. Hawai'i, like other state counties, is concerned about food sustainability, especially with the drought. So the County Council commissioned a baseline study of what food grows where on the island. We found the speaker's 2012 baseline data riveting. As rural as our island is, only 4% of agricultural land is in crops. Of that 4%, half is planted in macadamia nut orchards. That was an eye-opener.

The speaker's maps showed exactly where each farm crop grows, small pockets of land grouped in distinct areas. The most prolific area for vegetables is Waimea, much of it greens, tomatoes, and cruciferous and root vegetables. Waimea also grows prized strawberries. To the southwest lies the Kona coffee belt. South Hawai'i grows macadamia nuts, most of which are exported. We only eat 5% of the nuts we grow. They're too expensive for most people. The same is true for Kona coffee. In the lower east, papayas and macadamias dominate, with some bananas. Coming up to South Hilo, macadamias are again the big crop, along with bananas. The two dairy farms on the Big Island are located on the Hāmākua coast and North Kohala. The data are very detailed.

What surprises me is the sparseness of agriculture on the Hāmākua Coast. We have great weather and lots of agricultural land. Until the mid-1990s, sugar cane grew here in vast fields, replacing taro fields, fish ponds and forests. Since its demise, nothing replaced it on the scale that once existed, and the speaker said that nothing likely will. Large farms growing mega-quantities of one crop are an outdated agricultural model for Hawai'i.

He also articulated that you can't talk about "food sustainability." You have to define each food. For example, the Big Island is 100% self-sufficient in milk with our two dairy farms, while the other islands import all their milk from us or the mainland. On the other hand, we grow no grain. If the barges stopped coming, we'd be back to eating sweet potatoes and taro, the only starches growing here in large enough quantities at the moment.

We produce about 34% of our vegetables, much of it around Waimea, and 32% of our fruit. We also have home gardens, farmer's markets and neighbors sharing backyard produce that the study didn't capture. There's also very little pig, sheep or goat farming and no poultry farming. The speaker agreed that this statistic is misleading because lots of people have chickens, sheep and goats. But they aren't "farming" them. And, despite all our cattle, we supply only 17% of our own beef. The study also estimates that hunters supply about 20% of Big Island pork needs, bagging about 5000 wild pigs every year.

Besides milk, we're in the best shape on fish, harvesting 51% of what we eat plus more for export. But the other 49% of fish we eat is based on food preferences. One of the most common fish consumed here is salmon, a cold water fish. So this category could be more sustainable if we changed our eating habits.

The speaker draws the conclusion that we need to abandon the oft-heard phrase that "85% of our food is imported." If the barges stopped coming tomorrow, we'd be okay in some areas, but woefully lacking in others. Because we're so isolated, it's probably easier to understand how vulnerable we are to food sustainability threats. I wonder how the County Council plans to use this information from the study they commissioned.

Regardless, we, the people have solutions. Eat from local sources to encourage more farming, and eat in season, the way we did as kids in the Midwest. (In the 1950s, oranges were a treat in Christmas stockings because they were rare.) Reduce your caloric footprint by eating lower on the food chain with more greens and less meat. Speaking of which, I'm doing well on my flexitarian diet. I'm eating more fish, fruit and vegetables and I almost never have beef anymore – just a couple of grilled brats while in Wisconsin this summer.

Hmm, I wonder how much beer we make on the island. We have two breweries, but I guess that doesn't matter because we don't grow grain. Maybe I should stockpile beer under my house.

Cheers and Prost to sustainable eating.

10. GROWING DEEPER ROOTS

Their First Anniversary.

September 9. Last month we observed our family's first anniversary of moving here – their anniversary that is. Faye surprised me with her suggestion that we should celebrate. I think the girls are beginning to like it here. So we headed to the beach. Even BG! He rarely takes time off from his consulting job during the week and he's never been to Hapuna, so it was a treat to have him with us.

I confess to still being a novice at ocean swimming. Growing up in Wisconsin I had many adventures in local lakes, including Lake Michigan, but I didn't experience my first ocean dip until I turned 35. I can still remember my buoyancy, my delight at the taste of salt water and my enjoyment of that day's gentle waves. Yet the ocean was so immense that it scared me, so I spent much of my time on the beach gathering shells and inspecting tidal pools.

Since that inaugural ocean swim, I've had few other opportunities. That was mostly my choice. We rarely vacationed at the ocean until we moved to Wisconsin in 2000. After living in Georgia for

13 years, I could not bear the frigid Wisconsin winters without a warm-weather spring break. So we bought a timeshare in Fort Lauderdale, right on the ocean. For five years, we left snow, boots and mittens behind and spent two weeks enjoying the sun's penetrating warmth. By then I had to watch the girls, age 6 and 2, on the beach and rarely went into the water. As years went on, I became more wary as they became braver. One year the beach was full of tar balls from some far-off oil spill and Jade decided she didn't like the beach anymore. "That doesn't look sanitary." So we split duties. BG took Faye to the beach and I took Jade to the pool. That suited me fine.

In later years we used our vacations to scope out potential retirement locations. While every location was warm, not all had water, something that felt wrong to me. I had grown up five blocks from Lake Michigan and realized I *needed* water. Our search took us to the Big Island, but the resort we stayed at for our timeshare swap had no beach, just lava bluffs. We did snorkel in a shallow bay and I have a clear memory of BG and the girls pushing me around like tugboats maneuvering a floating barge. Last year I tried surfing but I had my beachboy instructor, Johnny, watching over me.

So I'm still working on my uncertainty about ocean adventures. My bigger problem is finding a swimming companion. The girls hang with friends when we go to the beach, so if I don't have anyone else along, I stay on land. This time I had BG and no excuses. I've found the trick to staying upright when getting in is to bulldoze my way through the breaking waves, but not too far out. Otherwise I'll enjoy a saltwater nasal irrigation when bigger swells hit. It happened six times yesterday and my sinuses are surprisingly clear today.

I'm naturally buoyant, but salt water bobbing is another thing entirely, a slow dance with the undulations. The current pushed us out of the guarded zone again and again, obliging us to bob our way back in front of the lifeguards. At one point, a large Hawaiian Green Sea Turtle casually swam between us. About two feet long, he floated within inches of me. I resisted the urge to touch him. There's a whopping fine for harassing a protected species. After two glorious hours of floating, chatting and occasionally playing with the girls, the onshore wind picked up. The water became choppy so we hauled ourselves out. Tired and wet, we basked in the sun and wolfed our picnic of huli-huli chicken, cucumbers, tomatoes, hummus and grapes. It doesn't get better than this.

Bobbing doesn't feel like exercise, but all four of us napped when we got home. It was a perfect ending to their anniversary celebration. I have to push myself to do this more often. Maybe we can go again on *my* first anniversary, October first.

Chick-Ns and varmints

September 11. We don't have a huge house: three small bedrooms and two baths plus a great room containing the kitchen, dining room and living room. I've been banished from this room now that school is back in session. Not overtly, but it's clear that my needs are way down the list. Unfortunately I need quiet to contemplate, compute, or compose, and just can't tune out the homework conversations going on at the dining room table. Somehow my girls can focus on their work while listening to music and Skyping with friends at the same time. This Skyping to do homework is a new thing. They're plugged into their friends for hours, often with periods of no exchange, just everyone trying the next problem. I hate it when they Skype. I've found myself joining more than one conversation with some boy while wearing less than I'd like for a video appearance.

On top of that, I can barely check my email much less compose when Faye is home, because she's on my computer instead of her iPad. It's her way of demanding her own laptop. It used to be that my work could wait until they went to school, but I've been doing a fair amount of editing lately. I need both my computer and a quiet place to work in the evening.

Casting my eyes around the house, I scrutinized the back lanai. I remember Stacy telling me to include that space in my mental calculations of how much house we need because people live out on their lanais. But none of us have claimed it. While Hawaiian mosquitoes aren't as large as those from Wisconsin, they are persistent. Still, it's big, quiet and has electricity.

So I asked my tattooed friends Kim and Thomas to screen it in or, more to the point, screen the mosquitoes out. Since it has a roof, this should be an easy project. They've already delivered the required materials. Now I'm just waiting for rain because they have a prior commitment that requires clear weather. I'll start my rain dance tonight. Wrestling my laptop away from Faye is a separate problem.

Thursday I took everything off the lanai to allow the guys room to work unimpeded. As I dragged chairs into the carport, I stopped dead in my tracks. There, standing on the Christmas boxes was Henrietta, startled at first, and then defiantly holding her ground. We both stood still, staring at each other. I blinked first and slowly backed out. Replaying the events of two months ago in my mind, I remembered my objective was to procure eggs for free, not raise a clutch of baby chicks. Thinking I could return to my plan, I stayed out of her way for most of the morning.

At 11:30 a.m. she was still there, sometimes sitting with her tail in the air, sometimes lying flat with her neck outstretched looking ready for the guillotine, sometimes standing. Of course there was no layer of grass to ease her bones, no box to hide her face, no fake eggs to inflate her ego. But I have to give her credit. She stayed until she finished the job. Around noon I found her standing next to her egg. For about 15 minutes she just looked at it. What was she was thinking?

By the time BG came down to take his midday walk, she had left. "Hey, there's an egg out here!"

"Yeah, Henrietta was back."

"Well we aren't feeding or watering or coddling that bird. In fact, we're going to take every single egg she puts out until she gets the message that she's not welcome here."

"Okay," I replied, thinking he'd changed in a big way in two short months. With that, he brought in her small egg and added it to the carton of fresh duck eggs.

Friday I put out a box for Henrietta. It wasn't her deluxe Johnny Walker box; that would constitute coddling. Instead I found one BG purchased from Petco when he had visions of a chicken palace. It's called the Chick-N-Nesting Box, and fits perfectly into the Chick-N-Barn and Chick-N-Hutch. I don't make this stuff up. Henrietta arrived in the afternoon, but I found her sitting next to the box. Apparently it did not meet with her approval. I didn't take Chicken Psychology in college but, given my current circumstances, that might've been more useful than many other classes I did take. By early evening Henrietta was gone and she had not left us an egg. I removed the Chick-N-Nesting Box.

But I put it to another use. By this time last year, we were harvesting five or six avocados a day and freely giving them away. I think I may have trimmed the tree too much because it's dropping only one or two every day. On top of that, no matter how quickly I hustle out there in the morning, or how often I patrol the area, most of the avos have been half gnawed by something. I first thought it might be a wild pig. The post office recently put up an anti-pig fence, so maybe they've migrated over here. But locals say that no self-respecting pig would leave any part of the avocado behind. That leaves a rat or mongoose as potential perpetrator.

Yesterday was the last straw. When I woke up I found a bounty on the ground, but had to discard four of the five avocados. I finally laid out rat poison to entice the vermin to stop eating my avos. But BG says I have to shelter it from rain. Enter the Chick-N-Nesting Box, upside down. Go ahead Varmint, eat it! Make My Day.

No one has seen Henrietta the last two days. For all I know, she was part of the harem that scattered when BG shot at the big white rooster visiting our yard. Maybe she got the message that she's not welcome. Too bad. When I combine one large duck egg with one of Henrietta's little eggs, I don't have to adjust my recipes.

Wildlife of a different sort.

September 13. My friends in Wisconsin think I'm living in a backwater surrounded by vermin. But I have news for them. There is nightlife here. I went clubbing with two friends from the Women's Circle, Julia and Joanne. I haven't done that since my divorce decades ago. I almost never drive at night, but this was worth it. We went to the Blue Dragon in Kawaihae. It's open to the sky from its central courtyard. They can pull this off because they're on the dry side of the island. We scored primo seats tucked under a fan. The evening was perfect. We could see palm trees outside towering above the walls and, after dark, the stars. We shared a couple of tasty appetizers, fresh Ahi sashimi and mushroom polenta with grilled asparagus. Fabulous! Then I ordered their blackened fish tacos with Big Island handmade tortillas. I always thought fish was a weird thing to put in a taco, but I'm a believer now.

The evening's highlight was the Honokaʻa Legacy Jazz Band. I didn't even know about our famous Honokaʻa High School Jazz Band until I read an article last month in the Hawaiian Airlines in-flight magazine. The school's music director, Gary Washburn, created a legacy of his own by transforming the jazz band during his 34 years here. He started with a few old instruments, then bought, borrowed and fixed enough more to put a band together. He taught his students current music of their choice and kids soon considered it cool to be in the band. Now they make CDs, play concerts on and off island and, in 2011, they won a Grammy!

The kids who kept playing after graduation are the Legacy Jazz Band along with Gary. Membership shrinks and expands as kids go off to college and come home for summer. They play because they love it. The dozen musicians were like a small orchestra, mostly brass and exceptionally good. Why didn't I already know about this? Why isn't this one of the first things a new resident of Honokaʻa hears? I had no idea, though I know Gary's wife from water aerobics class! The coconut wireless is usually pretty good, so maybe I'm not as plugged in as I thought.

I pondered those questions as I strutted out to the dance floor to boogie with Julia. I had fun but, more importantly, I *had* to dance – rain dance, if I wanted Kim and Thomas to screen in my lanai. Alas, I did not impress the rain gods. Today it's bright and sunny.

Snorkeling and trusting my gut.

September 16. Last week Dianne talked me into playing hooky from my work on the County Council presentation. "Ditch the ditch," she quipped. We drove to the island's west side, beyond Hapuna and Kona, all the way past Captain Cook for snorkeling. When Dianne asked me to go I didn't tell her that my only other experiences were 20 years ago on our honeymoon, and five years ago with my family. They were both in Hawaiian waters so I figured that counted for something. I had a mask and snorkel tube, though I was so inexperienced I didn't realize the mouth piece was missing, and I didn't know we'd be swimming in deep water.

Before we left that morning, I received a rare email from Grace's daughter-in-law, Phoebe, that sent chills down my back. She had a dream that night so frightening that she felt compelled to write. In her dream, she and my girls were swimming with Mae and me. Sharks appeared, endangering the girls. She didn't elaborate, but Phoebe's dream was so real to her that she asked me to keep the girls from swimming that day. The girls were going to school, but what about me? Did that message give me pause? Hell, yes! I shared it with Dianne but, ultimately, I wanted a snorkeling adventure that day and I honored my gut feeling that I'd be okay.

We met Dianne's friends in Captain Cook. They told me of their experiences swimming with dolphins in the bay where we'll go. Once, last year, more than 20 dolphins put on a show for them.

They've never seen a shark, though they suspect sharks are out there. I felt a bit braver.

We went to a spot called Two Step, next to the Place of Refuge, reported to have some of the best snorkeling in Big Island waters. The Pahoehoe type of lava at this site is smooth enough to walk on. The entry point for the bay is two giant lava steps, the first about two feet down. The step's landing is slippery with sea moss because it's often submerged, especially at high tide. It contains curious little one-inch holes.

"Don't put your fingers in the holes. They contain sea urchins that will sting you."

Okay, got that.

"Lay your hand flat on the step as you sit on it. Now launch yourself into the water."

That second step goes straight down – eight, ten feet? The good news is that "a wave will wash you back onto the first step, so you can scramble up to the top level. Remember not to put your fingers in the sea urchin holes. Now swim away from the rocks and put your face in the water. Enjoy."

With those instructions, I fell into the water and started floating. And, oh, did I enjoy! Bright yellow tangs, white-and-black striped fish, black fish, and yellow-and-white striped fish darted alone and in small schools. The more amazing sight was the profusion of coral, many feet below me, covering the ocean bottom: beige, brown, pale green and white. Much of it was brain-like, in a variety of colors and sizes. I also saw smooth coral and long skinny coral, like fingerling potatoes, held in a 3-D matrix. It took my breath away.

Actually, everything took my breath away because I didn't have a functioning snorkel tube: take a deep breath, put my face in the water; take a deep breath, put my face in; take a deep breath, put my face in. It tired me out and, with my snorkel mask fogged up, I was ready to quit after 40 minutes. Just as my companions said, a wave washed me onto the step and I easily pulled myself out. No sharks in sight. I pledged to bring BG and the girls soon, this time with flotation noodles, mask defogger and a new snorkel tube.

Fast forward to yesterday. It was BG's birthday. He skeptically listened to my idea about snorkeling and staying at the King Kamehameha Marriott in Kailua on Saturday night. That meant we could spend two days on the dry side doing stuff we can't do at home. He hates to celebrate his birthday, but I convinced him that I couldn't take the girls by myself. I'm just too unsure of myself, while he's an expert swimmer. This opportunity just happened to be on his birthday. He finally agreed. Oh, boy!

Think of downtown Kailua as Kona's Old Town. It has wonderful restaurants, live music, a fine sand beach and surf crashing against a seawall. It has a nightlife! After checking into the hotel we drove another 30 minutes south of Kona through a beautiful rural area with coffee plantations and small villages with antique stores and B&Bs. Unlike the area north of Kona with its lava fields, this area is lush. The main road (the only road) is at 1000 to 1500 feet, so these villages stay cool, much like Honokaʻa. We had considered moving there, but it was too far from the girls' school.

The exit to Two Step descended 1000 feet to the seashore. We scored a great parking place and picked our way across the lava. "Last one in is a rotten egg!" Armed with a noodle and functioning snorkel tube, I was far more confident this time. The girls were too cool to use noodles, but BG and I don't care if that makes us weird. Jade took forever to slip into the water. "Are you sure this is safe? The water's kind of cold. How do I use this snorkel tube again? I think my mask is too tight; no too loose." Finally we were all in.

The water lulled us with gentle swells and the sun softened through a layer of thin clouds. The beautiful coral was as colorful as I'd remembered, and the same fish darted around. This time I could see better, having lavished defogger on my mask. I also noticed many sea urchins at the ocean bottom, and Jade was certain she saw an eel. Her scream, even through the snorkel tube, let everyone else know too. Occasionally we'd see a young boy swimming below us with a long dart gun in his hand. Is that even legal? Was it protection from sharks?

We all had a great time. Yes! Mom scores a hit! Everyone agreed it was way cool. Even chill. Maybe even chillaxing! I'm not sure anything I've ever suggested rated that high. Thankfully, we saw no sharks. I still don't know the meaning of Phoebe's dream.

We were all pooped and quiet on the ride to the hotel. I should've accounted for that when I made my big plans for enjoying Kailua's nightlife. I had it all mapped out. We'd start at the hotel's restaurant, sitting outside overlooking the ocean and listening to the live music that started at 6 p.m. We'd share a pupu or two, then wander down to the Fish Hopper for more pupus and a view of the setting sun. Finally, we'd stroll to Huggo's for a live band and dessert.

I planned the expedition thoroughly but my organizing outstripped our energy and the heavy load of homework the girls brought along. After showers, we stumbled down to the hotel's poolside restaurant and promptly ordered four large pupus. We were suddenly ravenous and everything on the menu looked great. Music? What music? About 30 minutes into the feast, the girls announced that they were heading back to the hotel room to study. I would've protested but, after snorkeling and two glasses of wine, my eyelids stubbornly tugged downward, and I could see BG was no better off.

BG and I spent a little more time finishing the last bits of food (isn't that what all parents do?), listening to the musician and talking quietly about the day. We even held hands across the table. It wasn't what I'd planned for the evening, but it was still bliss. Despite lights blazing in the room when we returned, and the girls plying BG with homework questions, I fell into bed dead tired. As I drifted off to sleep I thanked God for Dianne showing me Two Step, for some great new memories of snorkeling, for BG's willingness to be talked into taking a break, for a chillaxing time for all and for no sharks in sight. Amen.

I can find Madison again.

September 18. I feel like I'm back in Madison, the school I loved, and code for the enthusiasm of my youth exploring new issues like women's rights, social justice, care for the environment and socialism. But it also embodied a crowded living room sitting with 15 new friends, watching Nixon on TV and crying for the many people killed far away. "Madison" was my first taste of righteous indignation on behalf of social and environmental injustice.

That indignation has simmered within for a long time. Regrettably I had to mask that part of me when I lived in places like Atlanta. Now, 40 years later, living in Hawai'i, I've found "Madison" again. This state leans liberal and I have time to pay attention to these issues and feel their impact on me, my family, my community and the world. How sad that, four decades later, we still have many of these problems with us. We also have new ones. Well, new for me anyway. Eating in a way that's more conscious of animal rights has been around for centuries. I only started that journey in March. And now my environmental concerns boil down to living sustainably. It's come to mean something very personal to me on this isolated island.

I spent last night learning much more about a related issue, Genetically Modified Organisms (GMOs). A group wanting to create a GMO-free Hawai'i hosted an event at the Honoka'a People's Theatre. The County Council has already legislated that Hawai'i is to remain free of GMO coffee and taro. But we have GMO papaya on the island. Is it possible to eradicate GMO papaya and start over? The big seed/chemical companies are using Kauai as a testing ground for GMO seeds. How soon before they want to create a presence here on the Big Island?

The evening began with a traditional Hawaiian blessing and symbolic conch-shell blowing, done at the beginning of ceremonies to herald the gods and ask them to join us. The conch blower invited us to join him in the lobby during breaks to watch him pound taro into poi using traditional methods.

We watched a documentary called *Genetic Roulette*. While it presented evidence of many problems associated with GMOs, I feel that, once again, the biggest is a lack of transparency on the part of our government agencies. The FDA chose *not* to regulate GMO foods, deciding that the producing company is responsible for the safety of these products. At the same time, the FDA doesn't require GMO food labeling. We consumers have been eating GMO foods for decades without knowing it! The good news is that we're at a tipping point with GMOs, the same way we tipped milk with growth hormones (rBGH) off the shelves a few years ago. But we have to make food shopping a political act, make grocery store chains hear our voices with our buying habits.

We also listened to a panel discussion. The Deputy Director of Hawai'i's Department of Agriculture spoke because the moderator had asked him to investigate what was happening at one of the two island dairy farms. He reported that it nearly went under until a new owner recently stepped in. This new owner inherited the feed crops already in the field, which were half conventional corn and half newly-planted GMO.

This news galvanized the audience. "We aren't supposed to have GMO corn here. We won't buy that milk. We need to boycott and protest." The exchange that cascaded from this announcement troubled me and I couldn't figure out why until this morning. The food sustainability lecture I heard ten days ago taught me that the Big Island produces sufficient milk to meet our needs. If we boycott this farm and it goes under, we have just made ourselves nonsustainable in the one food that *is* sustainable. Worse, all the "big store" milk that would replace it from the mainland is GMO. So we'd kick ourselves twice. It was much easier fighting for social and environmental justice when issues didn't collide. Or were we just naïve?

The remaining agenda was music. In Hawai'i, if an event doesn't have music and/or food, it's not happening. I had great fun seeing Hawai'i's rainbow dancing there. Half the audience was made up of recent transplants and the other half locals – Native Hawaiians and the descendants of the Asian and Portuguese people who worked the sugar plantations for a century. I saw people of every color and age on that floor. A mom danced with her blond toddlers, a Japanese grandfather danced with his young grandson. Young people did the jitterbug. Guys danced with each other. The warm-up band members joined the crowd and danced to the music of the featured band. Gray long-hairs and bald guys danced with their wives, and young guys in dreadlocks danced with plump old hippies. Everyone wanted to dance with the babies who were passed around. Local politicians worked the room. The poi pounder in the lobby blew his conch between songs and invited us to try some foods he'd made with poi.

Everyone rocked either on the dance floor or in their seats. We were participating. We were engaged. We were fully present. And what's interesting is that I've seen these people before. They show up when there's an opportunity to learn something or express their feelings about an issue. Stuff like this must have happened in College Park, Maryland, Alpharetta, Georgia and Racine, Wisconsin, but I didn't see it. Those populations were so big I never felt that I made, or ever could make, a difference. Here on an island, with a small population (2010 census: 185,000), I can. I can meet my political representatives and work directly with them on issues important to me. I can help craft legislation. I can be on the ground floor of new ideas and grass roots organizations. I can take time to be involved. I can live my life to fit my ideals. I can walk the talk. I can.

Yes, I've found "Madison" again. And it feels good.

11. MANIFESTING HAPPINESS

Tools to the rescue.

September 20. My friend, Gloria who quit her job, is frustrated about not finding a new position, and she's not sure what to do. She and others have asked for my "magic formula." It's not magic. It's a set of tools. I didn't invent them I but use them regularly. I suggested she read any of the many books that discuss transformation tools, for example, *The Secret* (Byrne, 2006). These tools are the key to my successful transition from being stressed out and unfulfilled to achieving my life's goals in an authentic way.

The work I did in Taos with Dr. Barbara C. and Dr. Barbara P. began my journey and my longer path with Rita. To this day I'm in touch with these mentors who still encourage me to consider what I want out of life, to develop a plan to get there and to live life to the fullest. You don't have to work with a mentor or life coach to apply these tools in your life, but I'd recommend that in a heartbeat because you become accountable to someone for your inner work.

I gave Gloria a condensed version of some of my most important tools. Here's the story:

First, I adopted a way of thinking. You have to stop reflecting on what you *don't* want, because the Law of Attraction shows that you invite what you think about. Turn negative thoughts into positive statements. *Think about what you DO want.* Instead of "I can't get a job," think "This 'sabbatical' is giving me the push (or the time) I need to do something different." Instead of "My neighbor is driving me crazy," think "Thank you, God, for sending my neighbor as motivation to find new friends." Speaking of your neighbor, here's another tool: QTIP – Quit Taking It Personally. The people driving you crazy are actually in their own heads. What they say to you is not about you, it's about them. You can afford to smile when they show up, take a deep breath and listen compassionately. And be sure to give yourself a mental pat on the back as they walk away.

My favorite tool to combat negative thoughts was one Rita called "What's the worst that can happen?" As an exercise for the lows of life's roller coaster, she had me carry out each argument to its logical or emotional conclusion. Basically, you take one of your worries and keep asking the question, "If it comes true, what's the worst that can happen?" Once you have an answer, ask yourself that same question again, and so on. You might find, as I did, that your answers eventually take you to a place you know can't be true, or take you to a place where what could happen is much easier to bear than the constant worry. Either way, the conclusion always reveals a result that wasn't as threatening as the initial concern. Here's one conversation we had:

"My boss doesn't value my department and I'm worried that he'll send us to Marketing and Market Research."

Rita replied, "What's the worst that can happen?"

"Well, I'm not doing anything that would precipitate a firing, but he could displace me to another job."

Rita, "What's the worst that can happen?"

"My people would be absorbed elsewhere, so they'd be safe, and I'd ride out that job until I could retire. But I wouldn't be happy."

Rita, "What's the worst . . . ?"

"I'm unhappy now, so I guess that's not worse than my current situation. If I retired, I'd execute my plan to move to Hawai'i."

Rita, "What's the worst . . . ?"

"Retiring early, I might run out of money before I run out of life."

Rita, "The worst?"

"I'd move back to the mainland and live in a cheaper place."

Rita, "The worst?"

"Okay, okay. I get that I don't need to worry about this."

Next, you have to *trust that what you DO want CAN happen to you.* Open your mind to something great happening. If you do catch yourself saying something negative or skeptical, say "CANCEL." The Universe will give you more of what you're thinking about, so be positive and trust that it can come true. This works for anything you want to manifest. Practice on little stuff before you tackle life's bigger questions.

Beyond believing it can happen, you also have to *ask for it.* Ask the Universe or God or your Higher Power for what you want. The key here is to think about *What*, not *How*. Don't worry about how it could possibly occur. That's God's problem. Just focus on what you want. Do more than think about it. Draw a picture or write it down, describing as many aspects as you can. Be specific. Embrace the bliss of the anticipation.

When you receive it, *be grateful*. In fact, start being grateful every day for what you already have, for all of your current blessings. Dig deep and go with small blessings if you can't think of any big ones, but be as specific as possible in your gratitude. Today I thanked God that I received only two changes for the PowerPoint I'm drafting. I recommend you write your blessings in a journal. The act of writing makes those blessings more concrete, and I'll bet you're in a better mood after you write them down. That's part of the point of doing it.

People may scoff. All I can say is that this process is a big part of what enabled me to be happy and to retire and move to Hawai'i. I still use this. I'll give you a small example. Two weeks ago a good friend called to say that she's bringing her family to Hawai'i for Christmas. I've been inviting her forever. After the call, I realized I needed to buy a sleeper sofa. All the couches I've seen are either too big to fit in our living room, too stiff to sit on comfortably, don't have a sleeper, or are a poor color for my space. I see lots of leather sectionals in dark brown and black, or formal behemoths in gray or cream. None of this fits my style.

So, while at water aerobics, I told Dianne exactly what I wanted:

- Six feet long, but visually small with bamboo or rattan arms.
- Fabric cushions, not leather.

- A print that is tropical but not overwhelming, and a color that matches my living room.

- Comfortable; the right amount of cushiony softness and the right depth so my feet are on the ground and my back is against the cushions while sitting, and comfy for naps.

- Contains a queen-size sofa bed with a supportive mattress.

I was in Kona the next weekend and, as an afterthought, I stopped at the furniture store across from Costco. There it was at the back of the store, on sale. Go down the list. The couch had everything. I talked them into knocking an additional $200 off, and they delivered it on Wednesday. Dianne came over to see it. "It's perfect! It's exactly what you said you wanted. You manifested this sofa!" Yup. This stuff works. And I'm grateful that my friends can now sleep here.

Let's go back to a harder question than choice of sofa. *What do you want out of life?* It's one thing to ask for something, but much harder if you aren't sure of your direction. That takes a bit more work. Again, much of my work happened while partnering with Rita. She had me do several exercises. These are all about *visualizing* your future, either with pictures or words.

If you like pictures better, start with creating a vision board. Rita gave me a circle with pie shapes labeled Family, Friends, Career, Money, Home, Fun/Recreation, Health, and Spiritual Growth. I added Locale because I knew I wasn't going to stay in Wisconsin, and I broke Family into two sections, one for BG and one for the girls. You can add or subtract pie pieces to fit your life. Then I glued that circle in the middle of a piece of poster board, the biggest one I could find. After that, whenever I found a picture I liked, I cut it out and glued it near the appropriate pie section.

You can add anything that strikes you: words, pictures, drawings. It's fun and brings out your inner child. I hadn't played with scissors, pictures and glue in a long time, but this exercise gave me permission. Maybe I'll do my next one with pictures from coloring books so I can color too! Keep the collage out where you can see it. Mine leaned against the bathroom wall across from the toilet. I had the opportunity to study it every day.

A couple of patterns soon emerged. The Money section focused on retiring securely and soon. I filled the Locale section with pictures of tropical scenes and pictures of us in Hawai'i. Health showed people swimming, walking on a beach and doing yoga in outdoor spaces. The Recreation section showed a full bookcase, scenes of people in caftans drinking coffee on a lanai, and a family playing cards on a porch. I recently pulled my Vision Board out again and was startled to see that the kitchen portrayed under Home is much like mine!

I created this poster in 2007, adding to it over the course of a year or two. This was long before I decided to retire early and definitely move to Hawai'i. The only sparse section is Career, an area I'm still trying to manifest to this day. Ironically, there's a little quote in that section I found in a magazine. It says, "During the summer I work much fewer hours – I go to the beach the rest of the time." I just noticed that I'd crossed out the word "much" and replaced it with "many." And here I am, starting an editing business and having the liberty to go to the beach any time because I didn't rush into a full-time job. While it was sparse, the Career section still spoke to me. Finally, under Spiritual Growth, I inserted a quote that reads, "Within you is the divine capacity to manifest and attract all that you need or desire." Try making your own poster. What can you lose?

Rita taught me another exercise to figure out what I wanted. Write the script to a "movie" of my life, the part that I haven't lived yet. You write as if it's already happened. The act of writing helps you connect with unarticulated thoughts. If you just write and write, some of the most amazing stuff comes out. It's like your pen connects to your inner desires. You don't think first, then write. You write first, to see what you're feeling. Then you study it. I love the movie I wrote, because I'm living it – living the dream!

If writing about your life intimidates you, then start with the next six months. Rita had me do this often. "Six months from now, when we are wildly successful . . . " I always wrote what I thought was way out there. Then, six months later when we read my essay together, I found I'd always manifested far more than I had thought possible. So I progressed to wilder and wilder statements. The outcome was always the same. When I asked, I received.

Finally, I have a few of my own thoughts on saving and therefore *having* money. This seems to be many people's stumbling block, especially if their goal centers on retirement. I had a great teacher in my dad. And it might interest you to know that I only started saving for retirement at age 35. It's never too late to start.

- *Write* your goals. The biggest determinant to achieving your financial goals is whether you write them down or not. This technique has actual research behind it.

- *Discipline.* I don't buy on impulse. When I see something I want, I walk away. If I really want or need it, I'll come back to it later. Better yet, I don't go shopping unless I have a list. BG and I have a saying, "Looking leads to wanting, wanting leads to buying, buying leads to the poorhouse." This habit can be a problem in Hawai'i, where things disappear out of stores fast and can be out-of-stock indefinitely. Most people's motto here is, "if you find it, buy it." Yet I'd rather wait. If it's gone when I return, I didn't need it. My only exception is if I've manifested something based on a need or desire and I've consciously thought about it ahead of time, such as my sleeper sofa. When I see it, I buy it immediately. But I guess that item was actually on my mental list anyway.

- *Save* your raises *automatically* in a 401K or other fund. You'll never miss it. I didn't have a "realized raise" most years that I worked.

These are only a few of the tools I use, but they are the essential ones. This reminds me that I need to put together another "movie" of my life. I don't think I have an answer yet on what I'm going to be when I grow up! By the way, I inspired at least one Racine person with this advice. Sue dusted off the children's book she'd written, added her own illustrations, found a publisher, and now she's selling her book and giving copies to libraries. One of them is in Honoka'a.

More proof.

September 21. Gloria wanted additional proof that these projection techniques work. So I provided her with the "movie" I wrote in June of 2007. It shows the amount of detail to include so that later you can see if you really manifested your future or wrote something so general that any outcome would've filled the bill.

Note that I wrote this "movie" before we had finally settled on Hawai'i as a place to retire (though it sounds like I was ready).

We were still visiting other locations. This was also two years before we visited Honokaʻa. I've included notations in brackets *[ ]* to let you know if that section came true or not. You be the judge.

Diane's "Movie": My Perfect Life, Six Years from Now

Date of writing this movie: 6/2/07. When I'm wildly successful six years from now, August 2013, I'm living the life I want *[yes]*. I just turned 61 in May *[I actually retired earlier]*. Jade is 18 and has just graduated from high school. Faye is 14, and has just graduated from eighth grade *[she skipped a year]*.

This is the summer we moved, right after the girls finished school *[we moved two years before this date]*. Our retirement location lies far enough south to have daylight on both ends of my workday when winter comes. No more going to work in the dark and coming home in the dark! *[Yes, though I've chosen to work from home where my only commute is from the coffee pot to my laptop.]*

We're living in a climate that's pleasant year-round *[yes]*, warm enough to swim in the community pool regularly, but not so warm that we sweat taking our walks *[yes]*. Fresh fruit and vegetables are plentiful all year at local farmer's markets *[yes]*. We live in a pleasant multicultural community *[yes]*. Everything is close by: we can walk to church *[no]*, work *[yes, we work from home]*, the library *[yes]*, bank *[yes]* and to local markets where shopkeepers know us *[yes]*. We feel safe in our neighborhood and already know our neighbors *[yes]*.

Despite these amenities, we're also close to nature with nearby parks and natural areas *[yes]*. We spend much time in our own backyard where vegetation draws local birds *[yes, birds and chickens!]*. I grill in the backyard often *[yes, front lanai]* and, most of the time, we eat outside *[No, BG hates eating outside. Why did I think that would change? I can only write my own script, not his.]*. I have a lovely garden *[plural, yes]* full of low-maintenance perennials *[yes, in that I don't have to plant anything; the perennials are all here, but I have to keep chopping them back]*. I also have enough sun in the yard to have a small vegetable/herb garden *[yes]*, including lots of lavender *[yes]*. Given the weather, I can putter in my garden nearly year-round *[yes]*.

Our home has a beautiful water view *[yes, I can see the ocean from my back lanai]*. We're also near a creek *[yes, a gulch that has water when it rains]* within earshot of its lovely gurgling sounds *[yes]*, and with a direct route to get there *[yes]*. I have more time than ever to read as voraciously as I did in fourth grade *[yes]*. I love the library *[yes]* and my big porch where I can curl up and read, even during frequent rainstorms *[yes, as soon as my handymen add the screens]*.

The house is blessedly low maintenance *[yes]*. One of the best things about moving was the ruthless way we cleaned out the clutter of 24 years of married life *[me, yes; BG, no]*. We're now living with the things we truly cherish and need, using the definition of "need" sparingly *[yes, I am]*. Our home has lots of character *[yes, a plantation home]* and none of the upkeep of an older house *[yes, built in 1935, rebuilt in 1994]*. It has an open, airy and comfortable floor plan *[yes]* with lots of light streaming in from every window *[yes]*. Floors are either lushly carpeted *[no]* or have under-floor radiant heating *[no]*, inviting bare feet year-round *[no, we need socks in winter]*. The kitchen invites visitors *[yes]* and we entertain from there *[yes]* with a natural flow to the porch and backyard *[front porch, yes; backyard, no]*. Windows open in a way that we can have them open at night *[yes]* and they're placed to catch a nice cross breeze that cools the house naturally *[yes, no AC or heat]*. Everyone has their own bathroom *[no, the girls have to share, but BG and I each have our own bathrooms]*. Mine, of course, has a big old tub *[it could be bigger]* in which I can soak and read. And we finally have a bedroom that faces east so the sun's light wakes us in the morning as it streams through the windows *[windows face north, but sun comes in during summer]*.

The Holy Spirit told me to follow my passion for words and I'm doing that through editing *[yes]* and teaching *[no]*. I'm enjoying a new career *[yes]*. I'm making more money than I need *[not yet]*, especially because our retirement savings have grown beyond our wildest expectations *[yes, considering the Great Recession]*. We have enough to live on *[yes]* and we have enough in the girls' college funds *[yes]*. I've been able to concentrate my talents on something I love *[yes]*, and give back *[yes, community activism]*.

My children have developed into healthy, smart, lovely young ladies *[yes, and mature, too]*. I enjoy a warm loving relationship with both of them *[yes, Fish philosophy]*. While they still turn to BG for help on their homework *[yes]*, they turn to me for advice in other areas of their life *[yes]*. This is despite the ups and downs of their emotions as their hormones surge *[yes]*. Jade will go college in fall *[yes, next year]* so, in the past couple of years, we traveled often as part of her school search *[yes]*. The years Faye spent at Prairie School have prepared her to do well in the school she'll attend in fall *[yes, even skipping a grade]*. Given her social nature, I'm sure she'll have no trouble integrating into the new environment *[yes]*. She's already made friends with some nice kids *[yes]*. It's great that we were able to find such an academically strong school here *[yes]*.

Besides traveling to visit colleges, we finally have the time and money to travel abroad frequently. We go back and forth between Europe and the Far East *[not yet, but we have a year to go with this movie]*. It has been especially rewarding to take them back to China *[not yet]*.

My health has never been better *[yes]*. Because of the nice climate, I walk more than ever *[yes]*. After losing weight over the past 5 years *[yes]*, I've stabilized around 175 pounds *[no]*, and there is no sign of diabetes or heart disease setting in *[correct]*. Of course the bounty of fresh fruits and vegetables helps, as do fish and seafood grilling *[yes; notice that this describes my flexitarian diet!]*. I eat breakfast every day *[yes]*, a vital habit developed as I lost weight *[yes]*. And my stress is lower *[yes]*, I exercise *[yes, water aerobics three times a week and yoga at least once a week]* and I'm loving my work *[yes]*. My arthritis is no worse now than it was five years ago *[in fact, better]*. And I have a great massage therapist. I go twice a month *[not yet]*.

I have found a wonderful yoga teacher *[yes]* and attend class three times a week *[mostly once a week]*. Yoga continues to feed my spirit *[yes]*, as does the church we attend *[yes]*. It's a lovely small congregation *[yes]* and we've been welcomed with open arms *[yes]*. This location is also important to my spiritual well-being *[yes]*. It's clearly a sacred place *[yes]*. I could feel it the minute I first came here *[yes]*.

BG is happy in his career like no other time *[BG seems to enjoy his work more now]*. This move has been good for his self-esteem and his earning power *[yes]*. The backyard has become an important place for us to have wonderful conversations once again *[not yet but my handymen will soon screen in the back porch]*. Sharing coffee in the morning with the paper *[no]* and trading stories with the girls about what we're reading is also important family time *[yes]*, as is supper *[yes]*. Even with the girls' busy schedules we manage to have supper together five of seven nights *[yes]*.

I have new friends *[yes]*, attending yoga classes with some *[yes]* and seeing others at church *[yes]*. It's great that my sisters and Mom have been able to visit *[Grace came twice; Mom died before we moved]*.

I love my new doctor *[yes]*, dentist *[yes]*, hairstylist *[yes]*, house-cleaner *[no, but now that I have paying clients, I'll look for one]* and all the other professionals we need. It was so easy to find these folks *[yes]*. Everyone is so nice here *[yes]*. I feel at home with the political tenor (more liberal and environmentally concerned) *[yes]*, the community's religious tone (more liberal) *[yes]* and the degree to which local government is non-invasive *[yes]*. Property taxes are reasonable *[yes – actually cheap; we pay more than $9000 on the house in Racine and less than $700 here!]*, and politicians haven't gone crazy with butt-into-your-business laws and rules *[don't know yet, though the state is less transparent than I'd like]*.

I'm so happy that we made the plunge to change our lives and move here *[yes]*. It's been the best thing to happen to all of us in a long time *[yes]*. I am at peace. *[YES!]*

Wow. You need to understand that I only recently came across this "movie" script. It's not like I carried it around while I looked for communities, schools and homes. I manifested these things without constant reference to it. Can these tools change your life? I don't know, but they changed mine.

Honokaʻa Peace Parade.

September 23. Honokaʻa is known for a few things. One is the Parade and Festival for United Nations International Day of Peace, sponsored by the Honokaʻa Honpa Hongwanji Buddhist Temple. Faye and I went to the temple with my friend Amy when she was here in January. After the service, Faye decided that she would become Buddhist at age 18. I'm happy that she's exploring her future that way.

The story of this day starts with a few kids from the Honokaʻa Buddhist Temple, not much older than Faye. In 2007, the United Junior Young Buddhist Association lobbied the State of Hawaiʻi to recognize the United Nations Peace Day, by then more than 20 years old. They succeeded and now it's official. Honokaʻa has celebrated with the parade and festival every year since then. Many US communities have followed Hawaiʻi, but we were the first. I've looked forward to this parade since I heard about it from Stacy before I even moved here. Yesterday was the day.

My family will tell you that I hate parades. Racine had the longest-running July 4th parade in the state and took pride in putting on a great event, but I only went twice in eleven years of living there. It was too hot to sit in the sun for hours. In fact, stinkin' hot and humid. People came from miles around and parking for the downtown parade extended all the way to our house in the historic district. They came early to locate good viewing spots before the parade started. While we could walk the eight blocks to the parade route, we still had to leave early to find good seats for our short little girls. But it was the stinkin' factor that kept me away – the hot sun, the windless, humid air, the slow drip of sweat down the back, the whining for vendor drinks to cool us down, the inevitable need to go potty, then crying about losing our seats because we did – and that was just me. Little kids, heat, humidity and I don't mix. Just ask Jade and Faye.

Fast forward to the Honoka'a Peace Parade. It's sunny and cool, with highs in the 70s. The trades are blowing. We only need to walk a block to the parade route and there's plenty of room. The fact that we don't have to stake a claim on a viewing spot means we don't have to sit for hours in the sun. We walked to the Honoka'a People's Theatre and I finally met the doctor who refurbished it as he set out cushioned lobby chairs. Dr. Keeney was much younger than I'd imagined and quite handsome with his white hair and friendly grin. I scored a chair right in the shade of the building's overhang, with no one in front of me, a perfect spot. And I don't have to watch a tyke in training pants who'd squirm away from me every chance she got. This is my kind of parade.

I wish I could tell you that the "we" is me and the girls. Alas, despite their constant complaint that "there's nothing to do in this town," they punted. And BG doesn't attend community functions if he can help it. So I went with Dianne and Mitch. Too bad for them – they missed a fabulous event. This town is happening!

The parade started with the usual police and fire department vehicles. In other places, throwing candy from a car or truck is a serious offense punishable by a scolding that "a flying Milk Dud could poke someone's eye out." Apparently the State of Hawai'i hasn't yet banished this practice. I waved and caught candy, but also shouted "throw money!" I guess money CAN hurt you if you're hit with it, so no one in the parade hurled money at the crowd. On the other hand, if you don't ask, you don't get.

The Royal Court strolled by with their conch blowers. We actually have real royalty, descendants of the ali'i that American citizens overthrew in 1893 with the help of marines from the USS Boston. This was no fake Renaissance Festival Royal Court. This was the real thing, lovely Hawaiian ladies of all ages, walking at the front of the parade.

We heard high school marching bands, but not from Honoka'a. One thing Gary Washburn said he would not do when he took the Music Director position 35 years ago was train his musicians to march. He felt it was more important to put all his effort into developing their musical talents. That took guts.

Honoka'a's Elementary School kids were out in full force, handing out fans they'd colored and stapled to Popsicle sticks. The Honoka'a Senior Center sponsored a flower-bedecked float holding the Senior Club playing ukuleles and singing *You Are My Sunshine*. A group of young unicyclists showed off their skills riding in circles as the parade progressed. We saw keiki hula dancers, teenage punk dancers and Japanese ladies performing bon dancing. We saw taiko drummers, taekwondo groups, and monks chanting for peace.

Our current County Council representative waved his way down the street. Apparently he lives around the corner from us and is a Packer fan! I love this small world. Even the woman who hired Jade and Faye to babysit was there with her belly-dancing class. I took belly-dancing for two years back in Racine. Maybe I'll join her class and be in the parade next year. I have all the jingling and swirling gear.

There were actually more people *in* the parade than watching it. Dianne, Mitch and I cheered each group. Next year we'd like to have a Third Thursday Thrive group join in. I also like Mitch's idea of putting together a Retired People for Peace group to march behind the Workers for Peace group. He suggested we carry our abandoned briefcases, opening them occasionally to pull out candy, money, or confetti made from old memos. Speaking of which, I gave one last try at the end of the parade, shouting "throw money" to the last car. To my surprise, the driver leaned over to her glove compartment, scooped out small change and flung it out the window, another example of manifesting what I want. I swept up 34 cents.

In the afternoon, I went to the Peace Festival at Honoka'a Park. Faye backed out just as we were leaving, but I took Jade and her friend Emily. As we walked up the hill, I swore I could hear Elvis. Rounding the bleachers we saw him on stage. Yes, younger thinner Elvis was here with black slicked-back hair and a tight aqua jumpsuit. He crooned all my favorite Elvis songs with all my favorite Elvis moves.

We made our way around the booths. I bought a Peace Day T-shirt, then stopped by the state senator's booth. I first met her while I passed out leaflets on saving the Hāmākua Ditch at the Council Candidate Forum. She recognized me. I told her that I supported her, but I hoped she'd learn more about GMOs. She thinks labeling will solve the problem. I mentioned the *Genetic Roulette* video and she wrote it down saying she'd view it. I still can't believe how accessible politicians are here!

Elvis exited the stage and the Japanese bon dancers claimed the area in front of it. They invited everyone to join them. I held back for about 30 seconds. Then I saw Janet from water aerobics class and she motioned to me from the circle. I joined. The bon dance was sort of a cross between a hula and the Hokey-Pokey, less fluid than a hula but the movements clearly had meaning, such as planting and harvesting. I had fun, but my public dancing had consequences. Soon after I joined in, Jade and Emily quietly slipped away into the crowd.

Finally it was time for the Big Time Rhythm and Blues Band to take the stage. I immediately recognized them as the opening act at the GMO event on Monday! I told them how much I enjoyed their music. They invited people to dance, so we did. I loved the older couple with cowboy boots and hats, stiffly and formally doing a Texas two-step. More dancers joined as the fantastic singer belted out great tunes from my youth. Turns out she's an ER nurse at the Honokaʻa Hāmākua Health Center. We've got talent! Then she invited people to come up and sing backup on *Train of Fools*. I love that song, so I ran up on stage.

Sometimes my hearing is not so good. It turns out she invited a specific person on stage, someone who'd sung solo earlier in the day. By that time I was up there, the only other extra person. Thankfully, the bongos semi-hid me. I decided there was no point in being embarrassed, so I just sang and waved at my friends, following the lead singer's dance movements. I hoped to blend in, but my friends told me that I looked like a tourist who'd jumped the stage. Thankfully, Jade wasn't around.

When the song ended, I tried to slip away quickly, but the lead guitarist stopped me and asked if I played bongos. I hesitated a moment, seeing in my mind's eye my solid accompaniment, then a great bongo solo or even a voice solo, cheers for more, perhaps a future tour with the band, maybe even a record contract. It would be the boost I needed to sing professionally. It would be fun. It would be life changing. Alas, I don't know anything about bongos. Too bad. This just wasn't the moment to manifest my dream of being a performer. Besides, I really see myself as a torch singer. R&B is not my gig.

Not too far out there.

September 27. I just took an inventory of how I spent my time last week and began to think I might be a kook, or at least a bit on the fringe. Monday I started with yoga. Anita led us in a drumming ceremony and then taught us the Five Tibetan Rites of Rejuvenation. I spent the evening at the GMO event.

Tuesday I went to acupuncture because my knee was sore, probably from the twirling Tibetan Rites. My Chinese-medicine doctor prescribed regular moxa treatments for my aching knee. I'm a bit nervous about that because moxa smells a lot like pot. The last time I used it out on the lanai, my neighbor yelled at me. Either he disapproved or he wanted some. My doctor also started treating my migraines, poking needles into the base of my skull.

Wednesday was fairly normal, though I rose at 5:15 for a teleconference with a mainland client. By the time the kids woke up, I was pretty jazzed with caffeine. When I was off-normal before retirement, Faye would ask me, "Have you had your Happy Pill today?" Wednesday she said, "Did you meditate this morning?"

Thursday I rewrote the Hāmākua Ditch Presentation for the County Council meeting on October 2 . . . again. Four people are speaking and each one wants changes. This community activism is taking a chunk of time! I'm also helping Third Thursday Thrive keep moving, though it's all behind the scenes. This Thursday we had a speaker on bees, their importance to the community, why we should care that 90% of the Big Island's feral hives have disappeared and what we can do to help. Since we celebrated Peace Day all week, we called the event "Give Bees a Chance." Mitch, Teri and I sang "All we are saying, is give bees a chance" to introduce the speaker. Maybe it was all the honey tasting, but I didn't think our song was weird.

Friday I picked up a liver detoxification kit from my Chinese-medicine doctor and started the therapy on Saturday, just before the Peace Parade and Festival where I manifested money, danced the bon dance and sang on stage with a band.

In the Women's Circle tonight we're doing crystal therapy on each other. A person proficient in this work picks the appropriate crystal to match your energy or problem and rubs it on you. There's a Tango Trio I want to hear tomorrow at the Honoka'a People's Theatre. I'm also going to the Breadfruit Festival on Saturday to learn how to cook breadfruit from my tree. In two weeks, Dianne and I are going to a hypnotist. I certainly have manifested an interesting life, but am I getting too far out there?

Today I received my answer from an *AARP Magazine* article, "New Adventure, New Risks, New You" by Ken Budd. His premise is that people can become "happier, smarter, more confident . . . and more satisfied with life" by pushing boundaries, shaking things up, doing new things, and pushing out of their comfort zone. He says that boredom kills, literally, especially after 50. Wow, I feel much better about how I'm spending my time and living my life.

Umm . . . Unless doing this fringe stuff *is* my comfort zone. Maybe it's time to find a job and be occupied with something real.

Just kidding!

Chicken Dance.

September 30. BG is giddy. That's not a word I usually ascribe to him, but yesterday he finally hit a rooster with his BB gun.

Once again the damn roosters challenged each other right under my open window as I tried to nap. "Bloody chickens! BG, fetch your gun!" This time he was ready. Since the first time he tried to hit a rooster, he had "zeroed his weapon" and set up target practice with "the official 25-foot rifle target." I'm not a fan of guns but I love it when he talks military.

Stealthily, he slipped out the back lanai. He snuck up on the pair of roosters with their harems. *POP!* They scattered. Then things went quiet for a minute. *POP!* This time I heard *"Brock!brock!brock!"* and the sound of chickens running through the brush. He strode back in laughing. "I got one, the big white one. He jumped straight up in the air about two feet, jerked his wings, ruffled his feathers and looked all around, raising sand the whole time." BG did such a great imitation of the chicken dance that I laughed out loud with him.

This morning he performed a rendition of his great triumph for Jade, complete with an enhanced chicken dance. We laughed and savored the moment. Clearly his BB gun won't kill the roosters, but maybe they'll think twice about coming over or, at least, be quiet when they're here.

It's good to see Jade laugh. She's been so serious since school started this fall. She's stressing about college next year. Her full schedule this year includes two APs (Advanced Placements) and one honors class, volunteer work at the hospital's Physical Therapy Department, and the school musical. After four weeks of tryouts she landed the role of Sister Sophia, with a solo singing part, in *The Sound of Music*.

At the same time that she's worried about finding time to do all this, she ran for Red Cross Club secretary and won, she volunteers as Saturday night Mass lector and she and Faye just agreed to babysit a toddler every Thursday night from 6 to 8 p.m. They'll take turns. She says she needs money and the other things will look good on her college application. When I told Grace, she said Jade "sounds like her mother, juggling five things while balancing on one foot from the top of a six foot ladder." Harrumph. Maybe in the past . . . actually, it sounds just like me in the past and look how nuts that made me. I urged Jade to do less and simplify her activities, especially babysitting, to no avail.

Faye has made the transition to high school just fine. She's in honors Geometry and Biology and stays ahead of the curve on all her studies. But she thinks there's too much homework and too much drama, some of which is her own doing. Unfortunately I'm not at liberty to divulge anything. In fact, if I keep mentioning her, she threatens to stop talking with me altogether, just when relations between us are better.

I feel for them and wish I could help. But it's not likely they'll listen. They've been absorbing my unintended lessons their whole lives. It's only in the last several years that I've practiced my tools and manifested my authentic self and the happiness that goes with that transformation. I hope they have time to absorb some of this but, as BG often says, "You can't put an old head on young shoulders." Meanwhile, I'm holding my breath. When things melt down, I'll likely be babysitting on Thursday nights. On the other hand, $7 an hour isn't bad.

I can still juggle.

October 3. Life has heated up in good ways. I found a new client for my editing business. She's a small-business owner and I'm developing some brochures and signage for her. She's paying me back in massage. I already trade for acupuncture and sometimes for fresh produce. Now, if I can only find a beautician who needs my services, I'd be all set. Well, why not think bigger? How about a lawyer? We could use an updated will and a trust. I wonder if my dentist needs editing services.

I also have (drumroll please) a paying client. It's Rita! It's a small project, but maybe more will come. It hasn't even felt like work, but don't tell her that. She might ask me to pay her instead of vice versa for all the fun I'm having and the refresher on what she's taught me over the years. I love working with her.

After writing a frenzy of drafts on the Lower Hāmākua Ditch for our presentation to the County Council, I finally finished, just making the deadline for publishing it in the public record. The council met yesterday in Hilo. We were on the docket at 9:30 a.m. By 11 the small band of presenters and larger group of supporters were out in the hallway, high-fives all around. The council unanimously voted to support us. I was pleased to be pulled into the presenters' inner circle and thanked for my work. What a great way to mark my one year anniversary here! I've never been so deeply connected to the politics of any other place I've lived.

Interesting observation: before every topic at the council, a speaker representing Native Hawaiians entered a statement for the record. He basically said that this council has no legal jurisdiction over the Kingdom of Hawai'i. The illegal takeover of the sovereign kingdom is still a sore spot.

Tomorrow night I host the Women's Circle in my newly screened-in back lanai. Kim and Thomas did a bit of their own juggling to finish it on time. It looks and feels fantastic! They found an old-fashioned screen door that slams shut, pulled closed by a spring. That was important to achieving a cottage feel. It's the sound of summer, only the kids have been back in school for more than a month already. What a great anniversary present to myself – more livable space, more private space. And Faye has her own computer now so I'm not fighting her for mine.

I haven't had to juggle this many deadlines since before I retired. Yet it's all stuff I've manifested since arriving here. I guess I should be careful what I request.

Planting and protecting my crops.

October 7. Fall is here. Instead of the weatherman reporting where the tree colors are best at the moment, our signal for autumn is the report of the first humpback whale to reach our waters. Maui had its first a couple days ago. The Big Island's first sighting was on August 31. That guy was way early. He needs a tune-up on his radar.

I do miss hearing geese honking as they fly south for winter, but I don't miss cool weather or the damp and cold on rainy days. In fact, today I played in my garden, planting peas again. While prepping the ground I remembered what happened to the peas the last time: the chickens came over and ate them. Those they didn't eat, they pulled out at a tender stage during their scratching frenzies. I *must* protect my crops. What to do, what to do? The only thing that's been at all successful so far is the BB gun and that only scared them. I need a permanent solution.

Digging in the dirt, I suddenly hit on an idea and ran into the house to implement it. I advertised for a hired gun on Craigslist! Well, I didn't actually mention a gun. I said "capture." I've sold stuff on Craigslist but this was the first time I've used it for services. I don't know if rooster hunters peruse it, but I'm going to find out. The ad reads:

> I have noisy feral roosters that come into my yard every day with their harem of hens. I need someone to capture the roosters. You can have the hens, too. What you do with them is your business. I just want the roosters gone permanently. Will pay, and you get the chickens, too.

I hope this works. If it does, I'll finally have peas to share and "peas" of mind.

Back in Kindergarten.

October 12. This week I played with Dianne: yoga on Monday, Hilo on Tuesday, water aerobics on Wednesday and Kona on Thursday. We laugh a lot when we're together but we don't always play nice.

On Monday, as I walked to yoga, I heard beeping behind me. Dianne pulled her old green Beemer over and I jumped in. We were late arriving and Anita had a big class that morning with four new women plus the usual four. It was a serene practice until we crowded onto the floor to stretch our shoulders by moving our arms behind us. I could see Dianne's hand descend towards my mouth. Not wanting her to pull my tonsils out on her movement back, I gently nibbled on her fingers to let her know where her hand was.

"Ouch, she bit me!"

"You had your hand in my mouth!"

Soon we were giggling so hard we couldn't stop. Anita laughed, too, as she said, "This isn't kindergarten. No biting." At the end of class, Anita asked, "What was *that* all about?"

We both chattered but Dianne was louder, "She bit me."

I retorted, "She stuck her hand in my mouth. And I didn't bite, I nibbled." We laughed all over again. We talked each other into skipping water aerobics that day, and Dianne drove me home.

Tuesday morning I got an email letting me know that the County Council was hearing a request to "expand residential zoning to allow up to four hens per lot for the purpose of raising eggs for domestic consumption." All that time spent trying to tame Henrietta, it was illegal. But that means the roosters across the street are illegal too! Yes! I decided on the spot that I had to hear this discussion.

I contacted Dianne to see if she wanted to go. Of course, she did! She and Mitch raise chickens and she wanted to support the measure. As we settled into our seats at the hearing she said, "I probably shouldn't sit next to you because you might bite me." Ha ha. Interestingly, I found I could support this measure because it allowed only chickens in residential areas, not roosters. One woman suggested that they add Muscovy ducks to the measure because they don't make noise, they hiss. Another said that four hens is too low a number, because her family eats two dozen eggs every day! She needs 24 hens for that.

An older gentleman spent more time thanking the council for installing speed bumps in his neighborhood and requesting a traffic light at the corner than defending the chickens in his neighborhood. Later Dianne explained that he was "talking story," and following proper etiquette for moving to his point through a longer pathway that included the proper "thank you's." I'd once asked her to explain local culture to me and she said she couldn't. "It's all subtle stuff – you'll know it when you see it." Well, here was a clear example.

Many people took this opportunity to testify about noisy neighbor roosters and complain that they have no place to take their concerns – no agency has funding to confiscate the birds. When they try to complain, they're shunted from one department to another. One woman used her entire three minutes to play a recording of roosters crowing in her neighbor's yard. Everyone was sick of it by the time the county clerk called her time, exactly the effect she wanted. Another woman quoted the statistic that mature roosters can crow every ten seconds, while immature ones crows every seven seconds. Yes, I know those roosters. They live across the street from me.

We saw a divide forming on the council: nostalgia and sustainability on one hand, versus quality of life for hen owners' neighbors on the other. At least one council person flatly stated he will not support it when it comes up for a vote because his constituents are opposed to chickens in their neighborhoods. In the end, the council person who introduced the measure decided to table it to add other provisions such as a minimum lot size and setback, and maybe the ducks.

After the Chair cracked the gavel, I rushed into the hallway to find someone to answer my questions. Always the social butterfly, Dianne was already talking with the council's administrative assistant. She likes to introduce us as "Dianne and Diane – we make it easy for you to remember," and it actually does.

I told the woman about my situation. "Can I shoot roosters if they come onto my land?"

Absolutely not. No gun shooting in residential areas.

"What if it's a BB gun?"

She hemmed and hawed and finally said that some people shoot BB guns when no one looks but it's still illegal in a residential area.

Rats. Still, the good news is I now know those roosters are illegal; hens, too, at the moment. I think the Humane Society will loan people a cage to capture critters. I have a path forward.

We also stopped at one of my favorite stores on the whole island, a garden center that also sells Indonesian furniture. These juxtapositions don't even faze me anymore. I want a daybed for my back lanai so I can nap out there in the afternoon, or even sleep there on warm nights. I was pretty sure they might have something. Indeed, they had the most fabulous double bed in a wicker frame with a pointed roof. Dianne called it the Bali Bed. She loved it and has talked of nothing else for two days, but not for her – for me. She wants me to buy it. But even at 50% off, it's more than I want to spend. So, no thank you. But the stop wasn't wasted. I bought bib lettuce starters for my garden.

Wednesday we had water aerobics. As winter approaches, the pool water cools down. That's okay because we burn more calories in cooler water than in warmer water. Dianne told everyone the biting story. And she gushed over the Bali Bed. "You could write it off on your taxes if you do your editing from there. It's office furniture." I have to stop taking tax advice from her.

Wednesday afternoon she dropped by with a pork loin she'd marinated. "I have another piece at home. This was too much for just the two of us. You bake it for your family tonight." She also dropped off basil and rosemary for the roast and half a dozen lemons that are just ripening on her trees. In return, I gave her the four oranges I harvested from my tree the day before.

We stepped out to the back lanai to chat. Dianne motioned, "See how perfect that spot is for the Bali Bed?"

"No, the bed's too big. I couldn't open the screen door."

"But you could move the table down to the end and put the bed in the middle. Let's just measure the space," she countered.

I got the tape and we measured. I had to admit, "Yes, the bed would fit, but it would dominate the space. I couldn't have Women's Circle out here anymore. Besides, if I bought that bed, you'd be over here every afternoon for a nap. You just want to sleep on it."

"Yes, but it's also perfect for your porch," she said. "And we could all pile into it for Women's Circle." Sigh.

I made the pork roast with the rosemary and basil. It's not on my flexitarian diet but I was unprepared for supper. I also added a papaya that I'd harvested from a tree on an empty lot across the street. I made fingerling potatoes roasted with olive oil, salt, pepper, rosemary and garlic. The meal tasted soooo good. But if she thinks she can bribe me into buying the Bali Bed, she's got another guess coming. That night she sent me a picture of that bed. She's beginning to get on my nerves.

Thursday we went shopping in Kona. On the way, we delivered the girls to school. All the way to Waimea, Dianne described the bed to Faye, but now it was The Bali *Goddess* Bed. "This is not a mere Queen Bed or Diva Bed. It's a *Goddess* Bed." Faye was enthralled. Crap. I was so mad. But all was forgiven by the time we headed home again. On the way, Dianne and I expressed our gratitude for having found each other. She's not only my dear friend. She supports me, sustains me, and helps me thrive.

When I arrived home, Faye told me she wants to go to Hilo to check out the Bali Goddess Bed. I've been promising her a bed frame since we moved in, but the stalling point has been that she hasn't settled on a style yet. Does it have to be *that* bed? Damn Dianne. Next time I'll bite harder.

12. FINDING MY PASSION

"Look deep into my eyes. You are getting sleepy . . . "

October 16. " . . . very sleepy." That was my idea of hypnosis. Was I wrong!

Some time ago, Dianne convinced me to see a hypnotist with her. She knew Marga socially, but wanted to give the hypnosis a try. Dianne's been on a raw diet for a month and is ready to scale back, but she's afraid she'll abandon it entirely. She thought hypnosis could help her maintain about 80% raw food.

I'm game. I figure I can try this for migraines. They're less severe and occur less often than when I worked, but they still come around. Marga offered us a deal because there were two of us. She could do the teaching part and then put us into a hypnotic state together, just for this first session. I was a bit leery. I didn't want her to mix us up and wake to a craving for a kale and spinach smoothie. Marga said no worries, even though we both had the same first name. She'll also teach us how to do self-hypnosis.

Well, okay then, let's get started! She sent us her book on CD ahead of time. As I began to read, I thought of other things I wanted to "fix," so I added them to a list I prepared for our first session. Why not? Let's give her lots to tackle: eliminate migraines, lose weight, eliminate restless leg syndrome, stop waking up in the middle of the night and having trouble falling back to sleep, stop snoring and reduce napping.

Finally I added the goal of nailing down my passion for this chapter of my life. I still feel like I'm just playing around. So far I've eliminated a career in politics, a singing profession, teaching at the University and cleaning houses. I can't even keep my own house clean. I'm happy to be a community activist, but it doesn't pay anything. I like editing, but I'm not sure it's my passion. Maybe my subconscious will tell me.

The big day arrived and Dianne and I were ushered into a little gem of a condo, with a large leather couch that fully reclined. Marga explained that hypnosis is just a different state of consciousness and that we put ourselves into different states all the time: daydreaming, meditating, different stages of sleep. The point of going into a hypnotic state is to access the subconscious, where we store every experience we've ever had. This can allow us to figure out why we have migraines, are tired during the day, overeat and so on.

She reviewed the questionnaires we filled out. "Diane, I see that you have jimmy leg, you wake easily and you're tired during the day. It's probable the jimmy leg is the cause of waking at night leading to daytime tiredness and the need for a nap."

Sheepishly I admitted, "Well my snoring sometimes wakes me, too – it's rather loud."

"Well, that makes sense so far. But these are all symptoms. What makes you keep yourself close to wakefulness in the first place?

That'll be for a later session." Then she said something that truly piqued my interest. "You may not be able to rid yourself of migraines. Your body may send them to you as a warning for something else. In that case we wouldn't want to stop them."

Holy cow, I said something similar before I retired. I used to say that my body sent me bad colds when I overworked myself. My body insisted I rest. I could either schedule some rest or wind up sick. But wasn't that one of the main benefits of retiring? I was now on my own time, my own schedule. I can nap every day. I can say "no" to requests that overtax me. But am I really saying no? Hmm.

As for weight, she wanted to know if I craved carbs or sweets. If sweets, I want reward. My cravings are definitely carbs, meaning I want security. So it looks like I'll be digging up the "I'm not good enough" stuff again. Finally the payoff: she put us "under." Well, actually not. She says we don't have to go deep to make changes, that a light to medium hypnotic state is enough. I was fully conscious the whole time. We agreed to work on my weight and the grouped tiredness issues in this first session.

It started out with focused relaxing like any meditation session. No swinging watch, no Svengali eyes. She planted some suggestions. "You will enjoy eating less and slower. You will chew every bite 30 times with purpose and relish. You will be happy with smaller portions on your plate. You will enjoy a midday snack of healthy food." Then she tackled the tiredness. "You will stop worrying about whatever bothers you at night. That will allow your legs to rest and your snoring to cease. You no longer need to wake up in the middle of the night. You no longer have to worry that you will sleep so deeply that you will miss something. If there's a noise that alarms you, you'll immediately wake up, fully alert. Unless that happens, you won't need to stay on the verge of wakefulness and you can sleep soundly."

We came out of the hypnotic state fully rested and Marga gave us a CD to play where she talks us through a hypnosis session. I can strengthen the messages to my subconscious by repeating these and other suggestions every day. This morning I woke up genuinely rested, more restored than I've felt in a long time. I didn't wake up during the night as I usually do and I didn't take a nap! Now you could say that it was my subconscious just trying to prove her right. Exactly! That's the point! I don't care how it happened, just that it did. When I see her again next week I'll ask my subconscious what I want to be when I grow up.

Credibility.

October 20. *Friday:* I'm taking another step with my editing business – developing a website! I can hardly believe it. This is definitely stepping outside my comfort zone. At least it feels like a big step to me. But, then again, I'm pretty old school when it comes to technology. I've only had my cell phone for a year!

Julia's an expert website builder. She came over yesterday and we selected colors and fonts and some pictures. By the time she left I felt a bit overwhelmed with all the techno-speak. And all we did was play with the fun stuff. As she left she gave me an assignment to write copy for different pages. My homepage "needs an appealing, key-word rich paragraph describing who you are and what you do and why anyone would want to hire you . . . Ask for testimonials . . . You'll need to write a blog . . . " blah, blah, blah. Her voice faded away as if I'd turned the volume down, all the way to mute. I could see her mouth moving but nothing came out.

After she left I did what I always do when I'm stressed. I napped. Yes, despite the hypnosis, I still nap.

Later, refreshed and perky, I sat down to write thinking, "This will be easy." No. It was like trying to go back to sleep after waking at 2 a.m. (which I haven't done in five nights): tossing and turning and looking at the clock and turning on the light and going to the bathroom and putting my arms under the comforter and pulling them back out again and straightening out the comforter and listening for avocados to fall and plumping my pillow and reciting my meditation mantra and trying a different pillow and cursing the early rooster and still not falling asleep!

I don't understand it. I write every day, sometimes all day long. Why is it so hard to write about myself? Maybe I'm trying to write and edit at the same time. That never works. Deep breath. I finally admitted to myself what concerns me: I don't have the credentials for editing, or street cred, as my hip younger employees used to say. My degree is not in writing and my newspaper copy editing dates back to high school, 43 years ago! While I've spent lots of professional time writing and editing other people's writing, it wasn't the focus of my job. I did enjoy editing whenever I had the chance. I loved my red pen and the "track changes" function on my computer. But how do I get credibility? You don't get cred from loving something, do you?

So I put my big girl pants on today and started over with the "About" page. I think I could be a bit more playful on that page. The homepage is already serious. Here's what I've written so far:

About

Diane was a voracious reader as a child and practiced her growing language skills on anyone who'd listen. She wrote her first book at 13. Neighborhood kids sat around her living room waiting for her to finish each chapter so that they could read it immediately. She studied Latin in high school as a means of improving her vocabulary. She was the high school newspaper copy editor, where they called her "The Axe." For a kid, Diane was a serious language geek.

In the 1970s she spent her first year in college as a journalism major, tutored other students in English composition, and participated on an underground newspaper as copy editor. She became a radical language geek.

She detoured into science, writing a thesis and dissertation. She found the writing was easier than the research. She was a scholarly language geek.

During more than 13 years in research positions with the XYZ Corporation, Diane wrote 37 internal technical papers and eight external publications. She wrote and delivered 21 professional presentations at conferences, both nationally and internationally. She was a prolific language geek.

During the next 15 years of her corporate life with XYZ, and later ABC, she became a manager, where she had the opportunity to edit more than 300 presentations and reports of her employees annually. She taught them how to make their point, tighten their writing so readers understood the point quickly, and master the marketing of their message. She developed and taught a seminar on banishing passive voice from reports. They began giving her hard copies of their reports and stealing her red pens, in hopes of avoiding her helpful suggestions, but to no avail. She was a Samurai language geek.

In 2011 she finally retired from corporate life. She left Wisconsin and moved her family to the Big Island of Hawai'i. Now she can edit full time. Diane is a happy language geek.

Hmm, maybe this is too playful. Well I'm going to take my big girl pants off for the day and go to bed. Maybe I'll gain some clarity overnight.

Saturday: It struck me last night that most people don't receive formal training in their profession. They learn on the job. If I went back to school every time I switched job responsibilities, I'd still be in school! It's no different now that I've struck out on my own. I recall seeing a statistic that a person becomes a Master at his work when he's invested 10,000 hours. For grins and giggles, I added all my editing time and it's well over 10,000 hours. Yes, I have cred. Time to celebrate this milestone.

My editing compulsion.

October 23. Yesterday was a big day for me. I received my first check for an editing job and I sent out my first check to Julia for designing my business website. Same day. Must be some karma thing. They essentially cancelled each other out. Nonetheless, I'm very happy. My client has already discussed more work, and my website is live. I have other pages I want to add, such as samples of my work, but what exists now is sufficient.

I had BG look at it. He said it was too feminine. HA! Then we got it right! The audience he imagines is hard-hitting tough executives. Me too, but the executives in my mind are women. If you google ScheurellParadiseEditing.com, my site pops right up.

Julia thinks I should create a blog page for my editing website. She says it keeps the search engines finding new material on my site so I wind up higher on the search page. I'm not sure. I don't think I'd have enough to say about writing to keep a blog afloat. Still, I did create a blog entry in case I want to use it. Here it is.

> My editing is a compulsion. I can't help it. My eye goes right to a misspelled word, an extra space in a sentence, or a list of items that do not have parallel construction. I notice the use of a different font on one letter in an entire page. I cringe when a writer changes style mid-paragraph. I loathe passive voice, having read and edited hundreds of technical reports. Poor logic flow, mismatched subject-verb pairs and laboriously long sentences all make me wince. Convoluted sentences jar my equilibrium. An incomplete sentence jumps off the page.
>
> Its/it's, their/there, to/too/two, affect/effect: so many wrong choices! And, of course, I immediately see that wasn't a complete sentence. It needs a verb, but it begs for a subject as well. Let's try again: Its/it's, their/there, to/too/two, affect/effect: people make so many wrong choices!
>
> I've actually written to companies through their websites to let them know I found a spelling or grammatical error on it. I've never received a thank you. Maybe I need counseling or therapy. Or maybe I can turn my compulsion into editing help for you. Let's talk . . . or write!

Julia thinks it's hilarious and that I should put it on my sample page. No way. But does it work as a blog entry? I'm iffy about that, too.

Aspiration Angel.

October 26. I love to be Queen for the Women's Circle. Last week I reconstructed a workshop I experienced in the best class I've ever attended, a women's seminar in Taos, Passion for Leadership, Voice for Change. I've gone to many in my life, so that's saying a lot. We all have turning points where we need a push to make a decision, choose a new direction, or move on with life. Two of my special mentors, Dr. Barbara P. and Dr. Barbara C., hold a seminar every year, where many participants make these startling changes. Both times I attended, the women I met, the work I did there and these mentors transformed me forever.

In one of the seminar's workshops we made a spirit doll. The Barbaras use this creative exercise to motivate participants to take their heads out of the process, and to intuitively construct a doll as a representation of themselves: the parts lost to them, parts to which they aspire, and aspects they want to highlight. You have to admit, this is something a seminar for men would never do.

I enticed a handful of the more intrepid among the Women's Circle to make their own doll. The announcement read:

> I'm hoping to inspire us all to think about our aspirations and to fulfill them, regardless of our stage in life. Please pick out one of your current aspirations and bring it. You will NOT have to share it. We'll create Aspiration Angels or, for the more secular among us, Dream Dolls. You can embed or attach your aspiration to the angel you make. This is not about sewing perfect stitches. It's about having fun with creativity, scissors, glue guns, do-dads and yes, needle and thread if you wish. This process formalizes your intent to pursue one of your aspirations or dreams. I

have fabrics, stuffing, pipe cleaners and such, but feel free to bring your own materials.

For my gathering, I focused on the aspiration part of the exercise and had the participants explicitly attach the aspiration to the doll. It's good to be clear when asking the Universe for help, so I urged the group to be very specific. Based on the way their eyes glazed over when I shared mine, I realized I went overboard with the first draft: *I will grow my editing business to one day per week by December, two days per week by March and three days per week by May 2013.* It sounded more like a business plan, and a boring one at that – dry toast. Luckily I didn't finish my angel that night, so I continued to contemplate as I worked on her.

The group wanted some direction on what to do, so I pulled out my Taos dolls, mostly to show them how crude they can be. Naturally, they wanted me to tell the stories behind them.

I made the first doll, a puppet, right after my boss gave me a horrible performance review in 2004. How could I, the overachiever, "need development"?! That's like getting a D on your report card. That phrase seemed to nullify everything I had achieved in my life: the first in my extended family to earn *any* degree, working multiple concurrent jobs to pay my way through college and grad school (with honors!). Then there were the two semesters I sat in on Physical Chemistry before taking it for credit so that I could land an A and maintain my 4.0 GPA – painful to admit today. But there was more. How could I, the OCD organizer, start numerous chapters of professional organizations all while performing my job at the highest levels, and yet need development. Blah, blah, blah. Get over it, Girl! It doesn't matter. But, back then, I was crushed. I was embarrassed. I was livid. I was depressed. I was not good enough, AGAIN!

The week after this horror occurred, I attended the Taos seminar, withdrawn and anxious about revealing my dirty little secret. But while listening to stories of women who survived being fired, losing husbands or having heart attacks, I realized my problems were small potatoes. These women certainly didn't shun me because of this stupid performance review.

Nonetheless, I went into the doll-making workshop with an attitude. I'd decided to make a voodoo doll of my boss. I couldn't wait to stick him. I also made him without a mouth, so that I didn't have to listen to him. A miracle happened while I worked. I began to take in the seminar's message to find my own voice and be my own person. I realized I'd put every job-related disappointment, every slight that looked like a glass ceiling, and even my feelings about living up to my dad's expectations, into my reaction to this one performance review. I let my boss's judgment of me color my judgment of myself. And if I couldn't forgive, then I was no better than he. I decided I *could* climb above all this hurt.

As the evening wore on and the wine flowed, I felt better and better about myself, and wound up dancing with my puppet boss. I actually smiled for the first time in two weeks. At the end of the seminar, the women said I was the "most changed." By the time I boarded the plane to return home, my healing had begun and I looked forward to continuing the healing process with Rita. And now I love my little puppet, because he symbolizes the turning point in my life when I decided I didn't have to let other peoples' opinions of me matter.

I created my second doll at another crossroad in my life, spring 2010. By this time, I was friendly with the old boss, but had a new one, and was again having difficulty. I didn't love my work anymore. I still loved the people who worked for me, loved them unconditionally and didn't want to abandon them. But I was so unhappy. I'd saved enough to retire after my ten-year anniversary with the company. Yet I didn't trust the hours of calculations and the 13-page spreadsheet I developed that showed positive numbers on the last page.

I knew the seminar would help me to see things clearly, and it did. After earnest discussion and thoughtful meditation, I overrode my fears and decided to retire. All I had to do was stay at work until November 2010 so that I could "officially" retire with an insurance plan. Within the next three months, I bought a home on the Big Island and rented it out and, by October of the following year (2011), I was gone.

The doll I made at that seminar was my Aloha Aspiration Angel. With a long draped piece of Hawaiian print fabric as her body, she became a shawl I could wear on one shoulder, someone to look out for me and bless me as I started the next chapter of my life. She lost an eye in my suitcase on the way home, but she was so all-seeing and caring that I decided she only needed one. I still wear her every once in a while when I need comfort.

So what kind of doll would I make now? As I reflected, I realized that, until about four months ago, my life here had still been about completing the move, settling in, making friends and grounding myself. The looking forward part started more recently. What's my new passion? I have many passions. Which one will I choose?

My angel turned out perfect. She had a cotton back, to remind me of my working class roots. In fact, that fabric came from my grandma's favorite dress. The front is a rich red brocade I found in my mother-in-law's sewing basket, embodying abundance through hard work. She wears a necklace with a cross and a charm of Mary, symbolizing my mom's deep Catholic faith. I'm there, too. My angel has wild hair and glasses and she's a little rough around the edges. But it was my aspiration, the message on the stick that connected her head to her body, that surprised me. I just wrote it, not really knowing what would come out. It contained three statements: *I aspire to grow my editing business. I aspire to publish a book. I am a writer.* It was the first time I had written *I am a writer*, and it startled me. But I trusted my instincts and placed the stick into my angel.

Then, this week, meeting someone new, I astonished myself even more when I answered the question, "What do you do?"

Instead of my usual, "I'm retired," I said, "I'm a writer." It just flew out of my mouth. Holy cow! Am I a writer? I do love to write, but am I a *writer*? I'm not sure yet. I know I'm an editor. I've actually made money doing that. But my Aspiration Angel told me I was a writer. That's different. I've been trying that on like a new dress for more than a week now.

Of course, I'm a Gemini and I can change my mind at any time. Then I'd make a new angel with a new aspiration. But I don't feel like changing the dress yet. It's beginning to feel comfortable. In fact, you might catch me preening in front of the mirror.

Full Moon tsunami!

October 28. *Saturday*: I know people on the mainland are dealing with their own weather emergency at the moment with Hurricane Sandy. In Hawai'i, we're focused on the impending tsunami.

I'm at a concert at the Honokaʻa People's Theatre with six friends. The news of the tsunami has not yet broken, so everyone is oblivious to the potential disaster. It's a joyous night for the whole town. Our beloved Honokaʻa High School Music Director, Gary Washburn, will perform original works with his music buddies. We're all part of the creative experience; it's being recorded live for distribution next year. I've never seen the place so full, nearly every seat taken.

The opening set is typical of the music Gary performs with his High School and Legacy Jazz Bands: seven pieces of contemporary and classical jazz that he composed. The guys playing with him are all friends and seasoned professionals who, like Gary, have dedicated their lives to making music while living on a rock. Wearing maile lei and crisp white shirts, they all have that intense artistic energy that radiates to the packed house. The whole place is jumping, clapping, and moving with the beat.

At the intermission, the mood turns somber when the emcee announces that an earthquake in British Columbia is sending a tsunami our way. He tells us, "Officials expect the first wave to hit at 10:28 p.m., after the show ends. We're safe here at 1000 feet." He continues, "If you have loved ones in low places, Intermission is a good time to warn them."

BG and Jade are home. But Faye is staying with Ivy in South Kohala in an inundation zone. I call BG and tell him to alert Ivy's mom, Lillian. Then the phone goes dead. The cell tower is at capacity. Dianne can't reach Mitch, who's also not home. People are animated, worried. I see a small child crying; her mother weeps too. After Intermission the emcee carefully and masterfully redirects us to this joyful event and calms us down with a story about Gary and their 40-year friendship cemented with music. The lights go down. We fall silent. We're about to hear what we came to experience.

The second music set is very different from the first. Even the performers who join Gary on stage are not the same guys. This is Gary's opus, *Earth Life: October Full Moon*, an eight-movement suite for two pianos and percussion. The stage is impressive with two grand pianos and percussion instruments of all sorts: drums, cymbals, bells, chimes, gongs, a large singing bowl, bongos, shakers, tambourines and even coconuts.

The audience is subdued, intently tuned into the score. We try not to let the tsunami ruin this important evening for Gary. The movements are complicated. At one point, the drummer hit the cymbal with one rhythm, shakes a tambourine with another, bangs on the base drum with his foot with yet a third beat, and he taps his other foot, all at the same time! How does he do that? We may not have the technical skill to appreciate all that's involved, but we intuit and feel the power of the musicians' mastery over their instruments. They've been able to draw us out of our anxiety and into their world of music.

As the last note fades, the audience jumps up, clapping and roaring. The performers beam, bowing together, again and again. It's an unforgettable night for this small town. But the emcee announces a "meet and greet" with the musicians in the lobby and breaks the spell. My mind swiftly flashes to Faye and the tsunami.

I say good-bye to my friends and walk home briskly. Jade and BG have the TV on with its warning system flashing, "Civil defense authorities have issued a tsunami warning." We're 15 minutes away from the first predicted wave. BG talked with Ivy's parents earlier, but they weren't under an evacuation order. They were watchful, but staying put for now. Cell towers remain at capacity, so I can't talk with Faye myself. Luckily, they're not in the direct path of the approaching energy wave. Yet TV stations are reporting that tsunami waves can bounce among the islands, and those bounced waves can hit the Big Island's back side.

The TV screen shows cars pouring out of Honolulu, 100,000 stragglers heading for higher ground. Many are gridlocked. As the first wave approaches, the Oʻahu mayor recommends they abandon their cars and walk to higher ground. Downtown beaches are empty except for some foolhardy tourists standing on Waikiki Beach snapping pictures and waving beer bottles. Occasionally the TV station switches briefly to a neighbor island. But their focus, as usual, is Honolulu, even though the worst tsunami disasters of the past have been in Hilo, Waipiʻo Valley and Laupahoehoe on the Big Island.

Harried looking reporters huddle in front of the Pacific Tsunami Warning Center, capturing every scrap of news that comes out of the building. The wave model shows a directional energy headed straight for Hawaiʻi with nothing between us and the source. The Oʻahu mayor finally pulls police and emergency personnel out of all inundation areas, leaving those who defied the evacuation order to fend for themselves. Honolulu is eerily quiet.

This feels like times I've spent in the underground tunnels back at work when we had a tornado warning. Despite the worry there's a perverse excitement, a buzz. Or the anticipatory feeling on the night of a large blizzard. Would we have a snow day in the morning? Would the city come to a halt? Would we be making snow angels outside and cookies inside? But this is new. What does the day after a tsunami look like? Will there be casualties? Will houses float out to sea? Will the tsunami damage our harbors so that the barges carrying crucial supplies stop coming for some time? I wish Faye was home tonight and I silently pray for her.

Time ticks down to the predicted first wave. We strain to see something, anything, on the TV screen, holding our breath . . . Nothing, a few inches in Honolulu. Releasing our breath, we feel a tremendous sense of relief. The meteorologist reminds us that the third wave is typically the largest and does the most damage. Tsunami waves have a period of 15 to 20 minutes, so now we're waiting again. TV cameras peer into the dark, giving us a dim view of waves coming to shore.

After the arrival of the second surge, the meteorologist tells us that Maui reported the biggest wave so far – two feet. Still no word from Faye. Is she safe? With frayed nerves, I go to bed after the third wave, again small. Nothing about the situation is within my circle of influence, so I decide to wait until morning to find out what happened. I make myself relax and my mind goes back to the wonderful music I heard tonight, perhaps as a distraction against worrying about Faye. I fall asleep to the beat playing in my head.

Sunday morning: Lillian dropped Faye off at church in Waimea, halfway between both homes. When Faye got out of the car, I rushed to hug her. She was embarrassed, but I didn't care. From her perspective, the tsunami had been no big deal. They watched some of it on TV and went to bed after seeing a couple of movies. Mentally I resolved that if this sort of thing ever happened again, I'd go get her, wherever she was, especially if we had as much warning as last night.

We walked into church as a family and I thanked God for my girls and husband. Based on early reports this morning, the islands dodged a bullet: no gigantic waves, no major damage reports and no lives lost. At moments like this, one isn't thinking of building a career, planning retirement, hearing a concert, buying groceries, or paying bills. No, the energy of the community comes together in thankfulness, and we raise joyful voices in church. Praise God.

Braces on. Blinders off.

October 30. The girls were off school on Monday so I took Faye to the orthodontist for her new braces. She wasn't thrilled about getting them but liked the pink and purple rubber bands. I'm happy because with braces she finally looks her age. When we were college shopping this summer with Jade, I had to tell more than one flirting young man that Faye was jail bait.

While in Kona, we stopped at a thrift store where Faye found a bargain on a cover for her new computer. She and Jade both feel smart when they get so much for so little, and I feel good about influencing them on this aspect of sustainability: re-use. Okay, that's the high-minded message. Really we also love the hunt for a fabulous deal and nothing offers a better bargain than thrifting.

We headed to a Thai Restaurant for lunch, where we settled at a second-floor table overlooking the street scene below. The restaurant was Faye's choice. She's determined to travel to the UK, and she knows I won't take her if she doesn't broaden her palate. So she's experimenting. She's Made My Day. I admire Faye for knowing what she wants and figuring out how to achieve it. If I'd been as self-assessing and self-assertive when younger, I might've been a journalist instead of a scientist and then a manager. But that doesn't mean I can't apply my assessment and assertiveness skills now.

I've been digesting this thought of actually being a writer and making a living from it. Assessing the emails I've sent the past year, I see how I could use them as inspiration for a book, a collection of essays about the transition to my new life. Of course I saved my emails; my OCD paid off! My subconscious must have known about the book all along, but I had blinders on. I wasn't ready to see my writing potential or listen to my inner voice. Luckily my Aspiration Angel was very clear.

Some of the emails already read like essays, others need work. It was interesting to see how the writing changed as the year progressed. The early missives were shorter; I didn't have much time to write amid all the unpacking, painting and organizing. As I took time to "smell the puakenikeni bush," I found inspiration all around me and wrote about what I noticed and experienced, including changes within myself.

As I reread the emails, I also discovered that, though I've tried to relax into retirement, my basic personality is still competitive, obsessive about important things, indifferent about the rest (like cleaning) and passionate about life. I find that I can be all that, and at the same time be meditatively, gratefully, playfully, prayerfully, authentically whole. The qualities that allowed me to retire in the first place are also still here. I listened to Dad and saved my money, though I took more financial risks than he ever did. And he'd be appalled to learn that I shop at Goodwill; he had too much of that as a kid. I'm at peace with myself and with my God. I'm grateful for all my blessings. I believe that all I have is all I need. I appreciate and love my family more than ever. I don't need the approval of anyone but me. I love who I am. I believe in my abilities. I choose my attitude and I play. I Trust – Ask – Accept with Gratitude. I'm living the dream.

But am I navel gazing? Who else wants to read this stuff? And what genre is this? Travel? Autobiography? Self-help? Literally self-help: therapy through writing! I guess I won't know until I've organized it and tried to sell it to a publisher.

I'll need a good editor.

Manifesting Paradise: The end? No, the beginning.

November 4. It's time to put my beliefs where my mouth is and write out the "movie" of my next few years. It's risky to project my future. The only thing riskier is not doing it. So here goes:

The Movie of My Next Few Years: Manifesting Paradise

Movie date: October 31, 2016   Written: November 4, 2012

Holy cow! I thought October 2011 to October 2012 was a wild ride. I left corporate life, moved to Hawai'i, settled into my new life, became active in the community, started an editing business and wrote a book. Except for the activism and the book, I'd anticipated all of it in a projection technique I wrote in 2007. In fact, I didn't even know I was writing a book until I was already doing it. The next four years were even wilder. I had no idea how deeply my roots would grow into the unique world that is Hawai'i, or how far my passion for writing would take me.

I'd also anticipated other things in that 2007 "movie" that did not come to be. I didn't become a professor at UH Hilo or work for another corporation. No matter. What I did accomplish astounds me more than I can believe.

It all revolves around the book. I started out just writing email to friends who wanted to stay in touch with my new life. Soon they told me to write a book because my missives were so engaging. I didn't believe them. After all, my 2007 movie didn't mention becoming a writer, just an editor. Writing was a risky profession, not a good place to make money, and Dad was still talking in my head. But this was about more than making money. Once I grasped that I loved to write, that I could inspire people to think, manifest and laugh, I claimed it as my true passion. Yes, I enjoyed editing, but I loved writing. That was in October 2012. Who could have guessed where that would lead?

My first task was to manifest a publisher for *Manifesting Paradise*. I thought it would be straightforward: send the manuscript and secure a contract. I hadn't realized I'd need an agent to break into a publishing house. And because I didn't realize it, I didn't do it that way. I started by telling everyone I knew that I was looking for an editor and publisher.

Through my network I found a supportive editor who bled all over my manuscript while managing to encourage me to continue. The dozen women who read it told me the truth and I rewrote it again. That took up most of 2013. A couple of publishers turned me down but that didn't stop me. By spring the next year, I had a signed contract. In summer 2014, the printer produced the first run and I was a published author. The e-Book came out soon after.

Meanwhile I put my continuing essays on a new website as a blog. That was November 2012. My faithful email readers made the switch to the blog and encouraged others to read it. People who read the blog wanted to see the beginning of the story and bought the book. People who bought the book wanted to see how the story evolved and read the blog. My influence on community issues grew as my audience grew.

First hundreds, then a thousand people were reading my blog and buying the book. It caught the imagination of several important book clubs and received great reviews. It caught the eye of a larger publishing company where I finally landed. By spring 2015, I had my second run. With much satisfaction, I happily accepted an advance to write a second book.

Later that year, *Manifesting Paradise* landed on the New York Times Best Seller List, inching its way steadily upward. Reviewers compared it to Elizabeth Gilbert's *Eat, Pray, Love* (Gilbert 2006). Personally, I think of it more as Erma Bombeck. I had a blast doing the morning talk shows, even though winter settled in on the mainland.

In early 2016, the same week that *Manifesting Paradise* reached the number one spot, I signed a deal to put the first of several ads on my blog. I've been able to pick and choose so that the ads fit my community activism and I don't feel like I'm selling my soul. This year, 2016, has been bountiful. I joined a social justice coalition and we were able to push through some major legislation to benefit the disadvantaged and the environment.

This summer, I received an offer to turn *Manifesting Paradise* into a screenplay. The screenwriters said I could be as involved as I wished in the transformation of my work. I had long finished my second book and now had time to help them. A producer bought the rights and recently found the right director. Things are moving fast on the movie.

I hear that Susan Sarandon and Diane Keaton both want my part, but I think they're too thin to play me as I was in 2012. (They could play me now. I finally shed that extra weight.) I plan to be on set for the whole production. Luckily the Midwest scenes will be shot in May before the weather gets stinkin' hot and humid. And I can do the morning talk shows on the second book at the same time. We're filming the Hawai'i parts on location here on the Big Island. What fun! Plus it'll help the local economy. Everyone in town wants a part! Dianne wants Sandra Bullock to play her. She'll have to manifest that herself.

I also finally took the girls to Europe. (BG still hates to travel.) We spent one spring break in the UK, with Faye checking out colleges. We also spent one leisurely summer in Italy, living in a small village, eating pasta, traveling to see great art and learning Italian. Now I can swear with continental flair. It was a great chance to bond, given that Faye is poised to start college and Jade is deciding on her future steps. We'll travel to China or Australia next summer.

I've also taken the opportunity to turn my good fortune into philanthropy by donating half of my book profits to worthy causes. I started locally, funding programs important to me: food aid, assistance for at-risk keiki and teens, domestic violence, teen pregnancy, drug and alcohol education and treatment, sustainability, and non-GMO food production. Recently I expanded my philanthropic reach to the mainland. It's a great feeling to leverage my dough into doing.

The movie is scheduled to be in theaters in early 2018. We're going to have the red-carpet preview right here in Honoka'a at the People's Theatre. I donated money to the doctor to fully recondition the original seats for the big event. And it was tax deductible, because a group of us finally got the building on the National Register of Historic Places.

I am living the dream!

How's that for a movie? I finally stretched far enough. Yes, it's ambitious, even to me. But, as with my Aspiration Angel, everything I've ever projected seemed daunting when I first imagined it. Then poof, it comes to be.

Yes, I am a writer. Trust – Ask – Accept with Gratitude.

– Aloha and mahalo, Diane

DIANE'S DICTIONARY

' – the 'okina (oh kee' nah) letter in the Hawaiian alphabet that signifies a glottal stop, as in the word Hawai'i or Honoka'a. These are not apostrophes, but look more like a left single quote mark. (Hawaiian consonant)

'āina – (eye' nah) the land. (Hawaiian word)

ali'i – (ah lee' ee) a chief or noble. The ali'i were the Hawaiian upper class based on blood lines. (Hawaiian word)

aloha – (ah low' ha) hello, goodbye, and a host of other meanings related to being good to the 'āina and each other. (Hawaiian word)

brah – brother. Used to address your good friend or a person you don't know. Also "sistah," for sister. (Hawai'i Pidgin English)

chicken skin – goose bumps. (Hawai'i Pidgin English)

coconut wireless – the Hawaiian "grapevine" on which one hears the local news and gossip.

da kine – (dah kine') originally derived from "the kind." Refers to any person, thing, place or idea, especially when you cannot bring the word you are looking for to mind, like whatchamacallit. It is also used as shorthand for anything when the listener is likely to know what the speaker is talking about. (Hawai'i Pidgin English)

haole – (how' lee) one who is not Native Hawaiian. Hawaiians greeted each other nose-to-nose, breathing each other's breath. Newcomers did not, so the Hawaiians called them no (ole) breath (ha). Today it's used to describe white newcomers to Hawai'i, especially those who don't live with aloha. (Hawaiian word)

huli-huli – (hoo´ lee hoo´ lee) a chicken is that's been turned on a spit. Often shortened to huli chicken. Huli-huli is also the name of the basting sauce for these chickens. (Hawaiian word)

keiki – (kay´ kee) child. (Hawaiian word)

kiawe – (kee ah´ vay) 1. a thorned tree common on pasture lands and beaches. 2. to sway, to stream, as rain in the wind. (Hawaiian word)

kuleana – (koo lee ah´ nah) personal responsibility. (Hawaiian word)

lanai – (lah nye´) porch. (Hawaiian word)

lilikoi – (li´ li koy) passion fruit. An edible dull-purple or yellow fruit about 5 cm long, growing wild in many forests of Hawaii. (Hawaiian word)

mahalo – (mah hah´ low) thank you. (Hawaiian word)

mahele – (mah hay´ lay) portion or part. The Great Mahele was the apportionment of Hawaiian lands into sections for each Native Hawaiian. (Hawaiian word)

maile – (my´ lee) fragrant vine. Lei are often made from this vine and typically, but not exclusively, for males. (Hawaiian word)

makai – (mah kye´) towards the sea. (Hawaiian word)

malahini – (mah lah hee´ nee) newcomer to Hawai'i. (Hawaiian word)

mana – (mah´ nah) supernatural or divine power. (Hawaiian word)

mauka – (mau´ kah) towards the mountain. Inland. (Hawaiian word)

Mele Kalikimaka – (may lay kah lee kee mah´ kah) Merry Christmas. (Hawaiian words)

mochi – (moh´ chee) a Japanese rice cake made from pounded short-grain rice, usually sweet. The pounding creates the soft gel consistency. (Japanese word)

moxa – (mox´ ah) a burning "cigar" made of aged mugwort, used in moxibustion, the heating of acupuncture points to stimulate circulation in Traditional Chinese Medicine. (Japanese word; a different word is used in Chinese)

Pele – (pay´ lay) Hawaiian goddess of fire. Currently believed to reside in the Kilauea Volcano. (Hawaiian word)

paniolo – (pah nee oh´ loh) cowboy. The first cowboys on the island were Spanish cowboys from California and Mexico. The Hawaiians changed Español to Paniolo because the Hawaiian language has no "s" sound and Hawaiian syllables always end with a vowel. (So the word "Hawaiian" is not a Hawaiian word!) (Hawaiian word)

pau – (pow) done, finished, ended, terminated, completed, over. Hana means work or job. So pau hana means finished with work. But Hawaiian evolves just as all languages do and pau hana has also come to mean "happy hour." (Hawaiian word)

pidgin – Hawai'i Creole English language composed of Japanese, Portuguese, Cantonese, Filipino, English and Korean languages. Used as a form of communication among non-English immigrants speaking with each other and English-speaking people.

poi – (poy) pounded taro resembling a thick paste (usually purple). Popular Hawaiian delicacy. (Hawaiian word)

poke – (poh´ kay) a raw salad served as a pupu, usually consisting of raw ahi (yellowfin tuna) or other raw fish plus sesame seed oil, soy sauce, onions, chili peppers and other ingredients. There are as many variations as there are people who make it. (Hawaiian word)

puakenikeni – (pooh ah keh´ nee keh´ nee) a fragrant white-ish yellow flower. This word exhibits an interesting characteristic of having a section that repeats. Once you notice this, Hawaiian words become easier to pronounce. (Hawaiian word)

pupu – (pooh´ pooh) a snack or appetizer. (Hawaiian word)

reiki – (ray´ kee) a healing art of laying healing hands on the body to channel healing life-force energy to yourself or others. (Japanese word)

stink eye – a scornful look or stare. (Hawai‘i Pidgin English)

taiko – (ty´ koh) Japanese drums and the ensemble playing of same. (Japanese word)

trades – trade winds.

DIANE'S TRANSFORMATION TOOLS

These tools helped me change my life. Following each nontechnical description, I provide an example essay that demonstrates the use of the tool. This is not an exhaustive list; you will discover others. I'm adding to my toolbox all the time.

Aloha. The real spirit of aloha isn't just a greeting, but a way of seeing the world, a fellowship mindset. Aloha is about doing the right thing, especially for the ʻāina – the land – and living sustainably. It's about relationships, sharing and community and spiritual awareness.
   Aloha is real. p 33

Be authentic. Authenticity means admitting to yourself what's true for you, and deciding to live that way. It means letting people see the real you, even the parts you want to hide.
   Too young to retire. p 7

Be grateful. Genuine gratitude generates abundance. So start being grateful every day for what you already have, for all of your current blessings. Go with small blessings if you can't think of any big ones. Be as specific as possible in your gratitude.
   Still talking to God. p 36

Be present/Cultivate mindfulness. When you are present, or mindful, you have new eyes. You relish learning about the new things surrounding you. It helps you to be grateful because you are noticing your blessings. Being mindful helps you get one hundred percent out of everything you do.
   Spring in Hawaiʻi. p 85

Be there. Focus on the other person. Listen carefully, intently, with your eyes and intuition as well as your ears.

    Life's still a beach . . . or is it?   p 135

Celebrate success. This is part of stopping to "smell the puakenikeni bushes" but with a party attitude. Enjoy those milestones!

    Boomers rule; 60 is cool!   p 108

Choose your attitude/Think positively/Make lemonade. You can choose to be happy or choose to be grumpy. Research shows that, if you fake a smile when you're feeling grumpy, you are likely to start feeling happier. Choose to be happy at work and in life. I remember being accused of not only seeing the glass as half full, but overflowing! That works for me.

    Waking up to roosters.   p 12

Create accountability/Use a coach. Using a life coach or mentor is helpful because you become accountable to this person for your progress, and that accountability keeps you on track. There's more, of course, than just keeping promises. But I've found this is one of the key benefits of having a coach.

    Taos women's seminar.   p 42

Decide and take action. Stop wallowing in choices. Make a decision and get on with it. If it turns out to be the wrong decision, you can always correct your course. Getting on with life is better than analysis paralysis.

    Lessons through Mom.   p 114

Eat healthy and exercise. You don't need a definition here. But maybe you need some encouragement: get going!

    Going vegetarian-ish. p 89

Fish philosophy. This is a program a fresh fish company in Seattle developed to connect with customers. Refer to these tools: Be there, Choose your attitude, Make their day, and Play.

    Connecting with my girls. p 123

Get out of your comfort zone. I find that challenging myself gives me the courage to get moving toward my dreams. Yes, you can "Trust – Ask – Receive with Gratitude," but you also have a responsibility to be prepared and help that process along. Once I take that first step, the rest comes easier.

    Their first anniversary. p 181

Honor traditions. Traditions provide continuity among generations. They are the practices that cement meaning in your life. If you don't like your family traditions, or even if you do, create some new ones. For me, this tool was also about acculturating and learning the traditions of Hawai'i.

    Family traditions. p 139

Humor/Laughter. Laughter is the best medicine, all the better when poking fun at yourself. It's healthy to laugh out loud every day. Finding hilarious posts on Facebook is one of my favorite ways to LOL.

    Back in Kindergarten. p 220

Hypnosis. Hypnosis helps us access the subconscious where we store every experience we've ever had. We can use this process to figure out why we're thwarting our desires, or to help us manifest something new.

    Look deep into my eyes. You are getting sleepy . . .   p 226

Law of attraction. You manifest what you think about, so cancel negative thoughts and focus on your bright future. I like to use props to help me concentrate, such as vision boards, journaling, even crystals. See Visualizing/Projecting/Acting "as if."

    Finally free. p 138

Make their day. If you focus on other people, they feel the positive energy you bring to them. It's similar to the Marketing Principle of figuring out "what's in it for them," but this tool goes way beyond that. It's doing what you believe is wonderful for them without expecting reciprocation. It's sustaining others.

    Garden Party, Hawaiian style. p 87

Meditation. I take time for quiet reflection by attempting to empty my mind or focus on a mantra or on my breath; a great antidote for stress.

    Paintbrush meditation. p 67

Napping. If you need a definition, you really need a nap. If you think you don't have time to sleep midday, try a Power Nap: 20 minutes of draining your mind and resting your body.

    Lazy living – interrupted. p 28

Play/Fun. Any job can be fun. Parts of any job or task can be done in a playful manner. If you can play while working, it'll energize you.

    Playing while I work. p 127

Prayer. A prayer is any meaningful connection with your Higher Spirit.
    Putting things in God's Hands. p 52

QTIP. (Quit Taking It Personally) Learn to ignore what you *think* someone else is doing to you or thinking about you. Their action is really all about *them*, not *you*, so you can dismiss the thoughts and the hurt feelings that usually go along with your assumptions.
    Tools to the rescue. p 196

Self-care. Do the things you enjoy to keep yourself healthy, mentally alert, emotionally pampered, and in a pleasant healthful state. Make them part of your routine. Self-care is not selfish.
    Paintbrush meditation. p 67

Simplify life/Enjoy the simple life. Strip down to the essentials. Remove clutter from your mind and environment, eliminate unnecessary chaos and excess, and detach from thoughts of "need."
    Flea Market and remembered regrets. p 150

Support Group/Women's Circle. The women that I hang with every week have become my sisters. We sustain each other with emotional and physical support and love. If you don't have a Women's Circle in your locale, start one.
    Circle of women. p 57

Tackle limiting beliefs. Limiting beliefs are the stories we tell ourselves (for example, "I'm not good enough") that determine the course of our lives. Exposing these beliefs helps us replace them with supporting beliefs that reprogram our subconscious minds. (See also Hypnosis.) Rita taught me a number of methods to uncover limiting beliefs that no longer served me. Below are two of my favorites, What's my story? and What's the worst that can happen?

    Going out with a bang. p 23

What's my story? Write down all the things you want most and the reasons they are missing from your life. Keep writing. Then review it and look for recurring ideas. These are the limiting beliefs that are holding you back.

    Ditching my rock. p 19

What's the worst that can happen? Focus on one of your limiting beliefs (this also works for worries) and keep asking the question, "If it were true, what's the worst that can happen?" (For worries, the question is, "If it came true . . . ") Ask yourself the same question to your answer. Eventually your answers take you to a place you know can't be true, or to a place where what could happen is much easier to bear than the constant worry.

    Tools to the rescue. p 196

Traditional Chinese Medicine. Developed in China some 5000 years ago, TCM is a holistic approach to understanding the body. It connects body, mind and spirit. TCM practitioners use a wide variety of methods, including acupuncture, moxibustion and suction cups.

    Not too far out there. p 214

Trust – Ask – Accept with Gratitude. Trust that you will receive what you need. Ask your Higher Spirit for it, then welcome the gift with thankfulness. I have successfully used this process to manifest abundant blessings into my life.

    Tools to the rescue. p 196

Unconditional love/Forgiveness. Love others wholeheartedly, with no strings attached, even at work! Note that this goes way beyond forgiveness, but you need to practice forgiveness first. It's a baseline from which you can grow to love unconditionally. Allow yourself to be vulnerable, and trust that your love and kindness will be returned.

    My father's ghost is here. p 153

Visualizing/Projecting/Acting "as if." Imagining the future often creates that future by enlisting your subconscious to make the projection come true. Athletes visualize themselves executing and completing their sport flawlessly to ensure success when performing. This set of tools really works for me. Visualizing can be done just using your mind, such as visualizing white healing light flowing into your body. You can also project your whole self into the visualization by acting "as if." For example, if your goal is to lose weight, act "as if" you had already done it: how would you dress, carry yourself, flirt and greet others? Put yourself into that svelte body. And putting those future images into three dimensions or writing them down makes the outcome tangible:

    Spirit doll/Vision board. Create physical manifestations to imagine the future.

        Aspiration Angel. p 234

    Gratitude journal/Journaling/Movie of your life. Create written manifestations to imagine the future.

        More proof. p 203

Yoga and deep breathing. Yoga is not an exercise program. It's a physical, mental and spiritual practice performed to attain a peaceful, conscious state. Yes, yoga includes asanas, or poses. But my wonderful teachers also demonstrated that yoga is a way of life: patience with your level, love of what you're learning, courage to push yourself a little bit, self-care and so much more. Yoga is the breath. Yoga is mindfulness. I can't imagine my life without it.

    Translating yoga into surfing.   p 53

CAST OF CHARACTERS

I write about my life, not fiction. But that does not mean the people you will meet in the book aren't a bunch of characters. Let me say that more clearly. Everyone in my life is a character! All of these people are friends and have significant roles in my life. To help you keep track of who's who, here they are, in alphabetical order:

Alice: Wisconsin. Mae's younger daughter and part of the cousin cohort.

Amy and Kim: Wisconsin. Neighbors in Racine. Watch over our former home.

Anita and Bob: Hawai'i. My yoga teachers. They share the bounty of their garden with their students.

Dr. Barbara C. and Dr. Barbara P.: of Taos fame. Mentors and dream-supporters.

BG: Hawai'i. My husband and life partner. Packrat. Dam Engineer or Damn Engineer, depending on my mood.

Dr. Chuck and Marilyn: Wisconsin. My earliest mentor (Dr. Chuck) and first role model for a married professional woman (Marilyn).

Connie: Hawai'i. Wise, fun elder in the water aerobics class. Leads water aerobics when instructor is not available.

Dianne: Hawai'i. Savvy small-business owner. Often hosts the Women's Circle. Attends yoga, water aerobics, TTT and hypnosis with me.

Ed: Wisconsin. Grace's son and Rachel's dad. The oldest cousin.

Faye: Hawai'i. My younger daughter.

Gloria: Mainland. Sought my advice on manifesting paradise.

Grace: Wisconsin. My younger sister by 2½ years. She's the great mother hen for the whole extended family and a superior Nana.

Jade: Hawai'i. My older daughter.

Joanne: Hawai'i and elsewhere. Part of the Women's Circle. Julia's landlady.

Judy: Hawai'i. Part of the Women's Circle. Now cleans my house and keeps my dirty secrets.

Julia: Hawai'i. Part of the Women's Circle. My web designer. Gives great hugs.

Ivy: Hawai'i. Faye's best friend.

Kim and Thomas: Hawai'i. My tattooed handymen who work on the house and yard. They will do anything from soup to nuts except for major electrical and roofing. Please don't tell anyone about them – they are hard enough to schedule!

Lillian: Hawai'i. Ivy's mom and part of the Women's Circle.

Mae: Wisconsin. My sister, 9 years younger and fellow Scrabble addict. She's always been authentic; what you see is what you get.

Maggie: Wisconsin. Mae's older daughter and part of the cousin cohort.

Mitch: Hawai'i. Dianne's husband. Chicken farmer, kale grower and community activist. Pushes me into leadership positions on community organizations (Third Thursday Thrive).

Norah: formerly Wisconsin, now Minnesota. Grace's daughter and excellent role model for her younger cousins.

Phoebe: Wisconsin. Grace's daughter-in-law and Rachel's mother. Warned me about sharks.

Rachel: Wisconsin. Ed and Phoebe's daughter. First member of the fifth generation of our clan to go Up North to the lake.

Rita: Chicago. Mentor, client, dream supporter, and my Executive Coach. Rattled my cage when necessary.

Stacy: Hawaiʻi. My real estate agent. Helped me find my house in Honokaʻa. Connects me to people I should know.

Emmet: Wisconsin. Mae's husband and fellow Packer Fan. Picks up phone during Packer games to answer our stupid football questions.

Vitmer: Wisconsin. Grace's husband.

BIBLIOGRAPHY

Ban Breathnach, Sarah. *Simple Abundance: A Daybook of Comfort and Joy*. New York: Warner Books, 1995.

Byrne, Rhonda. *The Secret*. New York: Atria Books, 2006.

Fulkerson, Lee. *Forks over Knives*. DVD. 2011.

Gilbert, Elizabeth. *Eat, Pray, Love*. New York: Penguin Books, 2006.

Jeffers, Susan. *Feel the Fear and Do it Anyway*. New York: Fawcett Books, 1987.

Kenner, Robert. *Food, Inc*. DVD. 2008.

Klauser, Henriette Anne. *Write it Down, Make it Happen*. New York: Touchstone, 2000.

Lundin, Stephen, Harry Paul, John Christensen. *Fish! A Remarkable Way to Boost Morale and Improve Results*. New York: Hyperion, 2000.

Melrose, Jeffrey, Donna Delparte, and the University of Hawai'i at Hilo Geography and Environmental Studies Department. *Hawai'i County Food Self-Sufficiency Baseline 2012*. Prepared for Hawai'i County Department of Research and Development: http://geodata.sdal.hilo.hawaii.edu/GEODATA/COH_Ag_Project.html.

Pollan, Michael. *The Omnivore's Dilemma: A Natural History of Four Meals*. New York: Penguin, 2006.

Smith, Jeffrey. *Genetic Roulette*. DVD. 2007.

ABOUT THE AUTHOR

Sarah Anderson Photography.

Diane Scheurell, Ph.D. was a child of the '60s, raised in the working-class industrial town of Manitowoc, Wisconsin, on the shores of Lake Michigan. Like many of her peers, she had liberal ideals as a young adult, influenced by the zeitgeist of her 14 years on campus earning her bachelors, masters, and doctoral degrees. She had good intentions to follow those ideals, but they slipped away while she immersed herself in the corporate culture prevalent in the '80s and '90s. She knew something was wrong, knew she needed to reclaim her truth, and finally did using a combination of mentor-teachers and transformation tools. Recovering her authenticity and her inner peace, she escaped corporate life and started a new life on the Big Island of Hawai'i where she has put down roots.

Manifesting Paradise is Ms. Scheurell's first book. See the story continue at her blog, www.ManifestingParadise.com.